Methodism and the Future

Facing the Challenge

edited by
Jane Craske and Clive Marsh

Foreword by Gareth Jones

CONTINUUM

Continuum

Wellington House
125 Strand
London WC2R 0BB

370 Lexington Avenue
New York
NY 10017–6550

First published 1999 by Cassell

Reprinted 2000 by Continuum

British Library Cataloguing-in-Publication Data
A catalogue record for this book is available from the British Library.

ISBN   0–8264–4972–7

Typeset by Kenneth Burnley, Wirral, Cheshire
Printed and bound in Great Britain by TJ International Ltd,
Padstow, Cornwall

Contents

Foreword

One of the weaknesses of the academic lifestyle is that one finds oneself within institutions that are somehow separate from the realities of everyday life. When this happens, it becomes very easy to forget one's roots. Sometimes one *wants* to forget them. For myself, as a student in Cambridge and then a junior research fellow in Oxford, it seemed a positive virtue to forget that I was from the Black Country. And yet this book has taken me back to that world in a way that I had not imagined.

Back in the Black Country in the 1960s and early 1970s, I was far more conscious of the Methodist Church than I was of the Church of England. Not only did there seem to be a large number of Methodist churches, but they also seemed to possess a vitality and a tradition that was welcoming and embracing. In short, there was a genuine fit between the Methodist spirit and the character of life in the Midlands. Whether this was to do with Methodism's practical qualities and the hardness of life in an industrial society, I do not know. But I do know that it was something palpable in the religious life of my world around Wolverhampton.

That same spirit inhabits this book. It has been a delight to read, and a constant challenge to everything that I thought I knew about the Methodist Church. I have argued and debated in my head with some of the contributors, and nodded agreement with others. Some I have thought right, some I have been convinced are wrong. But with each of them I have been absolutely certain that I was reading something genuinely *Methodist*. For over 250 years that church has been a tremendous witness to the Lord in these islands, and as we enter the next millennium this book bears testimony to the vibrant future that Methodism possesses.

Methodism and the Future has enriched my thinking just as the Methodist Church enriches the world I come from, and I commend it as a valuable contribution to the contemporary discussion of Christianity's future in Britain.

GARETH JONES
Theological Consultant to the House of Bishops of the Church of England

Acknowledgements

This project began in the summer of 1997 and many people have helped to bring it to fruition. We thank those who supported it by giving initial reactions (positive and negative) and words of encouragement in response to draft plans. It was honed into shape as a result of the insights of many, as all the best collaborative projects are. We are grateful for the time and effort people gave, whether by returning phone calls, networking on our behalf, reading drafts, discussing aspects of the topic (formally or informally) or pursuing references. We are grateful, too, to those who considered writing, or began writing – only for workloads or other pressures to overtake them – and fully appreciate that life is short; this book, after all, only features amongst the first words on a topic, not the last.

We are sad that the range of authors is not broader. It is especially a poignant reflection on the current situation in Methodism that a higher proportion of those women asked to participate felt unable to take up the offer, or had to withdraw, due to many pressures upon them. But writing isn't everything. We simply hope that the book will prompt many others to join in lively discussion and action as a consequence of reading it, in whatever context, style or forum is appropriate.

We thank the Evangelism Office of the Methodist Church, members of the Harborne Group and members of the young adults group at Hinde Street Methodist Church, West London, who took a keen interest at various stages. We also thank those who wrote in response to our letter in the *Methodist Recorder* in December 1997. With apologies to anyone we may have overlooked, we thank directly: Fleur Anderson, Ian Andrew, Jil Brown, Keith Bulcock, Andrew Bull, Derek Cargill, Gareth Evans, Richard Griffiths, Sarah Hindmarsh, Brian Hoare, Ian Howarth, Nick Jones, Paul King, Rachel Lampard, Julian Lewis, Jill Marsh, Julie Norris, William Porter, Anthony Reddie, Chris Roles, Kathryn Schofield, Mary Shannahan, Geoff Sharpe, Martin Turner, David Vanberg and Wendy Whitehead. We wish to thank Ruth McCurry at Cassell for seeing exactly what we were driving at in the project, and for taking the risk in publishing it. We thank the contributors themselves, for their drafting and re-drafting, their meeting of tight deadlines, and for being willing to give of their time, skills and experience to the project. Finally, we wish to thank Margaret and David Makin for granting their permission to us to dedicate the book to the memory of their daughter, Rachel, who was a personal friend to many of the contributors.

JANE CRASKE AND CLIVE MARSH
11 November 1998

The contributors

Richard Andrew is a Methodist Minister in Sheffield. He is married to Debbie and has two children, Thomas and Rebecca. After four years in industry he trained at Wesley House, Cambridge. He is in the final stages of completing his doctorate on Karl Barth and the theology of mission.

Adrian Burdon is a British Methodist Minister presently working as a Mission Partner with the Free Wesleyan Church of Tonga (The Methodist Church in Tonga). He is the Principal of the Sia'atoutai Theological College, where he teaches both Liturgical and Methodist studies.

Elizabeth Carnelley is an Anglican Priest in the Diocese of Manchester, working half-time in a parish and half-time as Director of Reader Training. She studied theology at Durham, Cambridge and Oxford. She is a jazz singer and is interested in feminist theology, urban theology and Hinduism.

Beverley Clack is a Senior Lecturer in theology and religious studies at Roehampton Institute, London. She has published articles in feminist theology, has co-authored an introduction to philosophy of religion, and edited a Reader in misogyny. She is married and lives in Oxford.

Jane Craske is a Methodist Minister in circuit in Manchester, who also teaches half-time in theological education at Hartley Victoria College. Her previous circuit appointment was in central London. Before entering the Methodist Ministry she was a secondary school teacher. She has a particular interest in feminist theology.

Andrew Hindmarsh spends his weekdays as Director of Academic Planning at the University of Sheffield and the rest of his time enjoying the company of his wife Sarah and their three small children. He grew up in the North East of England and studied zoology and then animal behaviour at the University of Oxford. He acquired an interest in organizations while undertaking postgraduate study of marketing and organizational behaviour.

Clive Marsh has been in Methodism for seventeen years, having stumbled into it at university when he went looking for Anglicans. Since then, he has been – at various times – a circuit steward, a church steward and (for ten years now) a Local Preacher. He is involved in theological education in university and church contexts and lives in Rotherham with Jill, a Methodist Minister, and their two children.

Stephen Plant is married to Kirsty. He grew up in Doncaster, has lived in Tanzania, studied in Birmingham, Cambridge and Germany, and served as a Circuit Minister in Hammersmith and Hertfordshire. He works as Europe Secretary in the Methodist World Church Office. He is the author of *Simone Weil* and is writing a book on Bonhoeffer's ethics.

Christopher Shannahan lives in Birmingham with his wife Mary and their children Bethany and Jonathan. He is a Methodist Minister in Handsworth and teaches contextual theology part-time at The Queen's College. He used to live and work in the East End of London. He follows West Ham and U2.

Nicholas Sissons has a special interest in inter-faith issues, particularly Jewish–Christian relations. He is a member of the Connexional Committee for inter-faith relations and has recently written a course on Judaism for the Open Learning Centre. After working as a Higher Education chaplain he is now in rural ministry in Sussex.

Martin Wellings is a Methodist Minister working in Northamptonshire. Having read Modern History at Oxford and undertaken research on the nineteenth-century church, he trained at Wesley House, Cambridge. In addition to circuit work he is also a prison chaplain and Secretary of the Oxford and Leicester District Synod.

Richard Woolley is the former Director of Studies at Cliff College, where he taught contemporary Christian issues. He is a Local Preacher and a part-time student at the Urban Theology Unit, Sheffield, where he is researching Christian Socialism in the late twentieth century. He is currently involved in primary education in north-east Derbyshire.

The 1950s was an era of low geographical mobility. This had many effects. It reinforced the clear regional demarcations within the country, and placed great emphasis on the local area, with its own local government, local policing, local entertainment, local transport. Networks of railways were still linking small towns, providing people with access to their employment and their relatives. In fact, the locality and neighbourhood were central for work, shopping and leisure, with the local cinema given central place in many small towns. Family relationships, too, echoed this local pattern. Many studies on traditional communities have described the importance of extended family living, with jobs being passed down from father to son, and mothers 'speaking for' their married children to the local landlord who could provide them with accommodation. There were fairly fixed gender roles within the family, and leisure time was often spent indoors with relatives of the same sex across the generations ... Along with low geographical mobility went low social mobility. By and large, people lived within fixed and distinct class positions. Powerful private ownership and hereditary wealth co-existed alongside widespread patterns of non-ownership and very low income ... Class lines were also reflected in education and voting patterns ... At the same time, intense poverty and hardship were often ameliorated by public provisions, especially in the area of welfare, council housing and health care ... In fact, for the most part, the 1950s were a period of national optimism, with almost full employment, and the flourishing of traditional heavy industries ... Yet change is hardly ever as planned ... many underlying assumptions, which were as yet unquestioned in the 1950s, were to come under substantial attack from the radicals of the 60s and early 70s: assumptions now described as 'class-bound, patriarchal and white'.[1]

Seen in retrospect the 1950s seem almost like a golden age of King Solomon, the sixties an era of moral prophecy of a fairly Pelagian sort. The period in which we have now arrived is quite another, an age of apocalyptic, of doom watch, in which the tragedies of an anguished world have become just too many to cope with, yet in which there is the strongest feeling that there may still be worse to come.[2]

Introduction

A passionate age

Clive Marsh and Jane Craske

Why this book?

What keeps people in church? More particularly: what keeps twenty-
and thirty-somethings in church when so many of their contemporaries
have never been in church and might never consider joining? In many
ways, that question forms the background to this present book. The contributions are all written by people who are under 40. Of the twelve
writers, ten are Methodists critically examining their own tradition in
contemporary perspective. Together, the chapters form a snapshot from
within one particular, struggling brand of British Christianity. The chapters reflect a shared belief that Methodism's heritage is likely to be of
some importance in the shaping of Christianity's future in Britain, but
that easy assumptions about *how* the Methodist past shapes the
Methodist present, *whether* Methodism should remain institutionally
distinct, and *to what extent* Methodism should influence Christianity
more generally, cannot be made. Though the book is therefore self-
consciously *about* Methodism, it is not a narrow book from a single,
obviously partisan perspective (i.e. either defending the Methodist
status quo, or arguing for Methodism's demise). But nor is it devoid of
strong opinions. Clear positions about Methodism or Christianity's
future are often stated in the pages that follow. As editors we have not
sought to harmonize these views. Nor does the book dodge posing a
straightforward challenge at the end: for something has to be done.

Our purpose in gathering the chapters together has been to offer a
collection of argued standpoints from people interested in the present
state, and future prospects, of British Christianity, and of Methodism's
place within it. As we do so, there is no point denying Methodism's
numerical decline. Early in 1996, news broke of the extent of the decline
in membership of the Methodist Church in Great Britain. The triennial
membership figures were made public, as usual, but for some reason the
figures in that year provoked more than a passing interest, and the
broadsheets were on to the story in a flash: Methodism was dying. Its
members were literally dying, and not being replaced in anything like the
same numbers from among the young. Methodism may have, or have

had, a strong youth emphasis. But it didn't appear that young people stayed around very long. For a whole host of reasons – at that stage, ill-defined, more speculated about than proven – people did not stick with the church into their twenties and thirties or, in general, did not join it if they had not been brought up in it. It was against that backcloth that this writing project began.

Statistics do not, of course, say everything, even whilst their undoubted force cannot be ignored. The circumstances of – and reasons for – 'church leaving' have been the subject of study since the 1996 publicity about Methodism (Richter and Francis 1998). But there remains a question about 'church staying'. Even when the decline is acknowledged, Methodism remains still alive and kicking, even if it may need a thorough shake-up.

We have reached a stage in our own lives when we are (just!) young enough still to be called young. Yet we are often referred to as 'young' in church life in a way which would not happen in our professional lives. And we are old enough to have gathered sufficient experience and expertise of church life, and of wider society, to be taken with appropriate seriousness. We are also witnesses to some shocking examples of the patronizing culture of British church life. And though ageism is neither the focus of our enquiries nor the simple driving force of our essays, we must nevertheless risk the charge in our attempt to raise the issues we do and, at times, in the way that some of the material is presented.

The rapid social and cultural change which has occurred in Britain over the last five decades merits close attention. We have come to realize just how different the experience of British society is for those born even in the late 1940s and early 1950s – let alone the 1920s and 1930s – when compared with those born in the late 1950s and early 1960s. It is this point we wish to press forcibly. We are, to use the sociologists' terms, 'baby boomers and baby busters' – terms we shall expand on further in the third section of this Introduction. Contemporary British Methodism seems to be so heavily marked by the culture of 1950s Britain that this feature of its life alone would be worth the closest scrutiny, even if this is not something we have been able to take up in detail ourselves. In his excellent recent study of modern Methodism, when discussing the end of the great preaching tradition, John Munsey Turner seems to agree that something happened at the end of the 1950s which has not yet been fully accounted for. He writes:

> Sangster, Soper and Weatherhead formed a remarkable Methodist trio in the 1950s, writing as well as preaching with distinction, but the great preaching tradition ended almost dramatically at the end of that decade. In the 1960s the crowds did not follow the great preachers any more. The reasons are

highly complex . . . there was . . . a mistrust of authoritarian oratory. Radio or perhaps pedestrian speakers like Baldwin, Chamberlain and Attlee killed it off, replacing it with 'fireside chats' like those of Roosevelt. Again, education-alists tended to write off preaching as an educational medium . . . The image, moreover, was often overtaking the spoken word as the mode of the message . . . By the 1960s, the spread of cheap radios and of television enabled people to hear the human voice (as Dr Alan Wilkinson put it) as verbal wallpaper. (Turner 1998: 54)

It is time, then, to begin to unravel and re-examine how the impact of that period in British history has taken shape and played a role in the shaping of British Christianity beyond its relation to preaching. More importantly still, it is essential to consider what Christianity looks like for those only implicitly and indirectly affected by 1950s British culture. For what if so many who have held – and perhaps still hold – power in the Methodist and other churches are effectively operating as if 1950s Britain still existed?

The quotation from Elaine Storkey, placed immediately before this chapter, sums up succinctly many crucial aspects of that cultural shift. We have moved from the easy assumptions that Britain is essentially Christian, that families (of a particular, presupposed structure and size) are the bedrock of social stability, that people live and think in very local-ized ways, and are employed locally. Gone is the idea that gender roles are always clearly defined. We have moved – even if by no means as far as we should have – away from the assumption that white culture has auto-matic superiority.

This book therefore offers a cross-section of views of Methodism and British Christianity (mostly from within) by people who were never even born when optimistic, socially stable, becoming-prosperous post-war Britain was interweaving with Methodism's own development in that period of strength. Though the chapters examine in many ways some standard topics (Methodist history, Methodist theology, worship, the evangelical tradition, socio-political concerns), the slant adopted by some of the chapters may be unexpected. Meanwhile, other chapters are distinctively concerns of the last three or four decades (church leaving, Methodism in the context of world faiths, the global church). Collec-tively, we have no desire to predict either the end of British Methodism, or to suggest its inevitable survival. We can only suggest from within – or from a position just outside – that its place as an aspect of current British Christianity is worth examining. And we offer our collective examination of Methodism's place in British Christianity to all who are interested in Methodism itself, or in Christianity more generally – whether from a religiously-committed standpoint, or as a sympathetic observer. As part of that examination, we are pleased to include the insights of an ex-Methodist, Beverley Clack, for whom Christianity itself became problematic, and whose version of Methodist Christianity was clearly unable to sustain her questioning in adult life. In addition, Elizabeth Carnelley, an Anglican, writes critically, but with affection, of a movement with which she has had considerable contact throughout her life.

The world of twenty- and thirty-somethings

We need to say something, even if in highly impressionistic fashion, about who 'we' are, not directly in terms of autobiography, but in order to paint a picture of the world of twenty- and thirty-somethings to which all the contributors to this book relate. A dozen white, English-speaking, religiously-inclined thirty-somethings, all of whom have received higher education and over half of whom are ordained clergy, is hardly the most appropriate bunch of people to talk on behalf of their age group in Britain today, let alone further afield. We acknowledge openly that our profile is limited and limiting. But if we do speak of 'we' as if we are somehow representative of our age group, it at least shows that we do not feel ourselves to be as radically different from many of our contemporaries as perhaps our churches may wish us to be. We are, however, aware that we are somewhat freakish in being attached to organized religion at all. Though it is not our concern in this book to explore the full implications of this, it is important to note for the simple reason that it is overlooked so frequently in church discussions as to 'why the young won't come'. For we are now at the stage where the answer is quite simple: 'the young won't come' for the simple reason that most young people don't.

Who, then, speaking representatively, are 'we'? Many of us have children ourselves, of course. Those of us who still live near our own parents like to keep the extended family very much alive (and the parents and in-laws are excellent baby-sitters). But many of us have moved around because of our employment. So our family patterns have changed considerably from what even we knew as children. We spend more time in the immediate family group, and have different kinds of links with people locally (often via our children's contacts). But we also keep up with past friends further afield. So lots of our free time is spent travelling to and from such friends. Many of us are not married, though have – or have had – long-standing friendships and partnerships. Some of us are fiercely independent and single, and are grateful that at last in society there seems to be more of an acceptance that people of both sexes can make such a choice. We are fairly upfront about sexuality, perhaps in a rather preoccupied way. We may simply be paying the price for previous generations' relative silence in such matters.

We spend a lot of time travelling, and those of us who have enough money tend to use our incomes to discover the world, even dashing from work on Fridays to catch a plane to somewhere exotic for a European short break. But there are many of us without the money to do that. Too many of those at the younger end of our age group, in their early twenties, end up in higher education but don't really want to be. And the quest to find satisfying work is a struggle even for those who are 'graduates'. It's usually possible to get some kind of income – and a fair number of our contemporaries seem to have worked at McDonald's, Burger King or their equivalent at some point in getting to where they are – but a decent income linked to fulfilling work is more difficult to come by. Those who are the high wage-earners, though, seem to be working all the time. Too many of our contemporaries seem to have sold their souls to their jobs. They are in need of a new kind of 'Reformation' because they have succumbed to 'salvation by work'. We have seen, too, often how over-work (because it's always cheaper to get one person to do two people's jobs, rather than two people to do the same work) stretches the people in work beyond the limit, and it makes us angry with managers and employers who speak easily of 'flexible working patterns', when sometimes it simply means being available at all times of the day at someone else's beck and call.

For those who do look beyond work, though, there are plenty of options. Leisure, health, sport, religion, shopping, entertainment: there is much of this in abundance. And this really is where religion comes in: it's a leisure pursuit which fights for a place (for those interested) in the middle of a crowded programme of televised sport, cinema, computer games, shopping expeditions, nights out, long weekends, team games and fitness drives. Or at least, the explicit 'collective worship' and 'meetings' aspects of religious practice fit in here. For that is where the time-pressure takes effect: there's always too much to do. In this context, if Christianity is to get much of a look-in, then it will have to demonstrate how the collective things are *worth* doing. And if these are worth doing, and are believed to be more than just isolated leisure pursuits, then a case will have to be made for how these collective activities (and whatever other individual activities should accompany the corporate pursuits) influence the rest of life. There's no escaping the fact, though, that at the moment, most of our contemporaries are shopping, visiting family and friends, sipping *café au lait* at the foot of the Eiffel Tower, donning a football shirt (to play or watch), or reading the newspaper on Sundays. They are not in church. And the truth is that even many of those who *are* in church feel a strong pull in other directions.

What of cultural life in other directions: politics, art, literature, music? We've tried to redefine what 'classic literature' and 'classic (or classical) music' are, simply because we've been a bit suspicious of who's been deciding what counts as 'classic' in the first place. Admittedly, we've probably gone over the top, and linked our own desire to redefine the terms too closely with consumer demand (the top 100 in bookshops and radio-stations' play-lists etc.). But this has seemed an important thing to do. Sometimes our interests have been openly functional (what makes us feel good? what is good to dance to?), sometimes nostalgic. We have, after all, lived through decades which must feature amongst the most heavily 'recorded' (and thus media-saturated) in human history.

As for art, there have always been the outrageous in any age, so there's nothing new there. And anyway, film is the main art-form for our age. We're perhaps less political, or less politically radical, than our immediate predecessors (those who were teenagers in the late 1950s and 1960s), but there's plenty of practical politics around. And recent opinion polls have revealed us – especially those at the younger end of our age band – to be more conservative and pragmatic than may have been supposed: we just want a job! (As an example of how stereotypes linger, though, it is worth mentioning that this very book was turned down by one religious publisher in part because of its conservatism. We wonder whether this was an inverted form of ageism, resulting from the assumption as to what 'young people' would or should produce.)

How we access our cultural comment is crucial, and may help John Munsey Turner in his thinking about why the preaching tradition has declined: we watch TV, get our news from the newspapers and, more so, the Teletext. We expect our cultural comment to come from *Have I Got News for You?* or *Newsnight* rather than from a Sunday sermon. The Sunday papers give us our review of the week's news. Some of us surf the Internet for things to read on topics that interest us, and get diverted in all sorts of ways by all that it presents to us. The would-be profundity of a local church – especially if entire services are left dependent on relatively uninformed preachers who perform badly and treat all their congregation like small children – seems poor by comparison with all this. The few of us who think theologically are even tempted to think that the Internet may have more to do with the Holy Spirit than the local church does. But then we recall that churches are about bodies too – not just minds and electronic links – and realize that we've got to do some thinking in this area, because so much religious thought clearly hasn't.

We have noticed, though, that it is local councils who seem to be doing most of the work of caring for people – in their bodies and their minds – and we are puzzled to have inherited a legacy of immense mistrust of local councils in churches. On closer inspection, we realize that this has something to do with the 1970s – the height of so-called 'secularization' – when Christianity (and probably all religion) was seen as a 'bad thing' and that if you were religious, it was best to keep a low pro-file. Now, though, it looks as though we've come through that, and it is the ardent secularists who are the dinosaurs. There is rightly still no place for mind-numbing Bible- or Qur'an-bashing. But it has been recognized that perhaps religions are quite important for social stability and well-being (a better term than 'social control'), and that partner-ships between religious bodies and local councils might actually be a good thing, and not just the result of economic necessity. So we're a bit puzzled at what all the fuss was about (and, indeed, why there's still so much suspicion around in churches).

These, then, are features of our world. Christians take their place in the midst of all this. Some reject much of it and wish to claim a place for their faith over against the world. Many accept that they are simply part of so much of it, for they are in the world. At any rate, it is, as we say, an impression of the kind of world out of which we write. But there is also a more analytical treatment of our contexts worth describing. To that we now turn.

The contexts of the book

Declining Methodist membership was the spark for this book. It is, how-ever, just one of the contexts within which it is written. As the potential group of contributors to this book was gathered together throughout 1997–98, it was constantly necessary to become clear about the many other contexts within which it took shape. What are these contexts?

The first which should be mentioned is the *changing face of Christian-ity* in Britain today. Echoing in a small way the nature of Christianity's growth around the world (which is considerable in some parts of the world, e.g. Korea, Central Africa), growth within British Christianity is occurring mainly among charismatic evangelicals (Brierley 1991: ch. 7). This growth should, however, be understood within a pattern of general decline in British Christianity, not only in Methodism, but across churches in general (*ibid.*: 201–6). Some sociologists interpret this evidence as indicating that: 'Christianity is becoming a more closed reli-gion' (*ibid.*: 206), and that its future is likely to be preserved among the emotional, the fanatical and the sectarian. The tenor of this present book is that Christianity should not allow itself to become a 'closed religion', but given the general context, the cumulative case presented by the various contributors will need to be argued plausibly and persuasively.

A second Christian context presents itself, however: *ecumenism*. The co-operation between Christians across denominations is either at a low ebb or at its most advanced, depending upon whom you speak to. Certainly there is often little enthusiasm for 'ecumenical events' at local or regional level, even while much high-level national and international work continues. But in many respects, denominational difference matters less than it once did. Among the younger end of the churches, there is often little respect for denominational distinctiveness. This is sometimes linked, though, with relatively little familiarity with denominational tradition, so the situation is two-edged. However, if Christianity is seen to be more significant than allegiance to a denomination, this can be a positive start to ensuring that God comes before any institutional church.

Ecumenism, though, is often taken well beyond Christianity. If *oikumene* means the whole household of faith, Christians don't have a monopoly on faith. Despite the complexity of the requirements of inter-faith dialogue, it is a logical next step beyond Christian ecumenism. This brings us, third, to the fact that Christianity is, of course, but part of a *wider religious context*. Christianity has always lived in a wider religious context, but since European expansionism intermingled with the spread of Christianity, encounters between Christianity and other religions have been commonplace, even if far from always positive. Today, in very concrete terms, the fact that people now live next door to Buddhists, Hindus, Sikhs, Muslims and Bahais, not to mention atheists, means that the religious picture is starkly pluralist. To call England a 'Christian country' in any simple sense will not suffice any more.

There is, however, a further twist to this wider religious context: the question whether a secular framework overrides the religious context anyway. Should the *secularization* of Britain be considered the primary context within which any study of religion (let alone Christianity) should be made? In other words, should we acknowledge that religions generally are private affairs, supported by relatively few, and of little public and political significance? The debate is a fierce one among sociologists, and its importance is not to be played down (Gill 1993; Bruce 1995a). It cannot be resolved here. As religiously-interested writers we are inevitably more likely to conclude that religion remains more important than sociologists tend to allow. For the statistics are themselves not as unimpressive as critics of religion make out: put all religiously-committed together, add to that those who profess some kind of 'personal spirituality', and it amounts to a fair percentage of the population, regardless of whether such 'religion' is easily quantifiable or very institutionally based. We must, though, acknowledge that this discussion forms one further context within which this book is written.

We have already made much of *the age profile of the contributors*. Aside from the question of the impact of 1950s British culture upon contemporary Methodism, which becomes a key issue for us, we must also consider the impact this age profile has upon the social and ideological context of the contributors. In sociological terms we are late 'baby boomers' (born 1945–60) and early 'baby busters' (born 1961–81). If Richter and Francis are right, all of us are interested in personal fulfilment and autonomy and are tolerant of a great diversity in lifestyles. Some of us (the boomers) have a distrust of leadership and institutions, emphasize the priority of experience over beliefs and the importance of individual choice, are generally optimistic, and display an attraction to spirituality rather than religion and a high degree of idealism (Richter and Francis 1998: 39–47). Others of us (the busters) take on the quest for personal fulfilment and the concern for tolerance. But we are also pragmatic rather than idealistic, suspicious of media 'hype', are immersed in sensory experience, and are willing to 'pick and mix' our spiritualities.

Those in their twenties and thirties find themselves caught up in *changing social patterns* in different ways from those whose teenage years were spent as late as the 1950s or the 1960s. In being 'tolerant of a great diversity in lifestyles' it is often supposed that today's twenty- and thirty-somethings may be more inclined to a view that 'anything goes', at least in the world of morals. This is far from true, as most surveys of social attitudes indicate. There is even evidence that the harsh realities of limited employment, and the more pragmatic approach to life which at least 'baby busters' tend to adopt, make for more of a moral conservatism than might at first be supposed. There is also in our context a much greater attention given to the sheer *difference* between people from diverse backgrounds. Whether we are speaking of pluralism in religion, politics, ethics, or of a recognition of the implications of diversity in sex, gender and race, the stress on variety is uppermost. We are conscious that the world in which we live is very different even from Britain in the 1960s, the decade which bore the hallmarks of active reaction to stable 1950s Britain, and first fully reflected the phenomenal change which the last half of the twentieth century has witnessed. Ours is inevitably a particular location in history. None of us can step out of our contexts, nor would we want to. But we can at least examine them critically.

We are, therefore, in our time, also caught up in the *critique of individualism*. We realize that things cannot go on as they are as far as the individual's right to assert his or her freedom at the expense of others is concerned. Though this recognition instantly raises afresh the question how the limits of freedom are to be clarified, and by whom, the posing of the question is seen to be necessary.

This has political consequences. It is no accident that we write in the wake of a striking example – whatever the quips about the Labour Government being the best Conservative Government the country has had in recent years! – of *political change*. It is too early to assess the full significance of Labour's victory in the British General Election in May 1997. But it is difficult not to conclude that one aspect of the desire for political change was a resistance to a particular kind of consumerist individualism, which proceeded without attention to communal well-being.

Finally, we return to *Methodism itself*. In the midst of all these different contexts, we write about this particular Christian tradition which traces its immediate origins to a context in eighteenth-century Britain, but claims a heritage reaching back to the first Christians. As contributors we are conscious of differing degrees of 'distinctly Methodist emphases' in thought and practice. But our position in relation to Methodism (inside or outside) is the specific context out of which we write. There have been those (e.g. John Vincent) who have been critical of attempts to emphasize Methodism's distinguishing features on the contemporary scene, on the grounds that there are matters more pressing. There are equally those (e.g. Geoffrey Wainwright) who are concerned that greater attention to Methodism's heritage and abiding legacy can prove a major contribution to the future viability of historic Christianity itself, at a time of major challenge. In a small way, our book is an examination of the space between those two contrasting views. And for readers whose first language is not 'Methodist', we have included a glossary of terms.

The challenge of the book

This is not, then, an exhaustive book. It was never meant to be a comprehensive study of contemporary Christianity, even in its (limited) Methodist form. It is not a fresh contribution to Methodist theology. Nor is it an apologia for a new form of spirituality for thirty-somethings. Its purpose is much more modest. It is a book written from particular, limited perspectives, giving an impression of Methodism, with an eye on its – and Christianity's – unknown future. We cannot but be constrained by the perspectives we represent. The book will have its faults, but those faults cannot be those brought about by the fact that we are not teenagers, or not aged 50, 60 or 70. From those viewpoints, Methodism – and Christianity's future – may well look rather different. We therefore urge readers not to criticize us for our standpoint, but to consider critically what we have written, and to examine their own standpoints, and the content of their own thinking about British Christianity's future as a result. In that way, the important conversations we hope to stimulate with this book will actually have a chance of taking place.

How I laughed at the news that the Methodist Church is facing 'meltdown'. Meltdown implies overheating, a surfeit of feverish activity. But there's not been much that's hot about Methodism since the turn of the century, the eighteenth century, when people in Scunthorpe and Skegness used to fall down in ecstasy at meetings, frothing at the mouth. I don't hear much ecstasy at my local church, unless you count the faint smiles that flicker across the face of the faithful at the sight of Jammy Dodgers rather than Rich Tea biscuits at post-service coffee. And did you hear the excuses as to why young people don't go to church any more? Get this. It's because of divorce. Yes. It seems that so many young people have to pay weekend visits to the parent that they don't live with, that they just can't get to church. I suspect there are plenty more basic things that make Methodist churches unattractive: entrance halls decorated like hospitals; Sunday School rooms with dreary pictures of Jesus knocking on the door holding a Victorian gas-lamp, or Boys' Brigade shields that make you feel like you've unwittingly enrolled into a public school; insipid tea and coffee served in beryl-ware, and endless sandwiches with potted meat in them; but worst of all, those noticeboards outside with posters printed on neon paper carrying unfunny slogans that scream, 'We live in a time-warp.'[3]

We'd love to get people of our age together to share a meal, to catch up with each other. But what we don't want is a 'church meal' consisting of quiches and potted meat sandwiches.[4]

Part I

Perspectives on Methodist theology and tradition

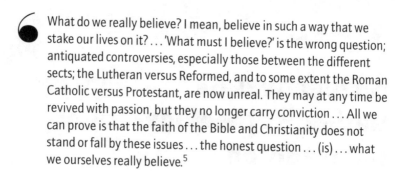

What do we really believe? I mean, believe in such a way that we stake our lives on it? . . . 'What must I believe?' is the wrong question; antiquated controversies, especially those between the different sects; the Lutheran versus Reformed, and to some extent the Roman Catholic versus Protestant, are now unreal. They may at any time be revived with passion, but they no longer carry conviction . . . All we can prove is that the faith of the Bible and Christianity does not stand or fall by these issues . . . the honest question . . . (is) . . . what we ourselves really believe.[5]

Methodists, particularly of British origin, retain from their origins an ecclesiologically significant sense of the 'provisional' character of their own existence.[6]

Chapter 1

An impoverished catholicity: theological considerations for a Methodist future

Richard Andrew

Introduction

The discussion paper 'The Making of Ministry', presented to the Methodist Conference in 1997, posed a question which lies at the heart of current concerns in British Methodism about the shape of its future: what does God require the church to be and do as it enters the twenty-first century? It is hardly surprising that such questions should be a central preoccupation at the present time. It is inevitable for a church in decline. Where once it could have relied upon the devotion and loyalty of significant numbers of the population, the present situation of British Methodism has caused many people to be anxious about whether or not it will survive in any significant form in the future. Few of us, I imagine, would be content with the prospect of becoming part of the heritage industry, repeating the patterns and conflicts of the past, like the Sealed Knot forever re-enacting the Battle of Naseby, of interest to tourists perhaps but scarcely of relevance beyond that (Bennett 1994: 355). Yet discerning a future direction is problematic. Any vision for the church is unavoidably linked to a specific place, time or tradition. The word 'Methodist' is an umbrella term. It describes a community which shares a common history but which in reality has a variety of views about the roots and norms of its common life, practice and identity. Methodism has its radicals, its traditionalists, its evangelicals, its lawyers, even its cynics, each with their own canon of saints and sinners, each converging and diverging from one another in surprising and often contradictory ways. One cannot help but wonder whether any of these diverse perspectives in isolation from one another will be sufficient by themselves adequately to prepare and nourish Methodism for the next century. The future of Methodism has become a problem for us.

In such circumstances how should Methodism think about its future?

Will the world remain its parish throughout the twenty-first century? How can its gifts and resources be placed at the disposal of the wider church and world? Is there even a role for Methodism in the future?

If such questions suggest a deep crisis of identity, their resolution must in part be determined by reflecting upon what we understand the distinctive character of Methodism to be. In other words, part of what it means to resolve the question of what God requires us to be and do involves prior reflection upon the nature of our identity as a church. Far from being a merely academic question, this concern for what is characteristic about us has enormous repercussions for the way in which we think of ourselves and of our relationships with the wider church and world. This chapter looks at one particular aspect of our ecclesial character. It suggests that this strange, fragile, sometimes beautiful thing we call Methodism has an essentially temporary character which is linked to a peculiar sense of what it means to be part of the 'catholic' church. Thus any process which seeks seriously to discern a future shape and direction for Methodism must take into account the need for a renewal of the distinctive character of our 'catholicity.'

Recovering a sense of what it means to be 'catholic'

Until comparatively recently, reflection upon the church (ecclesiology) remained one of the most undeveloped areas of Christian doctrine. This was in spite of the fact that the doctrine of the church had been used to provide theoretical justification for actual churches which had developed over many centuries, adapting to a variety of social, cultural and political contexts. Yet an understanding of ecclesiology yields insights into how the church may survive and flourish in relation to a whole range of competing and overlapping world-views. A central discussion in ecclesiology relates to the four defining 'notes' or 'marks' of the church. The church universal testifies in the Nicene Creed that it is 'one, holy, catholic, and apostolic'. These four adjectives provide boundaries for the self-understanding of the church and help to characterize what is essential to its vocation in the world. Of course, the Creed does not accord precedence to any of these characterizations nor does it define the way in which they are to be inter-related. Within this broad framework, however, it is the attribute 'catholic' that is most likely to be misunderstood. In the broadest terms it can be used to describe someone of wide sympathies. Thus we might speak of someone with 'catholic' tastes. In other contexts we might associate the word more narrowly with forms of church hierarchy or denominational allegiance with which we may or may not sympathize. For instance, we speak of those who are 'Anglo' or 'Roman' Catholic, associating the word 'catholic' with particular ways of being Christian. Indeed the Reformers were so suspicious of the word 'catholic' that they attempted to replace it in their translation of the Creeds with the word 'Christian' (Hefner 1984: 207). Yet it was not until the Reformation that the word 'catholic' came to be understood in such a specific and restricted way (Pelikan 1984: 245–6).

In fact 'catholic' is a complex word with a range of meanings. In simple terms it means 'on the whole', 'universal' or 'complete', as opposed to that which is 'partial', 'particular' and 'incomplete'. Alister McGrath indicates that the word 'catholic' went through three main stages of development (McGrath 1994: 424–5). First of all, the 'catholicity' of the church came to be closely connected with the notion of 'unity'. It described the universal church as the context which embraced individual, local churches. Each local church or specific denomination is a representative of the universal church. An individual church is not *the church* in total, even though it is fully part of the church as a whole.

In addition to this descriptive sense, the word 'catholic' came, secondly, to perform a prescriptive, and sometimes polemical, role. It described those who were deemed 'orthodox' as opposed to those regarded as heretical or schismatic and, therefore, beyond the boundaries of the church. In some Christian circles, it may be noted, the word 'catholic' is closely associated with the idea that unity in faith arises from subscription to correct formulae and, in some circumstances, has been linked to the idea of inhabiting a common culture and language (Lash 1986: 20). It is probably this view of what it means for the church to be 'catholic' that has proved most controversial in the modern period. It seems to leave little space for the '. . . complex and frequently conflictual process of remembrance, interpretation, discrimination, hope and enquiry, within which meanings and values are sought, affirmed and sustained' (Lash 1986: 21). Certainly the question of what constitutes doctrinal fidelity, and therefore 'catholic' faith in the second sense, remains a contentious issue among Christians.

Yet there is a third dimension to 'catholicity' that needs to be stressed. The idea of 'catholicity' also came to be linked to the geographical extension of the church throughout the world, a reference absent from its original meaning. In part this development in the understanding of 'catholicity' reflected the movement of the church from its initial, localized settings to its existence as a community in every part of the globe extending across a variety of cultural, linguistic and socio-political boundaries uniting Jew and Greek, slave and free. The adjective 'catholic' then has come to be intimately associated not only with the question of unity but also with the question of mission. It is this strand of 'catholicity', I shall argue, that particularly informs the Methodist sense of the term. Catholicity, unity and mission are interwoven elements of the church's self-understanding. The self-understanding of the church therefore relates to the widest possible understanding of catholicity. It entails embracing the unity of *all* humanity.

Conceived in this way, 'catholicity' states a fact about the church whilst hinting at its ultimate destination. It tells us something about what the church is, whilst at the same time intimately linking it with the attributes, 'one, holy, and apostolic'. At the same time, by raising the question of mission, it places the 'catholic' identity of the church in the closest possible proximity to the destiny of all humanity. The church universal must forever exhibit a form of *impoverished* catholicity until there is a new heaven and a new earth (Rev. 21.1–4). The church is in a state of continual becoming, renewing itself not only through its worship and domestic practices but as it engages with humanity and expresses itself through its mission. Nevertheless, in spite of its evident deficiency, 'catholicity' is the conviction that the church is universal in relation to humankind in all the different facets of its living even though it is limited by the constraints of a specific embodiment in time (Pannenberg 1972: 147).

So how are these senses of the word 'catholic' present in Methodist self-understanding? The answer in practice is that there is no single way in which the idea of 'catholicity' is understood in Methodist circles. This is hardly surprising given the plurality of our theological positions and the diverse sources of our ecclesiological history and inheritance. Nevertheless, if there are factors which mitigate against there being a single view of 'catholicity' within Methodism, there are some consistent strands that are worth noting. The sense that Methodism is a full participant in the 'catholic' church is an essential element of its self-understanding. In the Deed of Union, Methodism claims to cherish its place within the universal church and to rejoice in the inheritance of the Apostolic Faith. It holds to a mainstream 'catholic' position in the sense that it recognizes itself both to be a part of the universal church and to be historically and institutionally in basic continuity with it. The aspiration to visible unity between the various strands of the church is at least implied within this understanding, though we must be aware of what John Munsey Turner calls the 'theological imprecision' of much of the Deed of Union (1983: 338). Further, at the institutional level Methodism has evolved a structure that is both ingenious and novel in its approach. It parallels the relationship between local and universal church implied in the word 'catholic' through what it calls the 'connexional' system. Indeed in practical terms the principle of connexionalism, though understood in several different ways, has played an important part in the development and maintenance of Methodist institutional identity. The Deed of Union continues by noting that Methodism embraces the '. . . fundamental principles of the historic creeds and of the Protestant Reformation'. Thus, Methodism claims a place for the 'fundamental principles' of Christian faith in determining the character of its belief and discipline. In holding to the universal teaching of the church in this way, Methodism therefore claims continuity with the apostolic tradition, through loyalty to doctrine. Yet it does so, in line with the Reformation, by supposedly eliminating non-biblical beliefs and practices from its understanding. It is 'catholic' in a way that is simultaneously reformed. Nevertheless whilst the unity of faith plays a role which closely parallels the second use of the word 'catholic' outlined above, it does so in a fairly imprecise way. In practice confessional boundaries remain largely undefined in Methodism and open to considerable variation in understanding.

Methodism, however, has a particular kind of 'catholic sensibility'. It is a sensibility closely connected to our historical emergence as an 'enterprise of mission' within the universal church. I suggest that the idea that our identity is explicitly linked to a special sense of mission is likely to strike a deep chord of recognition in most Methodist meetings. It finds an echo in the words of the Deed of Union: 'It ever remembers that in the providence of God Methodism was raised up to spread scriptural holiness through the land by proclamation of the evangelical faith and declares its unfaltering resolve to be true to its divinely appointed mission.' *The consideration that Methodism has a special obligation or 'catholic' vocation to fulfil within, or on behalf of, rather than separately from, the universal church is one of the most urgent things we need to rediscover if we are to face the future with confidence.* The Methodist situation is a distinctive, arguably unique, one within the wider church. That Methodism exists at all as a separate church is in part an accident. Yet for as long as it remains a separate church it is constantly reminded that its identity is linked to enabling the whole church to fulfil its 'catholic' vocation in relation to the rest of humanity.

M. Douglas Meeks reminds us that we must do more than simply seek our identity from the present state of our churches if we are critically to practise the Methodist tradition today. Rather, he suggests, potentially 'dangerous memories' from our past must be allowed to surface in such a way as to challenge our present preoccupations. This may have the consequence of forcing us to change our present life situation radically. He asks simply whether one of our 'dangerous memories' is our origin as a movement within the church for its reformation and for the wider transformation of the world (Meeks 1985:16).

Is it possible that our primordial memories have something to teach us about our future direction? If so, in what direction do they point us? Certainly they provide an insight into the uneasiness which many

Methodists feel about their denominational identity. As it has moved through several configurations from past to present, Methodism has developed an ecclesiology whose purpose, in part, has been to provide justification for our status within the universal church, coupled '. . . with the denial that Methodism is a sect' (Strawson 1983: 183). The historical processes by which Methodism changed from a movement into a church are sufficiently well documented and rehearsed not to require repetition here (see e.g. Tabraham 1995). Yet it can never be forgotten, as Meeks reminds us, that the immediate context within which 'classical' Methodism developed was that of a religious society. For good or ill, Methodist identity will be forever stamped by two factors which had an enormous impact upon its subsequent history: its place within the Church of England and its sense of a special vocation within the universal church.

This point is reinforced in a perceptive article by Albert Outler which underlines this peculiar feature of Methodist ecclesial identity. Wesley, Outler points out, defined the essential identity of the church as act rather than form or institution (Outler 1964: 19). In other words, the essential features of his understanding of 'church' were missionary. Through a series of events Methodism emerged from being an eighteenth-century '. . . evangelical order in a catholic (or quasi-catholic) church' to become a low-church denomination that differed only subtly from other dissenting churches (*ibid.*: 21). Yet whatever Methodism subsequently became, '. . . its first and most decisive identification was as an enterprise of Christian mission, witness, and nurture' (*ibid.*: 14). Methodist ecclesiology cannot help but bear the imprint of our origin as a movement within a 'quasi-catholic' church. Methodism exists because of what Wesley saw to be an impoverished expression of catholicity in the national church. Its purpose was to renew the church, not to compete with it.

Methodism acquired a denominational history without intending to have one. Yet the memory of being an evangelical order in a 'catholic' church is so deeply impregnated that it cannot fail to influence the shape of Methodist self-understanding. Outler speaks of Methodism as a church 'harassed and embarrassed' by the tensions between being a church with institutions, concerned with its self-maintenance and management, and being a church concerned with proclamation, nurture and service (*ibid.*: 26). He concludes that Methodism's peculiar character is best served by operating within an understanding of catholicity in its widest sense. Only within such an environment can Methodism unfold its special vocation, since the concern with institutional self-maintenance distracts Methodism from its essential character (*ibid.*: 26–7). Methodist discomfort with our ecclesiastical existence is linked to a sense of our transitory character. Methodism was conceived as an interim project but 'the "emergency" . . . lengthened and the "emergency crew" . . . acquired the character of an establishment' (*ibid.*: 27).

Of course, Outler was thoroughly realistic about the future. Since we are now a church with institutions there can be no naïve harking back to a previous epoch which lacks the status of being authentically catholic. Rather the way forward is to a renewal of our catholicity, taking seriously the necessity of institutions but more importantly facing our obligation to be a church until there is a proper, valid alternative that more authentically represents our vocation to a fuller catholicity (*ibid.*: 27–8). In other words, those pondering the future of Methodism have a lesson to learn from our origins: the identity of Methodism is closely linked to our vocation which is directed towards enabling the universal church to discover a more authentically full 'catholicity'.

This point can be pressed further. Outler notes in his essay the distinctive way in which Wesleyan ecclesiology defines 'catholicity'. It is defined by its relationship to the universal outreach of redemption (*ibid.*: 19). *This, it seems to me, is the most important strand of the Methodist characterization of 'catholicity'.* Our 'catholic' sensibility is thoroughly informed by this sense of the universal outreach of divine love. The world is, after all, famously our parish (a point which Christopher Shannahan and Stephen Plant also take up in different ways in this book). Methodism's peculiar vocation brings the 'catholic' renewal of the church into the closest possible proximity to the needs and destiny of all humanity in its many different facets. Thus, the Methodist Church, though a particular institution limited by the constraints of a specific embodiment in time, physical location and always located within specific cultures, nevertheless understands itself to have a catholic, universal and comprehensive obligation. This obligation expresses itself most profoundly when the church engages in mission. It is essential to see that Methodism's understanding of its special vocation and mission is implicitly linked to its understanding of 'catholicity'. Though it is only one of the institutions that make up a society and numbers amongst its adherents only a minority of the world's population, the self-understanding of Methodism is intimately connected to the faithfulness that it embodies in its mission to the whole of humanity.

Renewing our 'catholic' vision

Methodism has always felt curiously inadequate about its theology. There is an apocryphal tale told of a distinguished former President of Conference studying under the famous Swiss theologian Karl Barth in Basle. On being told that his student was both a theologian and a

Methodist, the great man allegedly replied: 'Do Methodists have theologians?' It was once widely assumed that Methodism, and John Wesley especially, had contributed little to systematic theology. That view has come under close scrutiny in recent years and has undergone some revision. Nevertheless, it is probably safe to say that Methodism is better characterized as a set of emphases than as a theological system. It is possibly for that reason that Methodists sometimes choose to speak in theological shorthand:

> *All* need to be saved;
> *All* can be saved;
> *All* can know that they are saved;
> *All* can be saved to the uttermost.

The distinctiveness of Methodist theology is based on the conviction that all churches' identities, our own and others', are linked to the destiny of *all* humanity. Perhaps this Methodist shorthand ought to be interpreted in connection with our special vocation within the universal church. It has a distinctly 'catholic' sound to it, for it pushes the logic of 'catholicity' in the direction of its widest possible focus, the unity of *all* humanity. This expression of universality is inevitably linked to a sense of mission, directing the church out towards all humanity, seeking its definitive transformation.

Perhaps part of the requirement placed upon Methodism is to seek to discover where the logic of our 'catholic' vocation is taking us. The comprehensiveness that the vision of 'allness' implies has a scope that we cannot begin to imagine. It constitutes itself as a permanent task, inquiry and obligation. The logic of our theological vision needs to be pressed further. The 'catholic' vision is constituted not only by the unity of faith and the outreach of divine love; it also looks to the ultimate unity of humanity as the object of our common hope. For that reason, the renewal of our 'catholic' vision takes place as we continue to seek the humanity of God who as Creator, Redeemer and Sanctifier, is the encompassing source, goal and environment within which a 'catholic' vision of 'allness' might flourish. Ultimately, the 'catholic' question is one that is centred on Jesus Christ. As Ignatius of Antioch reminds us: 'Where Jesus Christ is, there is the catholic church.' Yet the 'catholic' vision is wider than the church as we know it. The New Testament pictures Christ as holding 'all things in unity' (Col. 1.17). This claim is staggering in its implications.

This confession is particular in that it is a claim about Jesus Christ and all the particulars of our cosmos – including us and you and me. But the confession is also catholic, universal, comprehensive, even cosmic. It speaks of Jesus Christ holding together not one thing or some things but all things – not only our liturgy . . . and our Bible . . . and Church . . . and our quest for the face of God . . . but ourselves and our world . . . It has to do with 'all things' . . . (Buckley 1992: 155)

Perhaps now is the time to take seriously how impoverished our theological vision has been. If our vision for the future is to be genuinely 'catholic', then each particular vision of the future needs to give a fuller account of what it means to trace the activities of God in Word and Spirit both in the church and in the broader dimensions of all humanity.

It is striking that the fundamental question that we return to in sensing a future direction is the question 'Who is the God of Jesus Christ?' This question invites us, however, to ask many more (more than can be examined within the scope of a single chapter). A 'catholic' vision requires us to ask, for example, how the '. . . God of the *particular* Israelite Jesus of Nazareth is the God of *all* humanity' (Buckley 1992: 16). A unified 'catholic' narrative requires a thoroughly Trinitarian vision, and this would be a further necessary line of exploration. In each and every situation we are to seek what God is doing in Word and Spirit for all humanity. This would inevitably take the form of a permanent inquiry into the humanity of God, Jesus Christ (Buckley 1992: 180). Focusing on the ways in which God is at work in Word and Spirit for all humanity allows us to identify a future which both embraces the world as it is, and encourages us to move beyond the current impoverishment of our 'catholicity'.

Conclusion

What does God require the Methodist Church to be and do as it enters the twenty-first century? My own view is that Methodism is in need of a theological renaissance that more fully appropriates the logic of our distinctive 'catholic' vision. Further, British Methodism needs to grasp the significance of its 'dangerous memories'. Methodism is an interim project directed at the reformation of the church and the definitive transformation of the world. Yet it is obliged to fulfil its vocation as a church for as long as the universal church fails to be 'catholic' in its ideal fullness. This could be an excuse for permanent separation. Yet as a form of impoverished 'catholicity', our distinctive identity could enable the wider church to achieve a fuller sense of its vocation to catholicity in relationship to all humanity. It may be that our destiny lies in a re-integration into the 'catholic' destiny of others. It could be that we remain apart even whilst we deliberately walk the same road. Yet in all cases defining a 'catholic' identity must be related to the unity of the gift of God in Word and Spirit to *all* humanity. That forms both the source and the goal from which we begin to discern the changes needed in our present embodiment. That is one way of interpreting what God wants the church to be and do as it enters the next century.

Some scholars . . . treat Wesley as a self-contradicting, confusing intellectual 'lightweight', and dismiss him with comments such as that of Ronald Knox, who said that Wesley 'is not a good advertisement for reading on horse-back'.[7]

. . . Wesley was not a contemplative man. The marks of incessant haste and urgency are everywhere in what he wrote and did. But this constant activity was everywhere informed and ordered by a clear and conscious understanding of the Christian truth, related always to the exigencies of his life and work . . . The sort of theology he approved was one in which practical consequences were appraised in the light of sound doctrine; doctrinal opinions were to be valued for their service to vital faith . . . In the name of a Christianity both Biblical and patristic, he managed to transcend the stark doctrinal disjunctions which had spilled so much ink and blood since
Augsburg and Trent. In their stead, he proceeded to develop a theological fusion of faith and good works, Scripture and tradition, revelation and reason, God's sovereignty and human freedom, universal redemption and conditional election, Christian liberty and an ordered polity, the assurance of pardon and the risks of 'falling from grace,' original sin and Christian perfection. In each of these conjunctions, as he insisted almost tediously, the initiative is with God, the response with man.

One might apply a faintly fuzzy label to this distinctive doctrinal perspective: evangelical catholicism.[8]

Chapter 2

Singing songs of freedom: Methodism as liberative *praxis*

Christopher Shannahan

Walking across the river

My personal journey of liberation began in the petrol fumes of the East India Dock Road in London's East End. I have lived in East London for most of the last sixteen years and it is this experience that has led to a revolution in my relationship with the church, its mission and traditions. Three moments have been stepping stones on my journey. These stepping stones have led to an increasingly clear conviction that the only Gospel-centred future for a twenty-first century church lies in an action-oriented theology of liberation.

Poplar Methodist Church has long been a focus for the struggle to forge a way of 'being church' which emerges from the oppression that marks so many in the East End. As a nineteen-year-old student I began to worship in Poplar and was captivated by the vision of the Minister at that time, Bryan Rippin. Here I saw a picture of a church rooted in the struggle for authentic freedom. It was in Poplar that I first began to ask serious questions about the way the Methodist Church does theology, the suburban style of its structures and the depth of its commitment to multiply-deprived areas like Tower Hamlets.

On returning to the East End in 1993 as a Methodist Minister myself, the questions that had arisen ten years earlier hit me forcefully in the face. Every day in Bow has been touched by the reality of life in one of the poorest urban areas in Europe. How does 60 per cent unemployment affect the life of the church? What is the church to make of the daily examples of racist violence and of the rise of the British National Party? How can we make sense of the mission of the church on estates where elderly folk live in Dickensian poverty just a stone's throw from the wealth of Canary Wharf?

The third stepping stone over the river has been my immersion in the struggle for racial justice. Everything changed for me in November 1990 when my wife returned from a Black Consciousness conference. It was a Damascus Road experience which has led to a revolution in our lives. The brutal realities of racist violence, the blunt instrument of derogatory language, the failure of the church to engage meaningfully with Black identity and heritage have sharpened as I have discovered an alternative history which provides the source material for a theology born of centuries of oppression and marked by a deep commitment to liberation. Such a dramatic conversion has led me to believe that urban Methodism will wither on the vine unless it begins from the text of the Black experience of oppression and the radical commitment to the broad struggle for human liberation.

Beginning where we are: forging a theology that can set us free

As I have walked reluctantly from one side of the river to the other, these stepping stones have been crucial in my slowly emerging sense of a future for the Methodist Church in Britain. It is from the base of these moments that this chapter is written. In a small way I hope that these thoughts can stimulate radical reflection and, more importantly, enable people to engage with others in the only struggle that matters: the struggle for justice.

Felix made the journey from Ghana to Britain in 1983, coming to study accountancy. Ten years later, under the pressure of Home Office enquiries and the hovering threat of deportation, Felix crumpled in body and in spirit. In 1996 however, he married a woman from the Methodist community in Bow and soon after their baby girl, Patience, was born. The family's contribution to church life was quiet but determined. Without warning a bombshell blasted Felix and Patricia apart as the then Home Secretary ordered that Felix should be deported as soon as possible. On the night before Felix's tearful departure we shared Holy Communion together. As we knelt in their small flat and the trains rattled by, the broken bread took on a whole new meaning. A broken family were fed by the broken body of Christ. For just a moment we were part of the long line of God's suffering people, stretching back through the early Methodist *Agape* into the mists of the Passover, that meal of liberation. So often domesticated, the sacrament of Holy Communion is, in its essence, a revolutionary act. As bread is broken and wine is poured out, the solidarity of Christ with those whose bodies are broken today by systems of oppression is symbolized. But, more than that, this meal is a summary of the church's calling to stand with the oppressed. In Felix's cramped flat we were upheld by the solidarity of Christ and challenged to find ways as his church boldly to forge a theology which depicts a God who still 'hears the cry of his people' and which enables us to stand with all those who are oppressed, not only sharing bread and wine but working for liberation together. This is our calling as we approach a new millennium.

If we are to hammer out a theology that can set us free, the church needs to unlearn outmoded theologies that have either emerged in situations that are alien to us, or in the rarified atmosphere of colleges and libraries with no reference point in the struggle for liberation. I am sure that we are called as a Methodist Church to plumb the depths of our heritage to forge a truly liberating theology that emerges from the experience of oppression in our cities, towns and villages.

Such Gospel-centred theology refuses to move in neat straight lines. As Juan Luis Segundo reminds us, a theology that will set us free must take our everyday experience as its point of departure (Segundo 1976: 7-8). In Methodism's search for a truly liberating theology our text is found in the harrowing experience of unemployment, amidst the sense of alienation when one's own community becomes a playground for Canary Wharf executives. We find our text in Bengali homes where petrol bombs burst into flames, among families torn apart by racist immigration legislation, and in polling stations that are swamped by BNP party officials with Rottweilers. As people of faith, our theology must be hammered out together as part of the task of discipleship. Segundo notes that our raw experience must only be the beginning of a theological spiral which leads us to analyze the situation in which we live and move. Through analysis we begin to see our experience in a fresh light and are freed to reflect on the Gospel and upon our Methodist heritage in the light of our fresh understanding. But the spiral continues to move onwards into informed action for freedom before returning again, in the light of fresh experience, to further analysis and reflection.

Gustavo Gutiérrez, the Peruvian theologian, puts it this way: 'Theology *follows*. It is the second step . . . Theology does not produce pastoral activity; rather it reflects upon it' (Gutiérrez 1974: 11).

Where are the theologians?

Like politics, theology has got rather a bad name. Mention of theology during a Sunday service can send people to sleep. Why? Because for far too long the message has gone out that theology is the business of some 'professional' religious élite preparing sermons or giving lectures. 'Theology? Well, that's for other people, not us. Anyway what's it got to do with Felix's deportation, or the pain of the family of Stephen Lawrence?'

If the Methodist Church is to be true to its roots where small class meetings hammered out theology in the light of their experience, we must rescue theology from those who peer at the Gospel through a microscope in total isolation from the experience of oppression and the broad-based struggle for justice.

During 1992 The Queen's College in Birmingham took the bold step of employing Robert Beckford as the first Tutor in Black Theology in a 'mainstream' British theological college. The appointment triggered a number of irate letters to the *Methodist Recorder*. Many of these letters were outraged at the very notion of 'Black' theology. It was suggested that theology ('talk about God') was unitary and neutral. Letter-writers suggested that theology is 'colour blind' and declared that the received theology of the church was value-free, untainted by personal experience or vested interest. James Cone is a Minister in the African Methodist Episcopal Church in New York. He is also the 'father' of contemporary Black Liberation Theology. In his writings Cone rightly insists that theology is neither value free nor 'colour blind'. Cone shakes us and reminds us that theology is a revolutionary activity. He says:

> Christian theology is language about the *liberating* character of God's presence in Jesus Christ as he calls his people into being for freedom in the world. The task of the theologian is to clarify what the Church believes and does in relation to its participation in God's liberating work in the world. (Cone 1975: 8)

Another critique of dominant theology is found in the songs of Bob Marley. The prophetic Reggae singer is one of the few widely accepted 'Third World' voices articulating a Black philosophy of liberation. Marley stands outside an identifiable Christian tradition, shaped instead by Rastafarianism. However, the church dismisses his voice at its peril. As Beckford rightly asserts, Bob Marley was a Black liberation theologian. His songs constantly draw on the Exodus motif from the Old Testament, reminding the 'slave-masters' church' of God's solidarity with the oppressed. It is also true to say that if the church is to have any credibility with urban (and particularly Black) youth it is vital to hear the voice of Bob Marley as he expresses the experience of oppression. His song *Crazy Baldheads* provides a good example of his critique (Beckford 1998: 119). Within Rastafarianism 'baldheads' were white Europeans and also Black people who had been seduced into the slave-masters' church. Marley is convinced that true liberation can only be won if

Black women and men undergo a psychological revolution, a view expressed in his hymn-like *Redemption Song* (Beckford 1998: 120).

If the church in Britain sincerely wants to ring in a new millennium singing songs of freedom we need to cast off the shackles of oppressive theology. A major contribution to our 'unlearning' has been the growing realization that theology has been used as ideological camouflage for oppression since the conversion of the Emperor Constantine in the fourth century. Ideology in this Marxist sense is the projection of particular group interests. Historically we have seen the group interests of the ruling class imposed upon the poor and depicted as 'the truth, the whole truth and nothing but the truth'. In reality this 'truth' has been an ideological stick with which to beat the dispossessed. An example of such projection was the theological undergirding of the slave trade during the seventeenth and eighteenth centuries. It is therefore necessary to put aside romantic notions of 'value-free' theology. As people of faith we all actively participate in the theological project as we reflect on the Gospel in relation to the context which shapes us. The admission that we all reflect out of our situation is not an admission of failure. Such contextual reflection is inevitable. What matters is where we are located in relation to the struggle for human liberation. As such, the following questions are of urgent significance for the British church:

• How can our theology increasingly emerge from a radical commitment to liberating *praxis*?
• How can our local church life revolve around a 'bias to the poor'?
• How can our worship begin with our experience and send us out as agents for God's freedom?
• How can courses in basic Christian education, or a Local Preachers' training course – such as *Faith & Worship*, undertaken by all British Methodist Local Preachers – equip preachers with such a radical theology?
• How can theological colleges, seminaries and courses take the mission of liberation as the departure point in the training of diaconal and presbyteral Ministers?
• How can solidarity with the oppressed and the struggle for liberation actively shape the policy and practice of the Methodist Connexional Team?

And for all good Methodists there are three points . . .

As we glance back through Methodism's family album we will find snapshots that can help us to piece together a liberation theology for the new millennium that is based around Wesley's call to 'go always, not only to those who want you, but to those who want you most' (bearing in mind that 'want' in the eighteenth century means 'need'; cited in Davies and Rupp 1965: xl). I am now going to introduce and reflect on three such snapshots in an attempt to get a flavour of the source material available to us in this exciting and frightening enterprise.

First, I shall reflect on one particular aspect of Wesley's catholic vision for the emerging Methodist movement. I shall consider, second, the Methodist understanding of the church, as expressed in particular in its emphasis on 'connexionalism'. Thirdly, I shall examine aspects of a radical, liberation-based understanding of Christ.

'The world is my parish': Wesley's catholic vision as liberation for all

It is clear that John Wesley was one of the unsung heroes in the struggle against slavery. Wesley's contemporary George Whitefield condemned cruelty to slaves, but Wesley pointed out that Whitefield 'owned' 50 slaves in Georgia. In 1774 Wesley published his *Thoughts on Slavery* in which he condemned the slave trade and called for its abolition. The last letter that Wesley wrote was a letter of encouragement to William Wilberforce in the struggle for abolition. The Methodist Church in America went still further in 1780 when it declared that all those who owned slaves or profited from the slave trade were acting 'contrary to the laws of God and man' (Davies and Rupp 1965: 65).

In the last years of our century a broad-based Christian coalition called Jubilee 2000 has emerged. The campaign calls for the year 2000 to be marked in Levitical fashion as a Year of Jubilee (Lev. 25). It forcefully suggests that the burden of unpayable debt in the Two-thirds World represents a contemporary example of slavery. Jubilee 2000 encourages those within the Methodist Church to re-visit Wesley's clear opposition to slavery and to assert God's will for the whole world to be free.

Forced, as he was, out of Anglican parish churches, John Wesley began to root himself in the wider community, among the poor and the dispossessed (such as the miners at Kingswood Colliery). As a result of this alienating experience, Wesley broadened his own vision. 'The world is my parish', he declared. In 1984 Tissa Balasuriya, the Sri Lankan theologian, re-stated the conviction that whilst our situation shapes us, we must resist the temptation to become trapped within it. Balasuriya welcomes and draws upon situation-based liberation theology, but he wants to go much further: 'Today the destinies of all peoples are closely interconnected . . . The whole planet earth must be seen as a context for theology' (Balasuriya 1984: 15).

Writing two centuries before Balasuriya called for a global theology of liberation, Wesley was prophetic in his worldwide vision. Inherent in a global theology of liberation is a high view of creation. The priestly authors of some of the early chapters of the book of Genesis proclaim that all people are made in the 'image of God'. In the eighteenth century many White plantation owners insisted that Black people had only been created to 'grow a crop'; had been marked by the 'curse of Ham'. Such racial stereotyping underwrote the centuries of slavery and undergirded it with racist theology, thus giving legitimacy to the economic reality of slavery. Whilst we may not name the 'curse of Ham' any more, churches up and down the country that depend on large numbers of Black members relegate them to subservient roles within the life of the church. When Heather Walton carried out her research for *A Tree God Planted* in 1984 she discovered a startling pattern of Black presence in numbers (42 per cent of Greater London Methodists were Black) and serious under-representation as church officers, Local Preachers, Stewards, District Synod Representatives, Divisional Officers and ordained Ministers (Walton 1985). Fourteen years later the picture is still far from rosy. In a decade when some White Methodists refuse to take communion bread from a Black Church Steward we need to hear again Charles Wesley's hymn 'For all, for all my Saviour died'. That hymn reflects an Arminian theology, the force of which is spelt out in Richard Andrew's chapter in this book.

Together with Wesley's global view, and his Arminianism, we can set three pieces of evidence of Methodism's formal theological commitment to a global theology of liberation and to the struggle for racial justice: the declaration of the 1978 Methodist Conference that 'Racism is a direct contradiction of the Gospel of Jesus', the study pack *Members of One Another* (1986) and the pack accompanying the 1996 Racial Justice Sunday material, entitled *One Race*. But such a Methodist heritage only matters if it enables us to be involved actively and reflectively in the struggle for liberation. Hymns, study guides, and reflections like this chapter are not the stuff of liberation; they are merely a reflection upon it and a stimulus to more of it. Our theology must respond to 'our-story'. Does it ?

As the music from *Eastenders* fades away, the newsreader describes that Albert Square loop in the Thames, the Isle of Dogs. It is a cold night in November 1993 and a local council by-election has been held in Millwall. The news sends a chill through the blood. Derek Beakon, a candidate for the openly racist British National Party, has been elected as councillor for the Millwall ward in Tower Hamlets. The bulletin ends and as Christmas approaches it becomes clear from the police's own figures that the incidence of racist attacks has shot through the roof. Spring 1994 brings with it a typically East End determination to re-visit the honourable tradition of opposition to fascism (echoing the battle of Cable Street with Oswald Mosley's Blackshirts in 1936). A Methodist Community Development Project, known locally as the Island Neighbourhood Project, which has been based among local people since 1980, helps to animate a 'rainbow alliance' of religious groups, community associations and Island folk from all ethnic backgrounds. Taking as its slogan: 'Celebrate the Difference', the alliance helps people to register to vote, takes folk to polling stations and protects the vulnerable from intimidation. Derek Beakon loses his seat.

This broad-based East End alliance represents just one example of an emerging cross-cultural liberation theology for Britain that reaches beyond denominational walls and into the world which Wesley saw as his 'parish'. As global travel becomes easier, as the world visits us on our TV screens, as many of us enjoy the privilege of living in cosmopolitan communities, we need to take a deep breath and dare to put behind us the parochialism which can lead to 'ethnic cleansing', to racist immigration policies and to encultured church-based racism. As Stephen Plant's chapter also argues, until we truly live out Wesley's vision of a worldwide parish, until we recognize that Methodism does not begin and end in Britain, we will never be able to forge a global theology of liberation for a new millennium.

As we consider our Methodist heritage afresh, these moments represent a 'breaking in' of God's kingdom of peace as described in Isaiah 11. Such stories provide us with the raw material for our reflection. Here is our text.

'We are one body': church and community in Methodist perspective
We turn next to Methodism's emphasis upon 'connexionalism'. Even if William Hague attempted, in July 1998, belatedly to soften the impact of Margaret Thatcher's (in)famous words, those of us who were formed in the Thatcher generation have lived with the notion that 'there is no such thing as society'. Across urban Britain we often live cheek by jowl, but inhabit isolated universes, often kept apart by iron gates and barred windows. We need to hear again John Wesley's conviction that there is no such thing as a solitary Christian.

In spite of the growth of Black-led churches (largely a response to racism in majority White denominations) and the House Church Movement, the broad sweep of the twentieth century in Christian terms has been marked by the ecumenical movement. If the centuries following the Protestant Reformation in the sixteenth century were marked by division then it is true to say that the present century has been marked by attempts to 'come together'. In such a climate it is useful for Methodists to re-consider our understanding of 'church'.

The East London Communities Organisation which is based at a Methodist church in Bow is a broad-based people's movement which brings together Methodists, Anglicans, Roman Catholics, Black-led churches, Muslims, Sikhs, Buddhists, schools and community associations. TELCO takes as its motto the phrase 'Acting together for change'. The organization strives to empower local people to develop a critical relationship with those in positions of power. This is the 'politics of the kingdom' and is based around common experience as Eastenders. The organization has worked in the area of unemployment (places of worship have been used as emergency job centres), health (working around the under-resourcing of local hospitals), parks (recognizing the significance of open spaces in an urban environment) and local politics (lobbying councillors and forging relationships with East London MPs). As we have engaged in common action emerging out of our common experience of oppression and powerlessness it has become clear that a theology for the new millennium has to be a discursive project which begins with an acknowledgement of our 'connectedness'. The strength of TELCO is found in its celebration of a diverse unity. A sense has developed that whilst we speak different languages and worship in different ways, we share a common humanity. It is this commonality that has led to shared action and has become the source material for the gradual emergence of a cross-cultural liberation theology which takes the East End of London as its reference point.

In the formal talks to come, Methodists have a lot to learn from our Anglican sisters and brothers. But we also have a lot to bring to the conversation about what the church is, and what it is for. The Methodist emphasis upon 'connexionalism' is an idea whose time has come. Linked as it is to Paul's notion of the church as a single body with many different but equal parts, 'connexionalism' can help us to step together towards Balasuriya's goal of a liberation theology that takes the whole earth as its context. The story of TELCO is one for the church to consider. The Methodist emphasis upon inter-connectedness must be read from the bottom up. Where people work together for justice, complementing one another's gifts, we can see a grass-roots ecclesiology that can be truly liberating. The emphasis upon our inter-connectedness can lift us out of the mire of theological and political parochialism. It can lift us out of our own context into a world full of diverse but complementary contexts. As Paul reminds us: 'When one member is hurt we all suffer' (1 Cor. 12.26). This means that racist violence is a matter for all

White churches as well as majority Black churches. Such commonality can be the motor for a liberated church where we are all oppressed whenever one person is oppressed and where I can only be free when all my sisters and brothers are free. This also means examining other contexts in church and society where exclusion is rife.

Jesus the Liberator

The final snapshot to consider acts as an example of how our understanding of Christian doctrine is transformed when the struggle for liberation becomes our plumb-line. Jon Sobrino's weighty book *Christology at the Crossroads* (1978) urges us to revolutionize our vision of Christ by examining our own situations of oppression and placing them alongside the Christ who lived out the archetypal theology of liberation. The debate about the person of Jesus is central to our future as a multi-ethnic church. But has the Christ who came to 'preach good news to the poor and freedom to captives' (Luke 4) become an agent of social control? In his book *Church in Black and White* (1993) John Wilkinson documents the use of the image of Jesus on Caribbean plantations to reinforce a sense of Black inferiority. As a White Christ hung above altars, Black congregations were told that Christ was 'the Word made flesh'. Goodness was located in the White Saviour and evil in darkness and in that which was Black. The early church father Gregory of Nazianzen suggested 'That which has not been assumed cannot be redeemed' (Kelly 1958: 297). To be 'assumed' as a result of the Incarnation suggests that we are drawn into the Godhead itself. Through the Incarnation we are drawn into a deeper relationship with the divine. Can Black Christians who live in a world where young men like Stephen Lawrence are murdered for being Black be 'assumed' by a White Saviour? Can such an image connect with the depths of Black identity ?

In 1933 Dietrich Bonhoeffer took up a teaching post in the University of Berlin. One of his first courses was on the subject of Christology. The key test as we reflect upon the person of Jesus, said Bonhoeffer, was: 'Who is Christ for me ?' Jesus, suggested Bonhoeffer, could only be the Christ if he is 'Christ for me': in other words if he has 'assumed' what it means to be me (Bonhoeffer 1978: 47–8).

Through an over-emphasis on the universal importance of the fourth- and fifth-century versions of Christology – Christology in its Nicene and Chalcedonian form – we have, I believe, frozen Jesus in time and space, rendering us powerless to react to contemporary experiences of oppression. The church has located Jesus in one particular culture, assuming that Graeco-Roman and White, Euro-American culture is neutral and universal. We have domesticated Christ and as a result this man who lived amongst the outcasts of Palestine has been separated from the experience of the oppressed in Britain today. As we move into a new millennium we need as Methodists to be part of the hammering out of a new Christology which finds its focus in the mission which Jesus sets for himself in Luke 4 and Matthew 12.

In his book *Radical Jesus* the Sheffield-based Methodist theologian John Vincent has begun to sketch out aspects of this new Christology. He writes:

> Jesus gave Galileans a voice. He heard their cry and made it his own. He took their stories and told them to others. He studied their folklore, their gossip, their loves and their hates and turned them into parables of the action of God himself . . . Jesus gives the inner city a voice now. (Vincent 1986: 25)

Writing out of his African–American experience James Cone articulates a radical Christology of liberation. In *God of the Oppressed* Cone asserts that an authentic Christology must forge a dialectical conversation between Scripture and contemporary experience. Cone insists that we must not fall into the trap of separating the Jesus of history from the Christ of faith. The Jesus of yesterday gives us a clue in our search for an authentic Jesus for today. Scripture makes it plain that Jesus was a Jew, part of a colonized community, which had lost a sense of its own direction and was struggling to articulate a hope that would transform life for ever (the Messianic Hope). Echoing Gregory of Nazianzen, Cone insists that 'Unless Jesus was truly like us then we have no reason to believe that our true humanity is disclosed in his person' (Cone 1975: 120).

It is Cone's conviction that *because* Jesus was a Jew we can say with confidence that Jesus *is* Black. Such a declaration will doubtless cause many to bristle, but I believe that Cone's assertion can help us to build a Christology to offer to the wider church and more importantly to the oppressed in Britain. Cone bases his Christological statement of faith on the Jewish identity of Jesus. He writes: 'He *is* Black, because He *was* Jewish' (*ibid.*: 134).

Cone reminds British Christians that to be Black in Britain is to live in a racist society where Blackness continues to be questioned. Historically the Black experience for the last five centuries has been one of oppression. Thus by insisting that Jesus *is* Black, Cone amplifies the message of the Incarnation. Christ's presence is not docetic. His solidarity with the oppressed is not theory. God is not pretending to be really present in the person of Jesus Christ. And because Christ 'assumes' the experience of oppression he necessarily 'assumes' Blackness. We can therefore say that because Jesus is Black he is also a refugee, a battered woman, an unemployed teenager. Such lessons need to be learned as the church in Britain searches for an authentic spirituality of liberation to take into the next century.

Robert Beckford has drawn on the liberation strand in Rastafarianism in his recent book *Jesus is Dread* as he strives to articulate a Christology that will emancipate Black Christians 'from mental slavery'. Beckford suggests that a source for a dynamic Christology lies in the assertion that 'Jesus is Dread'. Within Black culture 'Dread' speaks of 'mental de-colonization, freedom, power and upliftment' (Beckford 1998: 144). To speak of a Dread Christ is therefore to speak of someone who empowers Black people to engage with and overcome structures of oppression. '. . . a Dread Christ tells Black British people that the Jesus of history is with them as they protest, fight, celebrate and progress' (Beckford 1998: 146).

Such a conclusion is not the simple projection of Black Nationalism. If we take seriously Wesley's catholic vision along with Balasuriya's call for a global theology of liberation which responds to a multiplicity of contexts, the concept of a 'Dread Christ' can be used as a tool to interpret a variety of experiences of oppression. Here is a Christ who stands with the voiceless, empowering them to cry out. Here is a Christ who enables the poor to preach good news and the captives to burst their chains. Here is a Christ for the new millennium.

Facing the future with confidence

We have glanced at three snapshots from Methodism's family album. I believe that they can provide us with some of the resources to build a vibrant, reflective church which is rooted in the experience of oppression and the struggle for liberation. Always our reflection must be rooted in Methodist churches and chapels up and down the country, and in our Monday–Friday experience. If such a theology becomes uprooted it should be thrown on the bonfire of history and the search begun again.

During 1992 my wife and I lived for six months in the Caribbean. It was in Jamaica that we encountered two Methodisms. On the one hand there was an attention to hierarchy and 'proper' structures, a singing of 'In the Bleak Midwinter' even though it was ninety degrees in the shade. This Methodism was based on what the former President of the Methodist Church in the Caribbean and the Americas, William Watty, has called 'a culture of imitation' (Watty 1981: 19). Such a church has been modelled on distant British Methodism and is a contemporary example of the 'planter Christianity' of the eighteenth and nineteenth centuries.

However we also became immersed in another Methodism which was marked by a total commitment to Wesley's vision of 'scriptural holiness'. Here was a church of the ghetto, rooted in Trenchtown and Tivoli Gardens (inner-city areas in Kingston, Jamaica). Among the dispossessed urban poor, Hugh Sherlock, who died early in 1998, struggled for more than forty years to develop 'Boystown'. This project works among children and young men, rooting itself in Paulo Freire's vision of liberation-based education (Freire 1972), seeing education as a tool for liberation. Those in the Trenchtown ghetto who are hostile to the 'Babylon' that the 'baldhead' church represents treated Sherlock with warm respect. He was 'father' to the people among whom he lived.

It is against the backdrop of these two churches that we can view our own situation in Britain. Here too we can find 'two Methodisms' breathing the same air but heading in opposite directions. As we strive to build a radical liberation theology to bequeath to the wider church we must be ready to encounter road-blocks on the way. I would be deluding myself if I suggested that these reflections represent the mainstream of Methodist opinion. We are, however, at a watershed in history. I believe that there is enough evidence to show that the church in Britain faces two possible futures. We can guard what we have and rely on numbers to bolster our sense of 'success'. We can be seduced by the 'Faith in the City' ethos and set the worshipping community to one side, setting up community centres that have no recognizable connection with the depths of our faith. Or we can learn from the earliest Christian communities, from the Methodist class meetings, and from the Base Christian Communities of Latin America, and acknowledge that our calling is to be salt in society: a creative and agitating minority bringing life and freshness. Such a future depends on our willingness to engage with society as it now is and not as some would wish it to be.

The church that was raised up by God to 'spread scriptural holiness' has a future as we move into a new millennium. Our future may not be found in Central Halls heaving with worshippers. Our future must not be found in the maintenance of the Methodist Church as an institution as if that institution was the Kingdom itself. I am confident that the future of the church in Britain lies in a simple proclamation: Jesus has come to set us free, to 'break the yoke of oppression'. With this proclamation on our lips we can respond to this liberator Lord as we forge a dynamic theology of liberation that begins and ends in action for freedom. For, as the Apostle Paul reminds the Galatian church: 'Freedom is what we have: Christ has set us free! Stand then as free people and do not allow yourselves to become slaves again' (Gal. 5.1).

An agenda for action in the 'New Methodism'

Since the authentication of theologies of liberation is not found in a critic's review but in their ability to enable people of faith to reflect creatively on their action for freedom, this chapter would be inadequate without a 'recipe for action' that can be rooted in the local church.

- Think about your own community. What jobs do people do? How many people are unemployed? What is the ethnic mix of your community? What places of worship are there in your area? What kind of houses/flats do people live in? What facilities are there for young people and for pensioners? *Build up a profile of your community.*
- Encourage all those who lead worship in your Circuit/Deanery to *focus on the theme of 'Jesus the Liberator' in worship.*
- Take this a step further and *consider the practical ways in which people in your community experience Jesus as Liberator.* Find out what might prevent this sense of liberation.
- *Review your Sunday School or Junior Church material.* Does your work with children focus on the story of the Exodus, or the preaching of prophets like Amos and Isaiah, or upon Jesus' identification with 'outsiders'? If not, *think of ways to build this into your work together.* (Have a look at Anthony Reddie's *Growing into Hope* for an example of Christian education material which takes Black experience seriously.)
- *Form partnerships with other people in your community* to address local examples of injustice. Then spend time together reflecting on what you learned about each other and about your faith as a result of your shared action.
- *Set up a weekly prayer group* where you pray for your local community and for all those who are oppressed across the globe.
- Build on this and *link up with the local Amnesty International group* where you can join with other people in writing letters to prisoners of conscience and political leaders, calling for action to alleviate oppression.
- *Read the Bible together with friends* or in a fellowship group in the light of your own experience and the experience of all who are oppressed and in response to our calling to share freedom. Read the newspaper in conjunction with your reflection on Scripture.

The Methodist Church, as the founding documents at union in 1932 make quite clear, is an evangelical denomination and as such stands within that great tradition of classical Christianity.[9]

 The Methodist Church . . . stands for the best traditions of liberal, socially committed Christianity. It is a Church that encourages people to think, and to live with mystery, rather than force-feeding them with instant answers. There are plenty of people in contemporary society who are searching for meaning in their lives, suspicious of certainty, but deeply interested in the spiritual dimension. Perhaps the Methodist Church needs to be more serious about being true to its own nature, about exploring new ways of relating to people in their spiritual search, rather than giving in to the temptation to emulate churches which generally take a more conservative stance.[10]

 . . . Methodism has been and perhaps always shall be of many hues and different emphases.[11]

Chapter 3

Evangelicalism, post-evangelicalism and the future of British Methodism

Richard Woolley

'Evangelical' is a dirty word. For some it is used with great pride to declare that they are the true members of God's church; others use it to denounce, dismiss and marginalize. Some of those within and outside the boundaries of evangelicalism use it as a term of judgement. Many have laboured under its shadow. Yet, whatever its connotations, deserved or otherwise, evangelicalism has again become a major constituency within the British church in recent years.

The term 'evangelical' is used in a variety of ways, and in at least one of its uses is hard to define. The word derives from the Greek *euangelion* meaning 'good news'. All Christians are therefore 'evangelical' in the sense that all are people 'of the Gospel'. The term is also used as a synonym for 'Protestant' in some regions of the world. 'Evangelical' is used, too, to identify a group of Christians within the church who share a common outlook in theology or practice. It is this third use that is of main concern here.

For many, the label 'evangelical' carries with it overtones of anti-intellectual fundamentalism. Historically, evangelicalism has suffered from a lack of intellectual engagement and, equally, from an obsessive 'feel-goodism' that has stifled debate and creativity (McGrath 1996:11). This may be understandable, for a church that believes itself to be 'right' has little need to question, and a church that feels itself to be successful has little need to examine its *raison d'être*. Many who used to call themselves fundamentalist or conservative evangelical still hanker after the long-lost days when belief was a certainty and Christian principles were effectively carved in tablets of stone, to be adhered to unthinkingly. These were days of security, of knowing right and wrong, of being sound in theology and clear in practice.

For some, however, the charismatic renewal of the latter half of the twentieth century brought about changes to such an approach. The division which developed among those evangelicals who believed that God's Holy Spirit was working in a dynamic and refreshing way, and those who believed it was a deceptive work of the devil, caused a rift which has gradually begun to heal over the last fifteen years. But the rift established more clearly than before that there are differences amongst evangelicals. The changes which came as a result further enlarged the spectrum of theology and practice and challenged evangelicals to reconsider the fundamentals of their belief. In particular, evangelicals had to learn how to cope with diversity within their own constituency.

The nature of evangelicalism

Essentially, evangelicalism is about discovering good news. It can be characterized by a quadrilateral of priorities: '*conversionism*, the belief that lives need to be changed; *activism,* the expression of the gospel in effort; *biblicism*, a particular regard for the Bible; and . . . *crucicentrism*, a stress on the sacrifice of Christ on the cross' (Bebbington 1989: 3). This four-fold manifesto has remained constant over time, forming a permanent deposit of faith. The interpretation of these four pillars has, however, altered radically in recent times (*ibid.*: 271). Bebbington's suggestions have met with a positive response across the range of evangelical thought, and perhaps provide the clearest contemporary definition (Tidball 1994: 14). Indeed this broad formulation has been credited with contributing to a shift in understanding of and attitudes towards evangelicalism (Calver 1995: 199).

There are, however, other accounts. Stephen Mosedale suggests an alternative, yet complementary, definition of an evangelical that expresses the four traits in a more experiential manner: *a personal experience of Jesus* – which lays stress upon an ongoing and intimate relationship with God; *living under biblical authority* – which makes active Bebbington's notion of 'regard' for the Bible; *tradition in doctrine and ethics* – stressing a general belief in the unchanging nature of the church's standards as informed by Scripture; and *a belief in evangelism* – seeing this as a priority in the church's mission (Mosedale 1994: 57). This summary offers a contrast to Bebbington's in stressing a personal and developing relationship between the believer and God within evangelicalism.

Although Bebbington's quadrilateral has been widely welcomed, it is still very generalized and leaves much to be debated. Characterizing and categorizing evangelicalism rather differently, Nigel Wright suggests six strands: fundamentalist, old, new, justice and peace, charismatic and ecumenical (Wright 1996: 7). Even so,

It is important to realise that at no point in Church history has there been an agreed definition of what makes an Evangelical. No body or institution within the Protestant world has the power to make such a definition . . . (Wellings 1994: 47)

The lack of a particular definition is perhaps for the most part due to the fact that evangelicalism is constantly evolving and adapting to the developing context in which it is found (although some evangelicals would find this hard to admit). For example, there are many within the evangelical camp who think nothing of buying a Sunday newspaper, visiting the cinema or theatre, having a meal in a public house or enjoying a bottle of wine. A generation ago each would have been unacceptable to a far greater number of evangelicals. It is a fallacy to think that evangelicalism has ever been static.

Evangelical religion in Britain has changed immensely during the two and a half centuries of its existence. Its outward expressions, such as its social composition and political attitudes, have frequently been transformed. Its inward principles, embracing teaching about Christian theology and behaviour, have altered hardly less. Nothing could be further from the truth than the common image of Evangelicalism being ever the same. Yet Evangelicals themselves have often fostered the image. They have claimed that their brand of Christianity, the form once delivered to the saints, has possessed an essentially changeless content so long as it has remained faithful to its source. (Bebbington 1989: 271)

Bebbington's framework offers a broad definition that allows flexibility in practice and diversity in belief (for example in attitudes to the authority of scripture). In the present climate this is admirable and can enable more creative dialogue between sections of the church. It is a less dogmatic approach than evangelicalism has traditionally been perceived as taking. It is certainly more creative than being asked to sign a doctrinal basis in order to assent to being 'evangelical', whilst maintaining what can be called a set of core emphases. Around these core emphases, a tradition of Christianity, which can be identified as 'evangelical', takes shape. However, it is taking time for some evangelicals and many non-evangelicals (even anti-evangelicals) to accept that such creative flexibility exists within evangelicalism itself.

Traditionally evangelicals have not been good at change. Yet the current situation demands a re-evaluation of all that we do. Such an attitude is theologically consistent. Although Jesus remains the same, 'yesterday, today and for ever', this does not also apply to the operation of his church (Calver 1993: 152).

Evangelicalism in practice

Evangelicalism is about discovering good news, but some have in practice found its style and tone to be bad news. I shall argue that this is not what evangelicalism, at its best, is about. The problem with evangelicalism is that it has often operated on the margins of the church, whilst believing itself to be the centre, with all others on the fringes or beyond. Perhaps this was inevitable. Because there was no shared ecclesiastical discipline between its adherents, symbolic doctrinal tests were used to determine who was 'in' and who 'out' (Wright 1997: 109). Inevitably judgements have been made which have implied that some believers have a more valid faith than others. Such judgementalism has caused much hurt, the extent of which must not be underestimated.

From another point of view, there has been suspicion from those who perceived divided loyalties amongst evangelicals, para-church interests adversely affecting commitment to one's particular denomination. This has certainly been true within British Methodism since the Second World War, where evangelicalism's supporters have been viewed with scepticism and distrust. It is difficult to quantify the damage caused by such a perception, but the point must again not be underestimated. My assertion is that the general assumptions as to the nature of evangelicalism underlying the attitudes illustrated in these accounts bear little resemblance to evangelicalism's contemporary focus and form. Evangelicalism has, in effect, grown up.

> There is much that divides – but if we hold that oft-quoted ecumenical dictum, that we should do together all that we are not in conscience obliged to do separately, then we can undoubtedly make Christ known together. (McCulloch 1992: 86)

This can equally be the challenge to contemporary Methodism: to find an ecumenism within. Evangelicalism's concerns are central to Methodism itself. Methodist commitment to social involvement remains strong. Questions concerning how the Bible is regarded, the importance of the Cross and the need for conversion remain. Each is important within traditional Methodist doctrine and practice, even if their interpretation and status in the modern day are open to debate.

The resurgence of evangelicalism and its implications for Methodism

Evangelicalism has seen a resurgence in Britain during the latter part of the twentieth century. The Evangelical Alliance now claims a membership of around one million. Evangelical para-church organizations are at the forefront of Christian social action, with CARE (campaigning on family issues), ACET (in the field of HIV and AIDS), the Keep Sunday Special Campaign and Christmas Cracker (raising awareness of and funds for Third World projects) just some of those having received notable media coverage. TEAR Fund (the Evangelical Alliance Relief organization) is now listed among the 25 largest charities in Britain. The *From Minus to Plus* and *JIM* campaigns during the early part of the Decade of Evangelism, and the increasing popularity of the Alpha programme have further highlighted evangelistic activity within churches. It is clear that evangelicalism is a force to be reckoned with within the British church as a whole.

> Evangelicalism has become a mass movement precisely because evangelicals have been concerned to identify and promote its appeal. Its activist, immediate and somewhat individualist approach to the Christian faith has ensured that it has maintained a high presence and profile in a culture increasingly tending towards democratic individualism. (McGrath 1996: 14)

Clive Calver suggests that the growth of evangelicalism can be generally attributed to: 'Fresh styles of worship, an acceleration in church planting and a new commitment to social responsibility . . .' (Calver 1995: 199).

The English church census of 1989 revealed that more than one quarter of the 3.9 million churchgoers claimed to be evangelical. Perceived growth in evangelicalism contrasted with perceived decline in the catholic and liberal wings of the church. To some extent this mirrors a resurgence in evangelicalism within the worldwide church (Tidball 1994: 8). 'Churches Together in England' discovered that Methodist and United Reformed Churches were less likely than average to call themselves evangelical. Half the Methodist churches questioned said that they were 'middle of the road'. The average size of a Methodist church was 47, with 60 per cent being in rural areas and 56 per cent having congregations of fewer than 25 members (Finney 1992: 3–6). John Finney notes that whilst evangelical churches reported an average of 5.6 public professions of faith per year, 'middle of the road' congregations reported an average of only 2.9. From this one may conclude that Methodist congregations are less likely to see numerical growth than other Christian groupings.

Growth was particularly apparent in the charismatic and new church (or house church) sectors. These groups are characterized by an emphasis on the content of belief and on personal responsibility and accountability. It would seem that people find Christian communities that have a clear set of beliefs and goals attractive.

Methodism has many of the strengths of new churches built into its structures: the opportunity to meet in small groups to explore faith and pray; a pastoral network to ensure that no one is overlooked; a strong emphasis on lay leadership; a predominance of smaller churches situated in the heart of Britain's towns and villages. If the comment about smaller churches seems strange, it is worth recalling Gibbs' comment that: 'When a church grows beyond the single-cell structure it ceases to incorporate people spontaneously' (Gibbs 1993: 78). Megachurch, large congregations with a centralized leadership do not function as effectively as metachurch congregations – those based on small groups with a belief in shared leadership (*ibid.*: 244).

It was through these very structures that Methodism blossomed in the first place. The small group meeting was the place to be accountable for one's faith. It was a place for enquiry and an opportunity to offer prayer and encouragement. However, the advantages of such structures are not capitalized upon within chapels that have long since forgotten the reason for them, and that are 'middle of the road' in Christian belief. Methodism is a new church that has grown old. It has the potential to be revitalized, if its members form themselves into missionary cell groups and congregations, willing to serve the local community *and* witness within it. There will always be a dilemma as to whether one should be prioritized – and if so, which – and whether it is ethical to serve people in the hope that they will realize faith. However, this struggle is a part of what it means to be the church. An immediate challenge for Methodism is whether it can start again to meet actively in small groups and explore the nature of the Christian Gospel with an awareness that the quest for faith may be more important than the conclusion. The danger that a full church (or a growing church) leads to complacency (Finney 1992: 5) is not one that Methodists need yet concern themselves with. What is essential is that congregations begin to spend time working out what it means to have Christian faith in their particular context, so that they are clear what good news the church has.

A vision for evangelicalism

One of the great strengths of evangelicalism is its proactive approach to the Gospel message. It sees the church primarily as a missionary organization, a community of conviction, with good news to share with those with whom it can make contact. The stereotypes of Bible-bashing individuals and hit-and-run evangelists are, at times, well deserved. But this is the unacceptable face of evangelicalism, not what evangelicalism ought to be about. The danger is that *conviction* is confused with *certainty* (Wright 1996: 3). All Christians must assert that they see and know only in part, and receive assurance from God's Spirit. Each is on a pilgrimage, a journey of discovery. The fear that if they start to think and question for themselves they will end up as 'liberals' has all too often been engendered in the hearts of evangelicals. But it is misguided. The notion that conviction is far more important than certainty can be owned by evangelicals too. But conviction must be held with humility. Evangelicals, and indeed all Christians, cannot make absolute their own position, must renounce imposing their position on anyone and must respect the convictions of others (*ibid.*: 76). Our only certainty is knowing that there is a quest to engage in and a God to travel with.

In his survey of nominal Christianity, Eddie Gibbs found: '. . . the need for *teaching basic doctrines*, so that people know why they believe what they believe' (Gibbs 1993: 299). The danger with Methodism's self-description of being a 'middle of the road' denomination is that it appeals to few because it seems to stand for little. But people are still wooed by passion and conviction. Who wants to be a member of an organization where the members are clear neither about what they believe nor why they take part? This may seem a damning observation of Methodism, but some basic market research in a congregation is worth undertaking. How many members can begin to explain the implications of well-known parables or even give a fragmentary theological understanding of the crucifixion narratives? Christian believers do need to be helped to explore faith so that they can make informed decisions and develop their own theological perspectives. It may even be appropriate to speak of 'clear teaching' here. For some, such talk implies lengthy expository sermons and dogmatism. However this is not what is intended here. Congregations need facilitated learning, drawing upon the resources and knowledge available to them, with less emphasis upon 'preaching' and more upon a shared exploration of the Bible.

Contemporary educational emphasis upon reflection models rather than those of deposit (i.e. filling learners with the essentials of information that are to be retained) do not deny the unique place of scripture but open up possibilities for creative use of the Bible (Vincent 1992: 8).

Evangelicals may be good at drawing people into the church, but they are not always good at allowing people to 'grow up' and discover what finding faith actually means for their own personal situation. Contemporary evangelicals can be open to question matters of faith, they are aware of (and often subscribe to) contemporary approaches to biblical criticism. Evangelicals can be thinking, thoughtful people. To most 'within' this is self-evident: to many 'outside' this will be a revelation.

In the present climate evangelicals are giving themselves permission to think. Here we see a shift within evangelicalism, adding a seventh term (post-evangelicalism) to Nigel Wright's categorization of types of evangelical (Wright 1996: 7). Dave Tomlinson employs the metaphor of building with Meccano (Tomlinson 1995: 82). From the metal shapes available it is possible to create a variety of structures. Each person can create a different structure, but each is made using the same materials. It is not possible to mix Lego with Meccano. Similarly, Christians may take Scripture, tradition, reason and experience, the building materials of faith, but come to a variety of responses and interpretations. Bebbington's quadrilateral offers one starting point for establishing the construction kit. However, the kit may consist not of evangelical building blocks, but, rather, of knowledge and experience drawn from the broad spectrum of the Christian church.

The contemporary affirmation that all formulation of truth is partial and limited brings a mixture of faith and doubt, commitment and enquiry, confession and self-criticism (Tomlinson 1995: 102). This is uncomfortable; but it is not arrogant. The problem is that, on the whole, people often want to feel comfortable and secure, holding to familiar beliefs. In moments of crisis or uncertainty there is always a tendency to return to old certainties (*ibid.*: 139). People need to know that they have the permission to be uncertain, to voice and explore their doubts. Traditionally, evangelicalism has been appallingly bad at sanctioning this. The fear has been that without absolutes, a mindset that 'anything goes' will emerge. This need not be the case. The church can identify building materials without dictating assembly instructions. Openness can lead people to explore creatively, to thrive on doubts and questions within a supportive community of faith, without ultimately being governed by their insecurities.

It is plain that evangelicalism is not a single movement but rather an umbrella term for a cluster of organizations, bodies and churches with some common aims and shared practices. If the nature of evangelicalism is a coalition of believers with a shared focus then one development from this would be a coalition of the whole church, united by the search for the establishment of God's kingdom on earth: God is bigger than evangelicalism.

Plainly there is a tension here, between proclaiming an assurance of faith in Christ, and exhibiting a willingness to listen to and learn from others. There are great things happening within the church that have little or nothing to do with evangelicalism. Radical Methodists – such as those exploring the relevance of liberation theologies to contemporary living, as evidenced by Christopher Shannahan's contribution to this book – work within local communities and campaign on social issues with tremendous vigour and commitment. They have a great deal to share with the rest of the church about how to read Scripture, reflect and act upon it within local settings. Feelings of supremacy and arrogance that have traditionally characterized evangelical believers are no longer tenable. 'For everyone who thinks he has arrived at his destination has actually hardly begun, and he who continues searching is closer to his destination than he realises' (Tomlinson 1995: 62). The shared quest for an understanding of faith brings a degree of unity – within Methodism and within the wider church – that will have an impact within and upon wider communities.

Within the contemporary church the challenge is not for evangelicals to accept one another, but for all those who subscribe to the Christian faith to increase in understanding and acceptance of one another's beliefs. Those within the church who are suspicious of evangelicalism can be helped to realize that not all evangelicals conform to the stereotype, and evangelicals can be enabled to see that their party is now more diverse than it ever has been. This challenge is particularly poignant for British Methodists who need to re-examine traditions – evangelical, radical and catholic – and consider how such a 'broad church' can develop and grow.

A broad evangelical future

At the formation of 'Churches Together in England' in 1991 it was stated that:

> Every Christian has the duty and the joy of passing on to others the Good News of Jesus Christ. We are to be 'ambassadors for Christ' – sharing in his work, reflecting his likeness, and inviting others to join in the same pilgrimage ... We are called to dedicate ourselves anew to spread this word, and to prepare the way for the coming of his Kingdom of justice on earth ... But the Church itself must listen to Christ. We, too, need to hear the Gospel afresh,

be touched by its challenge and its power and continually transformed by its message. (McCulloch 1992: 9)

I have already argued that the challenge for the denominations to come together and explore what it means to be the church in the late twentieth century needs to be mirrored within Methodism itself. In ecumenical dialogue evangelicalism has something important to contribute, but not to the exclusion of other traditions.

In establishing mission partnerships with churches I often get the opportunity to meet people who have very little or no contact with the church. The question that I am asked most frequently relates to divisions within the church. The most satisfying answer that I am able to offer comes when local congregations work in partnership, sharing general aims and goals. If the mission of the church is common to all, but diverse worship and ethos is practised by respective denominations at local level, the resultant unity is a powerful witness. Where there is no co-operation the church all too easily becomes discredited and discounted. God does not exist in isolated singularity but in communion and self-sacrifice: God is Trinity, three persons, equal, indivisible and co-operative. The broad principles of evangelicalism are one way through which churches can unify and share collective goals and mission aims: committed to sharing faith, studying scripture together, acting upon belief, and focusing upon the life and work of Christ to explore how all of this relates to their community.

At times being an evangelical is confused with attendance at, for example, Spring Harvest or Easter People. It is confused with the singing of shallow, repetitive choruses, and worship that depends upon emotionalism. At its best evangelicalism draws upon the broad traditions of the church. It needs a depth of spirituality that it has sometimes lacked. At the same time its sense of the immanence and immediacy of God and its distinctive of a commitment to evangelism need to be maintained. Thus evangelicalism needs ecumenism, and ecumenism needs evangelicals.

It is clear that evangelicalism is making major contributions to church growth: this must be noted by a denomination in general decline. However, if the fruit of evangelicalism is narrow-minded, unthinking dogmatism then it will itself lead to stagnation. This will be characterized by those who find its limits stultifying; who long to think for themselves; who dare not question and who ultimately become disillusioned and leave. It is not enough to start people on a journey. People can only travel at their own speed, choosing diversions where they sense their usefulness. This is a path advocated by those searching to define post-evangelicalism. Some would argue that this is dangerous, for individuals may stray from Christian orthodoxy. But the need to explore faith in God within communities, and for such communities to learn from others is essential.

In Methodism the notion of connexionalism, as a way of describing the way communities relate to each other, is crucial. However, connexionalism may mean little in practice. Unless a Methodist member has been to Conference or served on the District Synod there is little chance of there being any useful sense of the network that exists within the church. Even then it may well be limited. And the danger exists that those who get sucked into the 'system' find their time so absorbed by committees and working parties that their ability to be activists within their own congregation and community becomes limited. *Charter 95* is a typical example of an excellent piece of work leading to challenges being brought to national church policy, with little trickle-down into local congregations. Congregations need to be active in helping identify and affirm the gifts of their members so that all may share in the work of Christ: some are teachers, others pastors, some are administrators and others evangelists. All contribute to the work of living, sharing and deepening Christian faith.

Methodism needs to grasp the fact that people are searching for something immediate, often with passion and integrity. Contemporary evangelicals have found a zeal, a passion for sharing their faith and making a difference within society, which is actually working. As McGrath says: 'there is no doubt that evangelicalism is of major importance to the future of global Christianity' (McGrath 1996: 241). Evangelicalism has an important part to play in the future of the church if this leads to the church taking a proactive role within and alongside society in evangelism and social action. These two components of the one indivisible mission of the church cannot be separated; one must not dominate the other. This is not playing with words. Evangelism is the inviting and in-gathering dimension of the total mission, whereas other actions represent the serving, self-emptying and humanizing dimensions (Bosch 1985: 82). These areas clearly come into their own when they begin to interact. Different parts of the church have strengths in different aspects of this mission work. There is a need for communication and the sharing of talents and resources so that all the church may benefit from being active in society in meeting people's needs and in witnessing to the precious quality of Christian faith.

Whilst reclaiming their title and restating their core emphases in order to make clear what they stand for at the close of the twentieth century, evangelicals would do well to acknowledge that they share a common quest with brother and sister believers in the Christian church and be prepared to join them in that quest.

> For evangelicals to regain a position of respect within society they would
> have to recover their own identity. They also need to engage in a radical re-
> interpretation of their objectives and beliefs and to emerge from the
> self-imposed ghettos and the subculture they have created for themselves.
> (Calver 1993: 144–5)

But this is not a call to return to the past. What is needed within
evangelicalism is not a simple return to old values but the ability to
build upon the past and press on into discovering what God is saying in
the present and for the future. This is not an easy task, but the nomadic
nature of Christian discipleship does not suggest a static faith.

A simplistic reading of recent statistics could conclude that the
future is evangelical. It is in this wing of the church that growth is greatest, whereas in other areas decline is apparent. However, whilst
evangelical groups may provide a catalyst for growth within the church,
they may not provide for the ongoing needs of all people. Each person
must have the freedom to explore the varieties of worship styles and
theological emphases within the church in order to find their
'spiritual home' and must be able to 'move house' if they wish to as
spiritual maturity develops. To presume that denominational affiliation
or church tradition remains static is to produce a recipe for
complacency and stagnation. Yet within the spectrum of belief that
exists, the challenge to witness to the life-changing power of God is
non-negotiable. If the church is worth joining, if it is worth remaining
in; if the Christian faith is really relevant to modern life, then it must all
be worth sharing with other people. It cannot be presumed that such
people will realize a Christian faith like ours, adopt it as we did or subscribe to identical beliefs to ourselves. But these are the exciting risks of
inviting others to experience God's presence.

Michael Riddell offers a striking call to make a fresh start in order to
allow God to work in his church, beyond the sectarian boundaries that
have developed:

> . . . the deep reinterpretation of the Christian movement necessary to this
> age has as its precondition the spiritual anguish of confessing failure. Only in
> the relinquishment of self-assurance, pride and confidence will there be
> humility to learn from the Spirit. (Riddell 1998: 172)

This challenge is worthy of consideration by all.

The future is not purely evangelical: the future involves re-education
about evangelicalism, and it involves a dynamic approach to Christian
belief. The future must involve small congregations based upon friendship and mutual support; it must involve a commitment to the Bible, to

making a difference within society, to sharing faith with others and maintaining a distinctive belief in the unique life and ministry of Jesus Christ and trying to discover exactly what it means today. This is the path being pursued by many within the church irrespective of tradition. Methodism must embrace this vision, committing itself afresh to internal dialogue and openness as well as outward ecumenism. The future is more creative and diverse than any of us have yet imagined – if only we can dare to engage in the process of moving forward together.

... Methodist ecclesiology ... has some distinctive emphases ...
first, an emphasis on 'relatedness' as essential to the concept of
'church', finding expression in 'the connexional principle'; second, an
emphasis, stemming from Methodism's societal past, on fellowship
and shared discipline, exercised through small groups, and, third,
the conviction that the Church should be structured from mission,
and able to respond pragmatically, when new needs or opportunities arise.[12]

Chapter 4

'Forgiven, loved and free . . .': the distinctive character of Methodist worship

Adrian Burdon

Can we identify a distinctive character of Methodist worship?

The ecumenical convergence of ideas concerning the expression of worship has proved so effective that the unique and distinctive character of Methodist worship is often masked. The worship of today's Methodists is, to the casual observer and frequent participant alike, often indistinguishable from that of many other mainstream Christian churches. The purpose of this chapter is to identify the distinguishing characteristics of our worship and to suggest what Methodism may contribute to contemporary Christianity's understanding of worship.

In popular opinion, one of the distinctive characteristics of Methodist worship is the use of hymns. The preface to the *Methodist Hymnbook*, published in 1933, proclaims boldly that we were 'born in song'. However, as most churches today have hymns as a vital part of worship, this can no longer be claimed as one of our distinguishing features. And as has been shown recently – despite the claims of popular Methodist triumphalism – the Wesley brothers did not invent congregational hymn-singing, however much they (Charles especially) may have contributed to its development (Watson 1997: 205).

Other people suggest that Methodism distinguishes itself by its preaching. Indeed, many of the preachers of Methodism stand out as great saints and sages, but other churches too can point to outstanding orators in their heritage. Our traditional preaching style is typical of many of the churches and religious groups that arose out of, or were revitalized by, the eighteenth-century evangelical revival. It cannot, therefore, continue to be claimed as a distinguishing feature.

Some might want to suggest that Methodist worship is distinctive in the way in which it links with, and expresses, a social ministry. Yet this is typical also of many of the churches that developed 'social consciences' in nineteenth-century England. These included Anglicans influenced by the Clapham Sect, a group of evangelically-minded members of the eighteenth-century Church of England who were great advocates of the missionary enterprise and notable for their endeavours to introduce anti-slavery legislation. The link between social ministry and worship is therefore not a distinctive feature of Methodism alone.

In the light of the suggestion that hymns, preaching and its link with social ministry do not necessarily signal Methodist worship's distinctiveness, one may be left asking whether Methodism has a unique expression, or distinctive character, at all. This chapter will assert that such an expression and character can be found in the historical formulation of Methodism and needs to be assessed in the extent to which it has remained distinctive. The results of that enquiry must then to be put to practical effect. We must begin by returning to the roots of Methodism in order to get our bearings.

The legacy of John Wesley

John Munsey Turner's *Modern Methodism in England 1932–1998* contains a clear and accessible picture of the developments of Methodist worship (Turner 1998: 47–59). However, Turner writes as a significant Methodist historian, rather than as a specialist liturgical scholar. Further thought must, therefore, be brought to bear upon his picture in order to interpret it for our purposes. Writing in a volume that commemorated the 250th anniversary of Wesley's 'Aldersgate Experience', Norman Wallwork suggested that 'John Wesley's legacy to the modern worshipping Methodist community consists of the principles that he established and the types of services that he introduced. It does not lie in the forms that he used, for . . . these have either been greatly revised, or have fallen into disuse' (Wallwork 1988: 81).

It is vital that we recognize the significance of Wallwork's statement. Two centuries of liturgical development and reform have passed since Wesley's day. He was creating a liturgical system for a religious society *within*, and not separate from, the eighteenth-century Church of England. However, we are concerned with the worship life of the contemporary body that is a church in its own right. The liturgical rites and worship forms familiar to contemporary Methodists are greatly developed from any that would be recognized by the members of the early Methodist Societies. Indeed, twentieth-century liturgical reforms have carried the worship of all churches far from the forms that would be recognized by their eighteenth-century participants.

To understand the liturgical expression of any church requires more than the study of texts and forms. Contrary to the view of an earlier generation of liturgical scholars who believed that it was in the study of the texts alone that the key to understanding patterns of worship was to be found, we must recognize that an understanding of the purpose and the passion that drives a community to worship is also required. A study of John Wesley's motivation will therefore enable an identification of the distinctive character of Methodist worship.

In the *Preface* to his first volume of published sermons he wrote:

> I am a spirit come from God and returning to God; just hovering over the great gulf, til a few moments hence I am no more seen – I drop into an unchangeable eternity! I want to know one thing, the way to heaven – how to land safe on the happy shore. (Outler 1984: 1.1-4-5)

The passion which propelled Wesley on his spiritual odyssey was the desire to know and to feel himself 'saved'. The compulsion, which drove him continuously, was to share that knowledge of salvation with all people. In other words, the motivation for Methodist worship was – and is – both soteriological and evangelistic.

Due to the later developments of liturgy and spirituality, particularly in the Anglican and Evangelical traditions, it is often forgotten that John Wesley's expression was distinctive. Even before the experience of 1738 – when he felt his heart to have been 'strangely warmed', and his religious life took on a new dimension – he swam against the tide of both popular and scholarly opinions. This was the age of reason when the heart was to be governed by the mind and the emotions were subject to the demands of rationalism. In an age when some people – e.g. Deists, Latitudinarians and Rationalists – sought to strip religion of much of its mystery, Wesley set out after the most elusive enigma of all – the 'way to heaven'. In doing so, he reflected the ideas of a previous age, and demonstrated a system of thought that owed more to the expressions of the sixteenth- and seventeenth-century Anglican divines than to the voices of his own time.

John Wesley's whole understanding of the efficacy of the worship-event was influenced by his inheritance from the traditions of the Church of England. In his standard-setting work on John Wesley and the sacraments, Ole E. Borgen has written that Anglican tradition, as expressed in the *Homilies*, the *Book of Common Prayer*, and the 39 Articles, forms the major source of Wesley's sacramental theology. (Borgen 1972: 281). It is important that we acknowledge, though, that he was adopting and developing such sources at a time when many of his contemporaries were turning away from them.

It is in John Wesley's motivation, then, that the distinctive character of Methodism and Methodist worship is to be found. That character is both soteriological and evangelistic, concerned to express the great truths of salvation and to bring men and women to an acceptance of them. A Methodism consistent with its historical origins must be concerned with aspiring to heaven, attaining holiness, finding salvation. Methodist worship is to enable the expression of such aspirations and to facilitate the encounter and exchange between heaven and earth.

This brief survey of the historical motivation and purpose of Methodism has enabled the identification of a distinctive character and expression of worship. Methodist worship was known to enable salvation at a time when many expressions of the rational age failed to recognize the practice of worship as anything more than mere human forms and customs. Methodist worship was evangelistic, reaching out and touching the lives of its participants, at a time when most churches appeared not to care for such an encounter. Methodist worship was a vital expression of a living faith at a time when the worship of the parish church was, largely, in the doldrums.

Before moving on to assess the extent to which modern Methodist worship retains its distinctive character, we must first consider briefly the relationships between worship and salvation and the matters of importance which flow from that relationship to the work of evangelism.

Does worship have the power to save?

Worship is not in itself a means of salvation. However, it is important that we do not lose sight of an important expression that was employed by John Wesley. Using the phrase found in the General Thanksgiving of the *Book of Common Prayer* (1662) – possibly formulated by Edward Reynolds (Cuming 1966) – Wesley sees worship as a 'means of grace'. In his sermon on the topic he writes of the transforming effect of participation in worship in general, and the sacraments in particular.

> By 'means of grace' I understand outward signs, words, or actions ordained of God, and appointed for this end – to be the ordinary channels whereby he might convey to men preventing, justifying, or sanctifying grace . . . I use this expression, 'means of grace', because I know none better, and because it has been generally used in the Christian church for many ages: in particular by our own church, which directs us to bless God both for the 'means of grace and hope of glory'. (in Outler 1984: 1.381)

At a time when the contrary was usually the norm, Wesley observes that by participation in worship our relationships with one another and with God will develop, faith will grow and, by the grace of God, the way to heaven shall be found. So, we can suggest that Methodist worship seeks to enable the people to appreciate the presence of their brothers and sisters, the presence of their God, and to appropriate for themselves the benefits of that encounter.

Worship, then, does not itself have power to save but is, nonetheless, in Methodist understanding, a crucial aspect of the way that salvation comes about. In fellowship with one another, we rehearse the story of our salvation, are confronted by what has already been done for us by Christ on the cross, and are challenged to respond with faith. It is in and through worship that we are transformed and saved. When writing about the nature of some of the church leaders of his day, Wesley asked, 'Do they resemble him they worship?' (Telford 1931: 3.309). He recognized worship as a transformative event, through and by which we are changed 'from glory into glory', from earthbound beings into a more vigorous reflection of the Godhead. This is the essence of our salvation that is enabled and expressed by our participation in worship.

In what way is worship an evangelistic event?

An important aspect of the worship of the first Methodist Societies was its evangelistic purpose. John Wesley is frequently associated with the suggestion that worship or, more particularly, the Lord's Supper, is a 'converting ordinance'. Rack suggests that this unusual position was in all likelihood a case of Wesley permitting the seeker after faith admission with the hope that they might become converted (Rack 1992: 405–7). Although attendance at certain Methodist functions was restricted to those able to present a valid class ticket, there was always a space found for the serious pilgrim. The qualification for admission to the Methodist Society was not the experience of having been 'saved' but the earnest desire to be so.

The notion of the converting ordinance is not found in the ideas of the earlier Anglican divines: but it is consistent with a development of thought which springs from their works. Wesley's adoption of the understanding of worship as a 'means of grace', what Lancelot Andrewes called the 'conduits of grace' (Andrewes 1841: 3.199), does have implications for the proposition of an evangelistic purpose for worship. The consideration of the evangelistic character follows on from our consideration of the link between worship and salvation. Once worship has been identified as a 'means of grace' that transmits benefits for salvation, then the implications for recognizing it as an evangelistic event become clear. In terms of evangelism, the 'frontline' acts of pastoral care, social outreach or political concern, are always likely to be the most effective. However, the initial encounter with the community of faith must be followed by the invitation to worship. It is in participation in worship, where the story of our salvation is constantly rehearsed, where is found the means of grace by which our faith grows, that the 'way to heaven' is to be found.

The expression, in worship, of the evangelistic character of Methodism carries with it a great challenge. It is the challenge to be involved in a form of worship which enables people to be met – by God and other people – in their need. It is the challenge to help to create worship which handles the ancient truths of the Gospel in ways that speak to the contemporary situation. It is the challenge to be able to identify, and distinguish, what is essential to the contemporary proclamation of God's revelation to human beings through Christianity.

For John Wesley, the search for appropriate expressions led him to consider the spiritual treasures of many traditions and ages. He adopted and adapted a variety of liturgical practices in the hope that they would lead the people called Methodists into a living relationship with one another and with God. He held ancient gems of the catholic tradition alongside more recent pearls of the evangelical and reformed traditions. In the present time when, within British Methodism, 'catholic' and 'evangelical' have come to be regarded as mutually exclusive labels, it is essential for us to recognize that John Wesley held the two in juxtaposition. To be 'catholic' and 'evangelical' in John Wesley's time was, though, to be something different from what is understood today by those terms. The so-called 'catholic revival' in nineteenth-century Anglicanism, with its associated rise in ritualism, was to lead to a general misunderstanding of the term as it applied to John Wesley. The rise of Pentecostalism, especially that originating in nineteenth century America, would cause a general shift in understanding of what it is to be 'evangelical'. Wesley was able to make use of both traditions as the means by which he, and his people, might plot the route to that heavenly shore. We must also recognize that here, too, lies a distinctive character of Methodist worship. With these traditions held together, Methodist worship can be properly evangelistic.

So much for the historical identification of a distinctive character and expression of Methodist worship. The purpose of this volume is to help the reader address the question of what future there might be for British Methodism in relation to other Christian communities, whether together or apart. This chapter is specifically charged with the identification of the character of Methodist worship and the assessment of its continued viability as a distinctive expression. So we turn to address these issues, beginning with the acknowledgement of our continued confidence in the efficacy of worship.

Participation in worship and the Christian life

Founded upon Wesley's search for a personal assurance of salvation, the system of piety promoted by Methodism is for the purpose of enabling others to share the quest. In so sharing, in participating in worship, they become aware that they are in God's presence. Participation in worship is thus a vital part of people's spiritual identity and formation. When we consider the development of piety we are struck by the recognition that, for many of us, it is at precisely the point of worship that our religious identity is formed. It is not the workings of the General Assembly, Synod, or Conference, with which we identify ourselves but, rather, what happens Sunday by Sunday when we gather to worship.

The many aspects of the life of Methodism outlined in this volume find their source, and their destination, in the God who is made known to us in Jesus Christ and with whom we meet in worship. It is worship that makes the church into the church. Without participation in worship, pastoral care can be reduced to a social service. Without a dimension of worship, a fellowship meeting can become a tea party. Without the root of worship, work for social justice can become just political activism. These activities are good in themselves, but with the added dimension of worship they are raised to a higher plane. The identity of the Christian community is established and expressed most clearly when we gather for worship. It is here that our encounter with the living God finds its early and enduring expression. It is here that our interaction with the world finds its source and continuing inspiration. The many acts of ministry that bring the church into contact with the world find their stimulation in the reflection of the people upon their encounter with the living Lord.

Whilst there are many aspects to, and expressions of, the ministry of the church, it is in worship that we undertake our unique work and fulfil our distinctive calling. Participation in worship, more easily than all else, lifts us beyond the temporal and directs us towards the eternal. Whilst the many acts of ministry demonstrate our working towards that time when all creation sings, our worship is the vision that inspires and encourages us.

Such is the expression of worship that is consistent with the development of Methodism over the past three centuries. Yet we can question whether this is now distinctive, or unique to Methodism alone. John Wesley and his followers nurtured the flame of the Spirit in an age when the rational winds of challenge and change threatened to extinguish it. In later days, though, that same Spirit has found expression in the continued calling of all God's people. Restored relationships and renewed visions have led to an increase in the acknowledgement of common expressions of faith, and a deeper sharing of our distinctive characters.

Twentieth-century developments

Later twentieth-century ecumenical, liturgical and charismatic movements have enabled developments in forms and styles of worship in all churches, including Methodism. As this chapter suggested at the start, the ecumenical convergence of ideas and expression has often masked the distinctive character of Methodism. There has been a restoration of the use of liturgical forms alongside more imaginative extempore expression. There is wider appreciation of the different elements of worship and a greater expression of balance between preaching and other aspects of worship. It is now recognized that the way to heaven may be found and expressed in the movement of drama, the contemplation of music or hymns, the reading of poetry and Scripture, the impact of stillness and silence, as well as in the appeal of preaching.

The motivation of John Wesley and subsequent Methodists has been shown to be both soteriological and evangelistic. However, we can question whether this remains a distinctive expression unique to Methodism. There has, of late, been an increase in ecumenical evangelical mission activity, such as Billy Graham's 'Mission England' in the early 1980s. The publication of the hymnbook *Mission England Praise*, later renamed *Mission Praise*, was the single most significant act of this movement. It has triggered a wider appreciation of a greater variety of music styles within the worship of all churches including Methodism. Modern Methodist worship includes music of staggering variety as ancient hymns and more recent compositions feature together. Charismatic choruses are supplemented by chants from Taizé and 'socio-political' songs of Iona. Hymns from familiar British and North American writers stand alongside examples of world church spirituality as we sing Russian Kyries, an African Sanctus, Pacific praises, or Caribbean calypso.

There has been a great change in the style of leadership and the manner of participation in worship. Worship planning groups participate in preparation; representative groups participate in the presentation of worship; music groups bring a wider variety of instruments and voices to the accompaniment of 'worship songs'. Worship has, by and large, become much less centred upon the leadership of an individual, be they lay or ordained. Our *leitourgia* has begun truly to be the work of the people. Sociological considerations have led to a greater awareness of the needs of the casual visitor or infrequent participant, recognizing the continued challenge for our worship to be evangelistic. Even if it may be right to question whether some of these developments have sometimes led to a stripping away of some of the treasures of a rich tradition, worship need not inevitably lose its sense that all who are present are participating in a mystery.

Still, though, there are voices of discontent about the nature of our worship. There are always those who, rightly, challenge the way we do things and call us to assess, constantly, our effectiveness. In 1997, as part of a larger project on Methodism in Britain, a survey was made of all Methodist Ministers. The Ministers were asked if they agreed with, disagreed with, or were uncertain about the statements given in the following table.

Statement	Agree %	Neutral %	Disagree %
Methodist worship is often dull	65	15	20
Methodist worship depends too much on the organ	68	14	18
Methodist worship would be improved by new liturgy	55	24	21
Methodist worship would be improved by more 'worship songs'	52	26	22

Source: *Methodist Recorder*, 23 July 1998

John M. Haley comments that two-thirds of Circuit ministers, who have a large responsibility for worship, admit that Methodist worship is often dull. He suggests that one reason for this may be the second statement that indicates 68 per cent of ministers believe that worship depends too much on the organ. More than half think new liturgy would make improvements. More than half would support the introduction of more new worship songs. Haley adds the suggestion that 'whatever changes are made should surely reflect participation, life and vitality. Only in this way is the dullness that many Methodist ministers feel likely to be removed' (*Methodist Recorder*, 23 July 1998: 10). We must, though, turn the comments back to their originators. If the majority of ministers recognize that Methodist worship is often dull, and also recognize the way to overcome that dullness, why does it remain dull? Leaders of modern Methodist worship have the resources to be creative. We are not bound by act of parliament to a set of liturgical forms. We are not really even bound by tradition. So why has this situation come about?

To contemporary ears, writing about Wesley's motivation in such terms as have been outlined in this chapter may sound rather quaint and antiquarian. Religious language has changed its form and many of the traditional expressions no longer evoke a response. We do not often talk of being 'in search of heaven'. Salvation is more often expressed in the language of the street, and has more temporal, social, or political aspirations. Yet whether we like the expression or not, when we are gathered for worship we are engaged in the business of heaven. Our task is that of translation and communication. When people suggest that worship no longer speaks to them, it will sometimes merely be because they have forgotten – or have not been taught – the language. When people fail to grasp the meaning of the symbolism, it is because we have failed to tell them the story, and to introduce them to the world of symbols, that enables them to see beyond the sign to the signified.

In 1995 the Methodist Association of Youth Clubs presented a document that expressed a vision for the church. That the Methodist Conference, meeting at Bristol in that year, accepted and commended the document for the greater consideration of the church, is of great significance. *Charter '95* begins with the bold recognition that today's world 'needs a Church of vision and energy. It needs a Church that is pertinent, a Church of action, a Church that inspires new hope'. The *Charter* asks for 'radical, creative and relevant worship' which 'balances the best of both old and new' and which dares to 'devise brave and varying forms and formats'. We must recognize the important statement that is buried in the midst of the challenge, that the worship 'balances the best of both old and new'. There is a tradition to be honoured, but there is also a God to be served and a world to be addressed and challenged. We have ancient truths to express, but we are a contemporary people who must strive constantly to speak in ways that enable people to hear, to understand, and to accept what we have, in Christ, to offer. Haley adds that 'although there may be new liturgy and more "worship songs", and a variety of instruments alongside the traditional forms and organ, there needs also to be a sense of continuity with the past' (*Methodist Recorder*, 23 July 1998: 10). It is, therefore, necessary that we do constantly check our bearings, look to our traditions, and seek renewed ways of expressing the essential elements of the Gospel message. Maybe then 65 per cent of our ministers will not think our worship dull!

Methodist worship, in common with the worship of many Christian churches, is developing very quickly. The 1998 Methodist Conference, meeting in Scarborough, authorized the publication of the new *Methodist Worship Book*. The most significant difference between this and previous Methodist liturgical books is the breadth of variety, and number of alternative expressions, in the rites provided for the worship of the people. Amidst such developments, though, we should not lose sight of the distinctive character of what we have to offer. Such distinguishing features include our concern for fellowship, our constant rehearsal of the whole story of salvation, and our recognition that it is our gathering in community, in the presence of God, which brings heaven and earth together. The most distinctive feature of Methodist worship, however, was, is and shall forever be our concern for salvation and the evangelistic purposes that lead us to maintain a balance, and creative tension, between catholic and evangelical expressions.

Some practical conclusions for a Methodist future

We have identified that the distinctive Methodist character and purpose, known through a study of our history, does not lie in specific forms and patterns but in our distinctive motivation. That motivation is soteriological and evangelistic. Whether or not British Methodism has a separate institutional future, our task is to clarify what these Methodist insights mean for Christian worship in practical terms. In this concluding section, I shall point to some developments which are clearly in keeping with Methodist emphases, whilst also recognizing that the present challenge to thinking about worship in the future is greater than is often realized. This conclusion is thus a challenge not just for Methodists. All churches may agree that worship should be evangelistic and concerned with the rehearsal of the story of salvation. Emphasizing Methodism's priorities simply indicates that Methodist tradition will place salvation and evangelism at the top of the list. For Methodism specifically, the challenge is to ask whether it is still worshipping God in a way which honours its own heritage.

What, then, does such an emphasis mean for Christian worship and liturgy? It is important to be clear that what is *not* being demanded is that every act of worship be a 'crusade' service, or a 'seekers' service'. We must acknowledge the value of such services, which explicitly seek to build bridges between the church community and the wider community, and which attempt to put the activities of mission and outreach into words appropriate for worship. Such events cannot, however, satisfactorily become the staple diet or standard form of Christian worship. The danger associated with such services is that they can come to be used as a substitute for evangelism rather than a support of the wider mission of the church. There are, however, even so, very imaginative and important developments in this area. The Willow Creek experiment, a Chicago initiative which attempted 'to answer the question "What would a church look like if it was designed for those who don't come, rather than for those who do come?"' (Robinson 1994: 175; also Robinson 1992), has proved a bold and successful experiment. It has been taken up in Britain to some degree. Its critics say it remains too 'church-like' (in a negative sense) despite its own best attempts not to be. Positively, though, it can at least be viewed as one present attempt to do a very Methodist thing: to look at how worship and how those who are, or feel, excluded from Christianity might nevertheless be brought together. Even if Methodism has not supplied a fund of novel forms of worship, it has sought to enable the widest possible range of people to discover forms of Christian life and spirituality which connect with their background and lifestyle. The challenge to do this is necessary for Christianity in any generation.

In the midst of finding forms of worship which blend old and new, and which 'connect' with people, Methodism would simply be avoiding its own history if it overlooked issues of social exclusion. 'Social exclusion' must be understood in the widest sense here. Are our forms of worship explicitly or implicitly exclusive, keeping out, via the language we use, those with any kind of disability, those who are racially different from 'us' (whoever the 'we' are, who write the liturgies, or lead the worship), those who are economically poor, women, those who are not middle class? Again there are examples of attempts across churches to address such matters head-on. Ten years after the report *Faith in the City*, the Church of England began to publish material which addressed the liturgical needs which followed from its findings. One of a series of supplementary works which provided leaders of worship with more material to use, *Patterns for Worship* (1995), made a particular effort to include forms which related to a wide variety of users, respecting sociological and racial difference, and relating to urban settings. It may be still too early to assess how successful the book has been. Again, though, it is an expression of what is needed in worship which sounds very familiar to Methodist ears: the 'saved people' cannot simply use other people's words all the time. There has to be a balance between the words from tradition, and the words of the saved people, or else worship cannot easily be from the heart.

There is a further dimension to Methodism's attention to this 'connectedness' between a worshipping tradition and the real life of a worshipping people. Methodism has its own history of a struggle between well-to-do and not-so-well-to-do Christians. The tale is in part told by the basic tension between Wesleyan and Primitive traditions. But there is another narrative too: Methodism carries with it into today a legacy of social inferiority – still keenly felt in many parts of Britain – over against a more established and upper-class church. Methodism is no longer simply the 'poor person's church', even where a church/chapel social divide may still be felt. But Methodism could rightly claim to have been a 'popular movement', at least with some deep roots in the working classes at some points in its history. The extent to which worship, as the central activity of Christian practice, does or does not address 'popular culture' in its widest sense, constitutes a good test of whether worship is implicitly socially exclusive. As such, it must be a Methodist concern. Hymnody is full of examples of popular tunes being taken up and having Christian words written to them. It is a practice still used to stunning effect by the Iona Community. Not only are memorable folk-tunes used or adapted, the words themselves are carefully honed to provide a thoughtful form of Christian faith for today.

Even the Iona Community, however, faces the charge of being too middle class, despite its actual work, and despite the fact that the Community was well into Celtic spirituality long before the more faddish forms of Celtic mania! This suggests that worship which is truly in keeping with Methodist roots may have to look even more radically at how popular culture can be both expressed and used in worship. And it will need to do so at a time when 'popular culture' is far from easily identifiable as the culture of the 'lower classes'. Things are even more complex now.

Methodist congregations are, for the most part, made up of faithful men and women who gather week-in and week-out despite the whims and fancies that are played out in the pulpit. These congregational gatherings, heirs of the 'class meetings' of the past, are the contexts within which the constant challenge to growth in commitment has to be made. It is perhaps not surprising that in ecumenical settings, it is the covenant service – the annual service at which Methodists re-dedicate themselves to the service of God – which is often singled out as of especial value by those of other traditions. Here is a case where Methodists have a particular contribution to make. 'Methodist' was originally a pejorative term. Perhaps we are now at a stage where people aren't asked to commit themselves enough. Perhaps we need to help people find new words, in worship, to express on a weekly basis what is stated more fully in an annual covenant service: we commit ourselves anew to God, as a saved people.

Finally, we must not let a further aspect of the Methodist legacy of hymn singing go unnoticed. Hymn singing was about enabling the widest cross-section of people, many of whom would not have been able to read, to be 'lost in wonder, love and praise', and to be incidentally informed – via the skilfully-penned words of Charles Wesley's summaries of biblical insights – as to what Christianity was actually about. A Methodist challenge to creators of contemporary Christian worship, then, must ask what features, in the present, have the same function. We may, again, have to expect our answers to be very different. Being 'lost in wonder, love and praise' may find us needing silence, in a noisy, media-saturated age, rather than the sound of music. Equally, respecting the fact that words are not everything (and are simply not easily used by some), it may mean continuing the increasing, renewed respect for the visual in worship, as not just the preserve of the Catholic or the Orthodox. Whatever avenue is found, liturgical practice in the church – in the widest sense – must enable people to grasp the immensity of the eternal, and lead them to worship.

All of these suggestions could, of course, be linked with either eucharistic or non-eucharistic forms of worship. When we look at the ecumenical scene, we are struck by the rise in importance of the Eucharist. The main Sunday worship event of the Roman Catholic Church and the Parish Communion of Anglican churches are both centred on it. Some members of other traditions, including the Methodist, wish that they too could adopt such a pattern, pointing to John Wesley's insistent advocacy of constant communion, and his suggestion of it being a 'converting ordinance', as 'proof' that such an expression is desirable within Methodism. It is, however, possible to recognize that the Eucharist is a vigorous and imperative part of the liturgical life of the church, without relegating all other forms of worship to a place in subordination to it. Methodism's freedom and variety of expression is its glory, for it brings a flexibility within which worship can be truly evangelistic.

The challenge before us is one of how to maintain a balance between the expression of the great truths of our tradition and the appropriate contemporary proclamation of those truths. Sometimes, in our worship, we fail to recognize the need for such balance. Those of us who would be labelled 'evangelical' sometimes reject the developed tradition as being 'no longer relevant', and emphasize the contemporary. Those of us who might be labelled 'catholic' sometimes reject the contemporary as being 'trite and shallow', and emphasize the traditional. In reality some traditional forms are no longer relevant and some modern ones are trite and shallow! In reality also, many traditional expressions do still have life and much contemporary worship does reflect the glory of God.

Methodism itself needs to recover its historic balance between catholic and evangelistic emphases. Salvation's story must still be proclaimed and the people still encouraged to search for the way to heaven. Worship which does not enrich the mission of the church is reduced to mere navel-gazing, and mission which does not lead people to worship is a contradiction of the Christian Gospel. The challenge before Methodism is to find the balance between the treasures of our tradition and the glories of God's continued inspiring of his people – those things which enable God's people to worship in Spirit and in truth. This means that our worship should include elements of tradition alongside the contemporary material in such a manner that enables God to be glorified. We should maintain a balance between eucharistic and non-eucharistic forms of worship. The question asked of worship should not be whether it is old-fashioned, traditional, new, or modern, but upon whether it enables salvation's story to be proclaimed, whether it enables the people to worship, whether it enables the mission of the church to be enacted.

Such is the effect of the ecumenical convergence of all churches that this chapter, on the distinctive character of Methodist worship, can conclude with a quotation from a hymn by Brian A. Wren, a minister of the United Reformed Church. It is a hymn which expresses the vital aspects of worship as here outlined. It speaks of our gathering together, with joy, to meet God and to rehearse the story of our salvation. It acknowledges that Christ is made known to us, and we are brought closer to one another, in the breaking of bread. It expresses the praise of God's people and challenges us to a closer fellowship as we return to the world to proclaim the Gospel by word and deed.

> I come with joy to meet my Lord,
> Forgiven, loved, and free,
> In awe and wonder to recall
> His life laid down for me.
>
> I come with Christians far and near,
> To find, as all are fed,
> The new community of love
> In Christ's communion bread.
>
> As Christ breaks bread and bids us share,
> Each proud division ends;
> The love that made us makes us one,
> And strangers now are friends.
>
> And thus with joy we meet our Lord;
> His presence, always near,
> Is in such friendship better known;
> We see and praise him here.
>
> Together met, together bound,
> We'll go our separate ways,
> And as his people in the world
> We'll live and speak his praise.
>
> (*Hymns and Psalms* No. 610)

There are certainly signs in Methodism of a much more imaginative approach to Holy Communion, and co-operation between the leader and the congregation in the preparation of worship is increasingly common. Moreover, by these developments, time consuming though they may be, people are being helped not only to perceive what worship is about but also to 'own' it for themselves. Such approaches, however, may be much less exciting than the exuberant styles, found in some quarters, whose exponents would claim that they are more in touch with the post-modernist taste for the immediate, the tactile, the visual and the emotional all at once. In such complex circumstances, it is important never to forget that the search for Christian perfection, which lies at the heart of the Methodist tradition, must always concentrate on promoting personal maturity.[13]

Part II

Questioning Methodism's effectiveness

. . . there are challenges to be faced and warnings to be heeded . . . First, Methodist origins invite the question whether the Church's structures help its members to grow in holiness. If the class meeting has largely gone, what has taken its place? Second, the Methodist Church, like others, faces the danger of becoming ponderous and inflexible; structures adapted to one missionary situation become perpetuated as hindrances to missionary activity in another. Third, in replacing those structures, there is the danger of being guided exclusively by the pastoral needs of settled congregations turned in on themselves . . . Methodists . . . should not feel the need resolutely to defend the structures of the Methodist Church. This is true of much, if not all, traditional Methodist terminology, including 'Circuit' and 'Connexion'. The underlying principles, however, of interdependence and relatedness, reflected in appropriate local, district, and national structures, of small-group fellowship and discipline, and of a flexibility which enables the Church to be more effectively structured for mission, will, it is hoped, be contributed by Methodism to a larger whole.[14]

Chapter 5

Supports or shackles?: Methodist structures in the twenty-first century

Andrew Hindmarsh

The Office of President of the Methodist Conference is commonly referred to as 'sitting in Mr Wesley's Chair'. It is a phrase which empha-sizes the continuity of the Office with the founder of Methodism. However, closer examination of the institution of the Presidency reveals something of an irony. The Methodist Conference was designated by John Wesley as a means of governing the emerging Methodist Church after his own death. Those early Methodists were only too aware of the extent to which Wesley had dominated his movement: it was 'an absolute monarchy of the most rigid kind' with Wesley as 'the keystone of the marvellous edifice' (Townsend *et al.* 1909: 373). (Indeed Wesley could perhaps be regarded as the original exponent of MBRA – Management by Riding Around.) The response of those early Methodists was to elect a President for just one year so that there should not be 'another king in Israel' (*ibid.*: 383). Thus, the one-year Presidency was created to ensure that no one would ever again have the same degree of power within Methodism: in other words, so that no one would ever again 'sit in Mr Wesley's Chair'.

Every organization with a long history carries with it some historical baggage. There will be structures that seemed a good idea at the time, but that no one would introduce today, and, as with the Presidency, they will be justified in terms that are sometimes at odds with the reasons for their introduction. The basic form of Methodism dates back to the eighteenth century when there were already Conferences, Circuits, Districts, Superintendents, Local Preachers, Stewards and so on. There have been changes along the way, with some arising from the merging of different branches of Methodism and others from attempts to up-date the structures to reflect more modern patterns of life (such as changes to the nature of trustees in the 1970s). However, many of the fundamental features of eighteenth-century Methodism are still with us and we must ask whether this structure is appropriate to carry forward the Methodist Church into the twenty-first century. In doing so, there may well be lessons to be learned from other organizations which have also had to grow and develop in response to a changing world.

'Nonsense,' some might say, 'fiddling with structures is a distraction from the real work of the church.' The answer to that criticism is that structures do, in fact, make a difference to the ability of organizations to carry out their 'real work', sometimes a very large difference indeed. The engagingly titled *What a Way to Run a Railroad* (Landry *et al.* 1985) documents how many co-operatives formed in the 1970s fell apart because their structures in the end proved unworkable. An example from industry is the quality assurance and lean production methods that were invented in America. These were first taken up by Japanese industry to become an important factor in that country's dominance of some manufacturing industries in the 1980s. The same structures and techniques have now been re-imported into the West, similarly transforming industry here, such that Western companies are now able to compete effectively with the Japanese.

So structures are important; they do make a difference. The right structures can support the work of the church; the wrong ones serve only as shackles.

Modern organizations

Many organizations have been changing in recent years. In the private sector, increasing competition (not least from Japan as referred to above) has forced organizations to seek the most effective structures possible. In the public sector, declining resources and an increasingly demanding public have similarly produced powerful pressure for change. Three trends have been evident:

* towards the writing of 'mission statements' – clear declarations of the purpose of the organization;
* towards delegation – pushing decisions downwards to lower levels within the organization – giving people more control over their work and so increasing their motivation and effectiveness;
* towards 'flatter' structures – fewer levels within the organization. Large hierarchies tend to stifle innovation and inhibit rapid decision-making, so middle layers have been removed.

And there has been a greater emphasis on leadership rather than management, transmitting a vision rather than operating a system.

Indeed, strong leadership, creating a shared vision and culture, may be needed to hold together the more diffuse organizations created by the first two trends.

This raises a question for Methodism: is there anything to be learned from the structures of these other organizations, in particular from the trends of recent years? Universities provide one example where a clear 'Yes' has been given (Gill and Burke 1996), and it is an example with which I am familiar from personal experience. Robin Gill and Derek Burke are a theologian and a former Vice-Chancellor of a university respectively and they cogently argue that the churches can learn from the approach of universities to the problems they have faced in recent years.

The essence of the problem for universities has been an increase in student numbers at a time of declining resources, resulting in greatly reduced funding per student (a decline of over 40 per cent since the 1970s). As a Vice-Chancellor, Derek Burke had to lead his university as it struggled to cope with the severe financial constraints. At such times of change, the accumulated wisdom of the past may be of little use – new conditions will often require new solutions. His approach, in common with many other universities facing the same problems, was strategic thinking. The university had to have a clear view of why it existed so that it could set clear priorities and then develop specific and measurable objectives. Equipped with a clear purpose, a keen sense of what was important, and measurable goals for the immediate future, the university had a chance to survive and prosper. Without these things, survival would have been at best more difficult and at worst impossible.

The problem for churches has also been one of declining resources, with the numbers of churchgoers going down and a consequent reduction in financial resources. Gill and Burke argue that the response of the well-managed universities, good strategic leadership, should also be the response of the church. The church too should have a clear view of its purpose and its priorities, and have a clear set of measurable objectives. To start the process, they suggest a Mission Statement for the church:

> The central aim of churches in modern Britain is the communal worship of God in Christ though the Spirit, teaching and moulding as many lives and structures as deeply as possible through this worship. (Gill and Burke 1996: 49)

If this Statement were accepted it would be possible to define priorities and objectives to guide the church through its present predicament. For example, placing worship as the central aim implies that other activities, such as maintaining buildings or social services, have a lower priority, and the reference to as many lives as possible implies that strategies for growth should have a high priority. This in turn provides guidance on how the declining resources of the church should be used. The role of church leaders is crucial to the success of such a strategy. They must:

> provide and foster vision – theological, moral and strategic – and enable the vision to be realised by the whole church. It would be their job as strategic leaders to think, to plan prayerfully, to coax, to consider, to help others to learn, and, above all, to identify and enhance opportunities for qualitative and quantitative growth. (*ibid.*: 86)

In particular, Gill and Burke argue that a consensus style of leadership is inappropriate – leaders must lead, not attempt to get everyone to agree. In difficult times universities and churches must be able to change, and change will always be opposed by some. If consensus is sought, obstinate minorities will be able to block that change regardless of how much it is recognized as appropriate by the rest. Churches are littered with examples of how change has been prevented by traditionalist minorities.

There are thus two components to the strategy for churches advocated by Gill and Burke: leadership and strategic thinking. Leadership is about setting a direction and inspiring others to follow, about sharing a vision. It ought to come naturally to a church – preaching, too, involves inspiring others to follow a vision. However, to be effective, leadership needs to be coupled with strategic thinking. This takes the vision and turns it into a clear and precise plan. The plan will state the broad aims of the organization (where it is going) and its objectives (what it is going to do in the next year or two to help it get there). The objectives will be phrased in such a way that it will be possible to look at each one at a set time and decide whether or not they have been achieved.

The basic argument is that universities have faced a time of severe constraints and great change and those which have prospered are the ones which have had good strategic leadership. If the churches are to survive their current time of severe constraints and great change, they should organize themselves in the same way.

Anyone at all familiar with recent management literature would not be surprised by the argument of Gill and Burke. Aspects of their argument can be criticized: for example, they take little account of the fact that churches are largely voluntary organizations when volunteers have a rather different relationship with an organization than do paid employees. Also some of their attempts to read modern management ideas in the New Testament fail to convince. There is a real discussion to be had about whether there are underlying values to management ideas and whether these are consonant with Christian values, but this is probably not to be had at the level of whether Paul behaved like a chief executive. However, the central ideas in Gill and Burke about how to run organizations are far from unusual. Strategic awareness, clear thinking and strong leadership are commonplaces in other organizations, just as the management textbooks are full of stories of organizations which failed because they did not have clear aims and objectives with strong plans for fulfilling them.

The organization of Methodism

The messages from the secular world are clear, so how does Methodism measure up against them? Much of the discussion has centred on strategic thinking and leadership and so the key areas of Methodism to consider are the Presidency and the Conference. There is also, of course, a Vice-Presidency, but this does not affect the argument presented here. The case of the Secretary of Conference, another central figure, is also interesting, not least because considerable power is often attributed to the role despite its lack of formal power. However, the nature of informal power is that it is hidden from view and so difficult to comment on without close personal knowledge. This section will also take a brief look at CPD (the Constitutional Practice and Discipline of the Methodist Church), as this impinges on some of the other features of modern organizations, such as decentralized structures. However, a more detailed consideration of the lower level structures (Districts, Circuits and local churches) is not possible within the confines of a short chapter.

Is the President of Conference a strategic leader, or any sort of leader? We have already seen that the one-year Presidency was originally designed to prevent a single individual playing a dominant role in Methodism and, more recently, the one-year Presidency has been defended on the similar grounds that 'the President is a threat to no one' (Greet 1985). This would suggest not.

The President does have some formal powers. However, the section of CPD with the heading 'President's Powers' lists only three, and none of them is really a power at all. Elsewhere in CPD, there are specific powers but these are largely cases where someone in Methodism has to take some operational decision about a matter and the President is named as the person to do so. These matters mainly relate to ministers (stationing, discipline, etc.) and the conduct of Conference. The

President may be something of a Personnel Officer, but is clearly not a Chief Executive.

Could the President, nonetheless, be a more informal leader? Even within the constraint of a single year of office, the time spent travelling round the Districts that has traditionally been the lot of a Methodist President could be an opportunity to exercise some leadership. It could be used to persuade local Methodists to support a particular position, perhaps on an issue that was due to come up at the next Conference, and thereby influence the church from the bottom up. However, another tradition associated with the Presidency is that outgoing Presidents do not comment on the business conducted at the Conference at the end of their term of office. So after a year of travelling and talking with the Methodist people, the President is barred by tradition from influencing the direction of the church.

Thus the President has few formal powers and has a limited capacity to influence opinion. It seems that he or she is more or less literally what is claimed – a President of the Conference, and certainly not a President of the Methodist Church.

The Conference over which the President presides is described in CPD as 'the governing body of the Methodist Church'. In most organizations, a body with this role would be responsible for setting the overall aims and strategy of the organization. While many matters of detail might have to come to the governing body for formal approval, these would normally be sorted out by lower level committees or structures so that little or no debate was required.

The Conference Agenda is full of relatively minor matters that require a formal decision. Many of these (70 in 1997) are Memorials from Circuit Meetings and District Synods which come directly to the Conference (with only a Memorials Committee intervening to group similar items together and suggest a possible response). This feature of Methodism requires the Conference to spend time considering these matters, often referring them elsewhere to re-emerge the following year, rather than have them dealt with by lower level structures (in 1997 about 40 per cent of Memorials were simply referred elsewhere).

On the other hand, until very recently (autumn 1998) there has been little evidence of strategic thinking about overall aims and strategy. The 1997 Conference received a strategic plan for the Connexional Team, but a plan for the Head Office is not at all the same thing as a plan for the whole organization.

Thus the Conference lacks an adequate structure for dealing with emerging business. The business from Circuits and Synods comes directly to the Conference, with much of it being sent away again to be dealt with elsewhere. And it does not appear to spend much time on strategic issues. There is some evidence that the Methodist Council is beginning to adopt a more strategic role but it is too soon, at the time of writing, to judge how effective this may be.

Many decisions of Conference result in amendments to Methodist Standing Orders and this is one of the principal means by which Conference ensures that its decisions are acted upon. The Standing Orders reach down to local church level and, despite some recent liberalization, still define in some detail how local churches must operate. For example, it is decreed that the church stewards are not merely responsible for taking collections, nor for recording the amounts received before handing them to the treasurer, but must do so in a special book 'kept for the purpose' (CPD 1997: SO 634(3)). Thus CPD provides a tight rein on the whole of Methodism (at least that is the intention). *However, it is a limited rein because CPD is primarily concerned with how things should be done, rather than what should be done; it is more concerned with procedure than with policy.*

The limited power of Conference to affect local situations was acknowledged by the Report of the Commission on the Conference to the 1997 Conference, which states: 'The Conference and the Connexional Team may seek to stimulate vision and initiative locally, and offer resources to carry through the initiatives they take and own, but such initiatives will not occur simply because the Conference has adopted a resolution' (Agenda 1997: 193). If the Conference cannot effect change within lower level structures, it is not a governing body in the usual sense of that term.

One reason for this difficulty with the implementation of Conference decisions is that lines of accountability are not very clear, if they exist at all. Circuit ministers are accountable to the Circuit Meeting in the sense that the Circuit Meeting can refuse to extend an invitation, but this is remote from day-to-day concerns. A survey of chairmen of Districts (Rowe 1987) found that the chairmen were far from clear about where their accountability lay: about half either did not know or were unsure about it. Sir Michael Checkland (1997), when he was Vice-President in 1997–98, found himself on an appointing committee for one of the co-ordinating secretaries in the Connexional Team. His question about the accountability of the secretary elicited a long silence followed by the remark that 'that was a very difficult question'. Local churches, provided they do not contravene Standing Orders, are not obviously accountable to anything or anyone. Thus, there is very little in the way of formal lines of accountability within Methodism, resulting in little or no systematic management oversight of Methodist activity to ensure that all parts of the organization are following the policies of the organization as a whole.

The conclusion of this survey of some aspects of Methodist structures is that Methodism does not conform at all closely to the style and structures suggested by the secular models. There is little leadership from the centre, the Conference does not concentrate on strategic issues, if it considers them at all, and while the Conference can control procedural matters it has little influence on the policies of local units.

At first sight, Methodism does have some of the features of a modern, decentralized and 'flat' organization. Despite the emphasis on the Connexion within Methodist tradition, it is actually radically decentralized in many ways, and the almost total absence of hierarchy means it also has a very flat structure. However, even highly decentralized organizations normally exercise some direct control, usually by defining the extent of delegation or through agreed plans of action. And very flat organizations still have some degree of hierarchy to ensure there is oversight of lower level activity.

One of the major issues facing Methodism is its possible extinction in the not too distant future as its membership dwindles towards zero. An organization with overall aims and strategy would have something, probably quite a lot, to say about this. Commercial enterprises are faced with possible extinction all the time, as they are in constant competition with other enterprises offering similar goods or services, and must adapt to a constantly changing world. Successful ones have strategies in place to ensure that they generate new products or higher standards of service or expand into new markets, and thus secure that survival. There is little evidence, however, that Methodism has a strategy to secure its survival through the next century.

Shouldn't a church be different?

That is all very well, one might argue, but a church should be different. Management ideas are altogether too ruthless, being more concerned with the bottom line than with the lives of people, and this is something that the church should stand out against. Moreover, the church should be a theological organization and would be betraying its nature if it pandered to secular thinking. To the extent that formal structures are required, these should be based on biblical and theological ideas rather than those of the latest management guru. So if Methodism does not conform to secular models, that is actually a good thing; it should not be trying to import an alien management culture. This counter-argument, to the suggestion that Methodism should learn from secular organizations, must be taken seriously.

There are two main components to the counter-argument. First, the argument suggests that it is not possible to transplant ideas and techniques which are successful in one type of organization (such as a manufacturing company) into another, different type of organization (such as a small charity). Second, it is supposed that because the church is theological, its organization should therefore be rooted in theological, rather than secular, ways of thinking.

Charles Handy tells a story of a newly installed minister who tried to use his experience as an accountant in an engineering firm to bring some efficiency to a large suburban church. The minister looked at his new church with his accountant's eye:

> There was no proper reporting system; there were no clear goals or targets; no one was really accountable for anything; it was all talk and very little performance. He saw a clear opportunity to apply his past skills and training and devise a proper organization. (Handy 1990: 98)

His response was to reorganize the church along the lines of an engineering firm. He introduced formal divisions, finance, pastoral, education and so on, each with its own budget and with a divisional officer in charge of a series of project officers. He circulated job descriptions for these officers and invited formal applications. However, things did not turn out as the new minister expected.

> To his surprise few candidates applied, and those who did so were quite unsuitable . . . More hurtful were the letters he received from many stalwarts of the congregation accusing him of assuming dictatorial powers, of arrogantly denigrating all the good work of the past. Then the churchwardens resigned. They appreciated his sincerity, they said, but this was, after all, a congregation not a business. People had a right to offer their talents in the way they wanted to. (*ibid.*: 98)

Charles Handy does not tell us whether the story is fictional or true, but either way it stands as a cautionary tale. Some account must be taken of the context or culture in which any idea or method is to be applied. However, this cannot be used as an excuse to ignore management thinking altogether. Many very different types of organization, including universities as discussed above, have found that management thinking was crucial to their survival in a difficult and changing modern world. If they have all found value in management thinking, it would be very surprising if there was nothing at all that the church could find useful. Transforming the church wholesale into a commercial company or service organization will not work, but that does not mean there are no particular ideas or techniques that, suitably adapted, can be used successfully.

Pattison (1997) adopts a rather more sceptical approach to management thinking. He argues that management can in many ways be seen as a religious activity. While there is no deity to be worshipped, management is laden with faith assumptions, symbols, and paradoxes (and even a few gurus) of a kind that are more often associated with religions. He then subjects a number of areas of management thinking to a critique that focuses on the religious and ethical aspects of the ideas involved. His conclusion is that

> One of the threats to Christian . . . identity and distinctiveness could be its uncritical acceptance of managerial theories and methods. If management is a kind of religion, with its own powerful ideologies and assumptions about the world embodied in particular techniques, it demands proper theological examination and critique before it is adopted in whole or in part. . . . It is essential, then, that those who look to management as a solution to the practical problems of churches should engage in rigorous critical examination of its theories and practices, preferably before they begin decisively to shape groups and individuals. (Pattison 1997: 165–6)

Pattison is undoubtedly correct in saying that management ideas should not be adopted uncritically by churches. However, much of his critique of management itself fails to convince. For example, his criticism of appraisal and change management consists largely of saying that these are difficult things to get right, especially if you ignore what the management theorists themselves are actually saying. This is useful practical advice but hardly fatal to the ideas themselves.

Pattison claims that 'much of modern managerial practice consists of unproven and unprovable faith assumptions about reality' (*ibid.*: 28). This seems to ignore the extensive empirical literature in many areas of management, such as in the relative effectiveness of different methods of personnel selection (interviews, psychometric tests etc.). Also, given that many of Pattison's examples of bad management come from the National Health Service it might have been useful to discuss the overall effectiveness of the introduction of management techniques to the NHS. Micklethwait and Wooldridge (1997), for example, conclude that despite all the problems, the NHS reforms have to a significant extent achieved their objectives. In other words, the management ideas that Pattison criticizes in the NHS have actually been successful in delivering what was intended. Thus while Pattison is a useful balance to the enthusiasm of Gill and Burke, his scepticism does not significantly undermine the case that management ideas can be usefully adapted by the church.

The second argument against the relevance of management thinking is that the church must be theologically and biblically based in its organization. That, of course, is quite correct, but it is another thing entirely to conclude that management thinking is altogether different and so has no role to play. Indeed, a striking feature of contemporary management thinking is the degree to which it sounds theological. The common use of the term 'mission statement' for a statement of the core aims and values of an organization is the most obvious example. *A management consultant who was called in to advise the church would almost certainly begin by telling the church to do some theology.* Any organization must start with a statement of what it is and why it exists, and for a church that must be a theological statement, literally a statement of mission.

But it goes further than that. Peter Drucker, who is often regarded as the founder of modern management studies, has for decades argued that employees are one of the most important aspects of an organization and should be treated as a resource and not a cost (see, for example, Micklethwait and Wooldridge 1997). Standard textbooks (these examples are taken from Beardwell and Holden 1994) take this to heart and commonly use phrases that would not sound out of place in a sermon, such as 'developing the . . . creative potential of human beings', 'break down traditional barriers', 'where collective aspiration is set free', and the 'empowering of the individual'. If management is identified with the idea of profit over people, it is not the fault of the textbooks.

Other areas of the subject are also starting to sound theological. Higginson (1996a) discusses a strand of thinking about leadership which talks of leaders as servants and quotes another author as saying that one of the most pressing needs of our time 'is to develop the capacity to be more at peace with ourselves; to find a still centre of inner stability and calm from which we can think and act with greater clarity and creativity' (1996b: 64). Many Christians would have little difficulty in identifying such a still centre of inner stability.

It would be going too far to argue that modern management thinking is simply Christian theology in disguise. But it does seem as if the management thinkers are converging with some strands of theology in their assessment of the nature of people and how they work together. This is one of the strongest arguments against those who claim the church is different and so is free to ignore the developments in other organizations. Churches are, in fact, not so different at all. Just below the surface, the best of the Christian tradition and the best of modern management thinking have some remarkable similarities. As the church faces up to its possible extinction in the twenty-first century, it would be foolish to ignore the lessons of those organizations whose future currently looks rather more secure.

What can be done?

This discussion of Methodist structures has highlighted a number of areas where Methodism may have something to learn from other organizations, among which the most significant were strategic thinking, leadership, and accountability and management oversight. *Before suggesting some changes to Methodist structures, it should be noted that the structures themselves are simply a tool for the effective running of an organization; they do not determine the policies of the organization.* The same structures could be used to pursue a wide range of aims and objectives and, in the context of a church, with a variety of theological standpoints. Indeed Rob Frost (1997), who comes from a very different tradition from myself, has made some similar suggestions about the reform of Methodist structures. So here are three suggestions for the reform of Methodism. These are not the only implications of the argument of this chapter but are sufficient to start the process of transformation.

1. Give the Methodist Council explicit responsibility for strategic thinking
Strategic thinking at the connexional level is straightforward: the Methodist Council is the obvious body to have responsibility for this, not least because it seems to be moving in that direction anyway. A body the size of Conference is too large for such a role. However, strategic thinking is also necessary at all levels within an organization. There are obvious locations here as well – appropriate District or Circuit Committees and Church Councils – but there is not always a structure whereby the thinking can be converted into action. Districts cannot, for example, decide to redistribute ministerial resources between Circuits, however compelling the strategic reasoning. Strategic thinking would almost certainly need other structural changes for it to be effective.

2. Appoint a President of the Methodist Church
As for leadership, it seems that a President of Conference cannot be a leader for Methodism, though a President of the Methodist Church could be. Sir Michael Checkland (1997) suggests the Secretary of Conference could also have a stronger role as a Secretary-General of the Methodist Church, which together with a longer-term Presidency would create a much more effective connexional leadership. Some thought would need to be given to the balance of ordained and lay authority as both the President and Secretary currently must be ordained. Several lay Vice-Presidents who chaired major committees of the Methodist Council and stood in for the President when this was necessary might be one approach.

As with strategic thinking, leadership is not just for the centre of an organization: any person in a position of authority could (probably should) have a leadership role. District chairmen and Superintendents are obvious candidates for acting as more local leaders, though District chairmen currently have very little authority over what happens in their District. Again, careful consideration would have to be given to the balance of lay and ordained authority
.

3. Introduce a structure of management and accountability
If decisions are to be implemented effectively, there needs to be some structure of accountability and management oversight. This is not a straightforward matter for a largely voluntary organization, as Charles Handy's cautionary tale illustrated. However, the difficulties in implementing such a structure for the paid employees of the church – the connexional staff, ministers, lay workers, etc. – are considerably less. For example, a Superintendent could have formal responsibility for managing the staff in a Circuit. This responsibility currently lies, at least implicitly, with the Circuit Meeting, but committees, let alone large ones like a typical Circuit Meeting, are notoriously ineffective at day-to-day management.

Some might say that these suggestions look like a return to the domination of Methodism by a Wesley. However, this would be to mis-read the nature of strategic management. Wesley probably was a strategic leader in that he had a vision of the future, took action to move towards it and inspired others to join him. However, he was also an interfering manager in the derogatory sense. Wesley rode around the country making sure that the early Methodists did his bidding in every matter of detail. Good strategic leaders let others implement their strategy in detail; Wesley certainly did not. *In some ways, it is Circuit Superintendents, with their power over almost every detail of Circuit activity, who are in a constitutional position to be the modern Wesleys.* Whether they are or not, of course, is up to them.

And what would happen to Methodism?

It could be argued that, instead of suggesting changes to Methodism, we should be considering structures in a much more ecumenical context. Other churches are also examining their structures, such as the Church of England through its Turnbull Report, and perhaps these should be more ecumenical discussions. However, we can only start from where we are and that is with an institutionally separate Methodist Church. Given that the church in Britain is divided and the Methodist

Church does exist, reconceiving its structure is not a pointless task but an attempt to maximize its effectiveness. In theological terms, it is flawed human beings in a flawed structure seeking to handle responsibly the God-given time and talents of its employees and members.

So if the ideas for action in this chapter were put into effect, what would happen to Methodism? It would undoubtedly have a changed character. Strategic thinking would help it to become an organization with a clearer idea of why it existed and what it wished to achieve. This might give Methodism rational reasons for continuing as a separate organization. It would also help it to deploy its resources in appropriate ways that contributed to its clearer role.

A stronger leader would help Methodism to change in response to a changing world and provide a visible national focus. Of course change always brings controversy and so there would be a strong argument for widening the franchise for the election of the President to ensure a greater degree of popular support.

A stronger system of management and accountability would enable resources to be deployed more effectively (it would be someone's responsibility to ensure that happened and they would have the authority to do so) and would ensure that decisions made by the church were actually acted upon. It should see the end of Reports to Conference which point out that even Conference cannot change the church.

Finally, the successful implementation of these changes, while not being easy (significant change never is) would please at least one group of people: those (some of whom are in their twenties and thirties) who spend their weekdays in more tightly organized secular organizations and who find their evenings at church meetings increasingly frustrating.

I am a member of a minority group, I am a Methodist male in his 30s. I used to be a willing member of the Church Council, Circuit Meeting and District Synod and went three times to the Methodist Conference. Now I only go to Synod. Whilst the pressures of having a young family are part of the answer, the plain truth is I am disillusioned with the business, style and sheer waste of meetings within the Methodist Church.

Professionally, I am trained as an Electrical Engineer. I work in the Information Services Department of a major engineering company. I am responsible for a number of our outsource contracts and manage budgets for contracts and projects of around £10m p.a. As with many people of my age and position I end up working between 50 and 60 hours each week under constant pressure to deliver more for less. Given this background, the last thing I want to do at the end of a day of meetings is to spend a further two-and-a-half hours in a meeting where the majority of the agenda items should be delegated to one or two individuals to conclude and execute, reporting back as appropriate, leaving time for the important things such as initiating new work and stopping work that is no longer required. In my experience, these are the kinds of discussion that the average Church Council finds it so hard to engage in. They are also the point, it seems to me, when matters of faith and theology are so important: providing guidance on how to prioritize such tasks.

Furthermore, the majority of Church members have no idea of the kind of things I do in my professional life, the decisions I make (decisions that often affect people's jobs and lives) or the pressures of a modern business. The fact that we all know something about education or the health service is frustrating to those who work in it. Such people are fed up of everyone being an expert on what they do and how they should do it.

Faith, calling and conviction often appear to have as little to do with the activities of the Church as the understanding that many church members have of how they apply to the modern world of work. A professional male thirty-something is not the person to be in the average Methodist (or any other) church.[15]

Chapter 6

On leaving the church

Beverley Clack

Introduction

On 14 November 1971 the radical feminist Mary Daly staged a dramatic 'exodus' from patriarchal religion. As the first woman to preach in the 336-year history of the Harvard Memorial Church, she used the occasion to ask the congregation to reject the sexist language, forms and history of Christianity, and to follow her example in walking out of the church. Contrary to her fears that she would make such a gesture alone, what followed has become part of feminist history: 'hundreds of women and some men began stampeding out of the church the moment I finished' (Daly 1993: 138). My own 'exodus' from the church has been somewhat less dramatic. While Daly's rejection of Christianity suggests a dramatic break with the tradition, my own experience has been characterized by a gradual distancing from the Christian church. In this chapter, I will explore the factors which led to the belief that, if I were to maintain my integrity, I would have to make my own exit from Christianity.[1]

At the outset, it might be helpful to say something about the position I held prior to this 'conversion' out of Christianity. As a teenager, I was a communion steward at my local Methodist church. My social life revolved around church youth activities. Later I was a member, briefly, of the Methodist Church's Faith and Order Committee. Theologically, my Christianity was defined by the insights of liberal theology, which I was first introduced to during sixth-form studies. The significance of this introduction should not be overplayed: not all liberal theology leads to non-belief; a questioning approach to religious belief does not mark the beginning of the road to agnosticism or atheism. For myself, however, that path of questioning has led, gradually, to a sense that my deepest values do not sit easily with Christian doctrine.

As a sixth-former, exposure to the ideas of Rudolf Bultmann and his attempt to reframe Christianity in the language of existentialism led to a fundamental rethinking of key Christian doctrines. According to Bultmann, the first-century world-view which shaped the story of Christ was no longer relevant for twentieth-century human beings, and had to be reinterpreted in line with the scientific age (Bultmann 1960). Thus, the ideas of 'crucifixion' and 'resurrection' had to be defined in relation to the individual's own lived experience. The cross was of little relevance unless I saw my old, materialistic and inauthentic self crucified there with Christ. Likewise the resurrection was not, to use David Jenkins's much-misunderstood phrase, 'a juggling trick with bones'. Rather, it is an event which symbolizes the need to rise to the new self with Christ every day. As an undergraduate, the ideas of Paul Tillich did much to further this sense of the importance of the lived experience of faith. His collection of sermons, *The Shaking of the Foundations* (1962), which still have the power to challenge after thirty-odd years, highlighted the importance of recognizing and communing with the 'depth experiences' of human existence. 'Who am I?' 'Why am I here?' 'What meaning can be found in my life?' These were the questions which Tillich asked and with which it seems all people – Christian and non-Christian – must grapple.

If Tillich's thought described the reality of God in strangely abstract terms (God is the 'Ground of All Being', 'Being-Itself', one's 'Ultimate Concern'), a rather different account of God is offered in the work of Don Cupitt, which I first encountered as an undergraduate. For Tillich, God is that which supports and sustains us, that which underpins human existence. As such, for Tillich and Bultmann, God is an objective reality. Cupitt's thought suggests a radically different understanding of the meaning of 'God'. Rather than think in terms of external spiritual powers, Cupitt emphasizes the internal spiritual life. For Cupitt, God is a symbol for the religious life (Cupitt 1980). Thus, when we use God-language, we are attempting to express the depth and importance that the religious or spiritual life has for us. The differences between the kind of theologies offered by Bultmann and Tillich and that offered by Cupitt must, therefore, be acknowledged, for it would be wrong to suggest that all liberal theology must end with the concept of God espoused by Cupitt. But for me a common thread runs through the work of these disparate thinkers. For all three, personal experience forms the bedrock for faith. Likewise, doctrines are to be interpreted in line with current religious *and* scientific thinking, which means that religious belief must reflect the concerns of the contemporary world.

While still accepting the validity of the emphasis on personal experience, a certain unease has arisen regarding the extent to which the reinterpretation of Christian doctrines is possible, or indeed helpful. When I became a full-time lecturer and started to write my own theology, the need to constantly explain and justify my world-view as 'Christian' became tiring, and somewhat futile. I was frequently asked how my theology reflected basic Christian beliefs. This led me to ask myself at what point a religious position ceases to be 'Christian'. Is there a core body of truth-claims to which one must ascribe in order to be a member of the church? Such questions have become more pressing in recent years, forcing me to reappraise the extent to which my understanding and experience of the relationship between divinity and humanity, God and the world, can be – or, indeed, *should* be – defined by Christian terminology.

God and the world

In 1996, I left London to live in Oxford. The move from city to the country has been highly significant. A reconnection with the cycles of the seasons has happened in a way which was not possible during ten years in the city. The sheer beauty of the physical world, and the change revealed by the seasons, once commonplace and ignored, is now awe-inspiring. Alongside this appreciation of the cyclical nature of the world and human existence has come a growing awareness of *the world itself as sacred*. By using that phrase, I do not intend to convey the 'God's in his heaven, all's well with the world' pantheism of the nature poets. The sense of the world as sacred, which I now have, owes more to the poetry of William Blake than to that of William Wordsworth. For Wordsworth, only the beauty and order of the natural world is considered. So, in some words from one of his poems:

> . . . I have felt
> A presence that disturbs me with the joy
> Of elevated thoughts; a sense sublime
> Of something far more deeply interfused,
> Whose dwelling is the light of setting sun,
> And the round ocean and the living air,
> And the blue sky, and in the mind of man:
> A motion and a spirit, that impels
> All thinking things, all objects of all thought,
> And rolls through all things.

Wordsworth looks at the beauty and regularity of the physical world, moving beyond these elements to a cosmic mind at the centre of the universe. Blake, by way of contrast, considers both the chaos *and* order, ugliness *and* beauty, of the physical world:

> Tyger! Tyger! burning bright
> In the forests of the night,
> What immortal hand or eye
> Could frame thy fearful symmetry?
>
> When the stars threw down their spears,
> And water'd heaven with their tears,
> Did he smile his work to see?
> Did he who made the Lamb make thee?

In seeing the world as sacred, the reality of both ugliness and beauty, chaos and harmony, has to be accepted. Without such an acceptance, one falls into a sloppy sentimentality which has little to do with the physical reality of the universe. Alongside this appreciation and experience of the nature of the physical world has come a growing sense that the transcendent God of Christianity is at odds with that fundamental sense of the world as sacred. For a time, the idea of the incarnation tempered my unease with what I perceived to be the disjuncture between my felt experience and the formal Christian structure of my beliefs. The incarnation can be interpreted as the most open recognition that divinity and humanity, sacred and profane, are not polar opposites; rather the divine can be located in the human, and thus in the physical (Cupitt 1988: 19). Yet even this interpretation relies upon a story which suggests that the world has to be divinized by an act of God. In order for the world to be sanctified, God must *enter into* the creation; and that still seems at odds with my sense of the world as *inherently* sacred. No external criterion or judge is needed to establish this understanding of the world.

A recent trip to the cinema further exemplified this tension. The film *Contact* opens with a stunning sequence. Starting from the sun, the camera pulls back, taking the viewer through the solar system and out into the galaxy, until eventually one is left looking at the swirl of the galaxy itself. The sense of the smallness of self in the immensity of the physical universe is far from depressing; the sheer beauty of the cosmos suggests that the world/universe in itself is enough. I do not need to believe in an external creator in order to appreciate the wonder and power of that vision of the physical cosmos.

If Christian doctrine does not fit easily with such an understanding of the world, the image of 'the Goddess' suggests a rather different model for divinity. For some time I have been interested in the myths concerning this female image of the divine (see e.g. Long 1992). The very notion that divinity could be described in female terms is likely to horrify some, and suggests something of the fear of female powers prevalent in our male-dominated society. Merely to entertain the idea of 'the Goddess' is, for many, likely to raise fears of idolatry and strange, pagan practices. Putting aside such fears, I began to explore this image of divinity and found that certain interpretations of the meaning of 'Goddess' reflected more adequately my sense of the physical world. Naomi Goldenberg's work was especially influential (Goldenberg 1991). The myths of the Goddess suggest that the physical and the spiritual are not at odds with each other, but that the world itself is the body of the divine.[2] To use some words of Monica Sjöö and Barbara Mor: 'the Goddess IS the world – the Goddess is *in* the world' (Caputi 1992: 430). The divine does not transcend the physical world. Moreover, this is no sentimental account of the natural world. A tacit recognition is given to the ambivalent nature of the universe. The Goddess embodies good *and* evil, change *and* flux, in a way which the Western concept of God, associated with the Platonic account of the Good, does not. As Barbara Walker puts it, the significance of this distinction has far-reaching implications for attitudes to life and death:

> The older matriarchal religions were more realistic in their acceptance of death, making it the sage's duty to realise the ugliness, corruption, and decay in nature as fully as he might realise its beauty: to accord death the same value as birth. (Walker 1983: 216)

Of particular interest are the ecological implications which follow from such an account. The Goddess, read in this way, offers an 'eco-friendly' framework for spirituality. Under this model, spirituality does not involve a distancing of the individual from the physical world. Ecological writers have argued that Christian doctrine is dependent upon such a polarized view of God and the physical world. The spiritual life has been juxtaposed to physical existence. The body, and all that stems from it, is to be mistrusted. This account of human life can be traced back to the pre-Christian philosophy of Plato, where reality is divided into two: spirit is opposed to matter, reason is opposed to nature (Plumwood 1993). The physical world we inhabit is described as less important than the transcendent 'World of Ideas', and death is seen as a blessed release from the prison of the body. Despite the non-Christian roots of such dualistic thinking, ecological writers such as Lyn White have argued that the destruction of the ecosystem owes much to the way in which the Christian doctrine of creation has been interpreted (White 1967). According to White, the creation story divinely ordains 'Man's' domination of the natural world. So, in Genesis 1.28, we find God's command to the first human couple:

> Be fruitful and multiply, and fill the earth and subdue it; and have dominion over the fish of the sea and over the birds of the air and over every living thing that moves upon the earth.

Rather than take seriously the responsibilities of stewardship, there has been a tendency to use the story of creation to legitimate the destruction of animal and plant life for the benefit of human existence. Such a view of the world is supremely anthropocentric: humanity is the focus of the created universe, the measure of all things. In the works of Francis Bacon (1561–1626) this hierarchical understanding of creation is taken to its logical conclusion: the world is a resource for humans, to be pillaged by the human beings – explicitly, the men – who are its masters (Bacon 1620). By way of contrast, the model of the Goddess suggests that one's spiritual life develops not through distancing one's self from the world, but by being immersed in the world, finding in its structures and relationships the meaning of human existence. Our real home does not lie beyond the stars, and it could be argued that the model of Goddess offers an account of divinity more relevant to the ecological concerns of a new millennium than that grounded in the Western concept of God.

Christian and feminist?

If the Christian model of the divine no longer coheres with my sense of the nature of the world, another factor signalled the end of my allegiance to Christianity. As my interests and fundamental commitments have become more explicitly feminist, my ethical concerns are no longer regulated by belief in the church's Christ, but by the quest for justice and equality.[3] My fundamental concern is to pursue a way of life which gives expression to my belief in, to use Rosemary Radford Ruether's phrase, 'the full humanity of women' (Radford Ruether 1983: 19), with all the implications that this notion has for the structure of human relationships, both public and private. Central to this concern is the recognition of the knowledge which can be derived from *women's* experience. As a theologian and philosopher, my training has made me painfully aware of the extent to which women's experience has been neglected within the Western tradition.[4] The Christian tradition has been shaped – and to an extent in academic theology, continues to be shaped – by male experience of the world. Feminist theology has argued that our understanding of human existence could be revolutionized if, instead of using male experience as the prime means of knowledge, reflection began with women's experience.

The notion of what constitutes women's experience is notoriously hard to define. Which women are we talking about? All-too-often, feminist theology has reflected the concerns of middle-class, white women. Can there be any universal experience which all women – irrespective of class or race – share? Some have suggested that the experiences which all women share are the reality of oppression in a society which continues to value men above women, and the possibility of 'sisterhood' or *real* connection with other women. However we inter-pret this idea of 'experience', the main point to grasp is the concern to include the experiences of non-privileged, 'marginalized others' (Anderson 1998: 78) in our theological formulations. This can have a revolutionary effect on the way we conceive of human life and experi-ence. James Nelson, a Christian theologian whose ideas have been influenced by feminist thinking, suggests that reflection on the female body might offer a radically different account of the nature of human beings than that habitually offered by Christian theology. Indeed, he suggests that the processes of the female body support a cyclical under-standing of the world which runs contrary to the lineal account of history derived from male bodily experience. As Nelson puts it, 'women . . . know incredible body changing processes that men can never directly know. Whether menstruation or pregnancy and birth, these are processes over which the woman has little control: she can resist them or move with them, but such radical changes have their own momen-tum' (Nelson 1988: 75). Historically, fear of the changing female body contributed to the restrictions placed upon women by the church (Ranke-Heinemann 1991). Nelson argues that, on the contrary, reflection on the female experience of embodiment may help us adjust to our place in creation. So, death becomes less a thing to be feared as that which lies at the end of all experience, and more a part of the changing, cyclical pattern of life which is the universe. All of which suggests a rather different theology to that which has arisen primarily from the reflections of men on their life experiences.

Nelson is Christian, and while it is true that in recent years the churches have sought to include more fully the implications of feminist thinking, change has been painfully slow. The leadership structures of the church are disproportionately male when one considers the pre-dominantly female make-up of the average congregation. The language of liturgy and hymnody maintains an androcentric bias. The status of the Bible as the norm for Christian teaching and preaching does not allow for the detailed critique that needs to be made of the derogatory way in which women have been treated in the Judeo–Christian tradition. This critique is being undertaken by Christian feminists such as Rosemary Radford Ruether (Radford Ruether 1983), and Elisabeth Schüssler Fiorenza (Fiorenza 1983), which suggests that Christianity and feminism may not be fundamentally opposed. It could be claimed, however (with good reason), that their work has done little to inform the teaching of the church. This is not to suggest that things are better in the other institutional religions of the world; but the central place of the Bible as the 'Word of God' makes it immensely difficult to eradicate the sexism which taints the Christian 'witness'.

Phyllis Trible's work provides us with a fine example of why the place of the Bible is particularly problematic for feminists. In her *Texts of Terror* (1984) Trible offers an exposition of four biblical passages which tend to be ignored by the churches, or whose implications are dismissed rather too quickly by 'mainstream' theology. Trible highlights the stories of Hagar (Gen. 16.1–16, 21.9–21), Tamar (II Sam. 13.1–22), an unnamed concubine (Judges 19.1–30), and the daughter of Jephthah (Judges 11.29–40). Consideration of just one story suggests why these passages might challenge the idea of the Bible as 'holy Scripture' for women. In Judges 19 we have the story of an unnamed concubine from Bethlehem. She runs away from her 'master/husband', returning to her father in Bethlehem. Her master pursues her and seeks to bring her back to Ephraim. On the way, they stop at Gibeah. Offered hospitality by an old man, that night the 'wicked' men of Gibeah demand that their host deliver the master to them so 'that we may know him' (Judges 19.22e). 'To know him' is an ambiguous phrase; in this context it suggests sexual knowledge. The old man refuses to do such a thing: in the place of his male guest he offers 'the services' of his virgin daughter and the concubine (Judges 19.24). Such an offer suggests something of the low status given to women in this period: 'if done to a man such an act is a vile thing; if done to women it is "the good" in the eyes of men' (Trible 1984: 74). In the event, it is the concubine who is thrown out (by her own master/husband) to the men, who rape and abuse her all night. The next morning her master finds her, and, offering her no words of comfort, they set off again. Once home, her master cuts her body into twelve pieces to send to the twelve tribes of Israel in 'condemnation' of Benjamin and as a call to war.

How is this story to be understood as the 'word of God'? It is often treated as a tale regarding the hospitality laws; but this gives the story an androcentric interpretation. The old man's actions are 'justified' because they protect the male guest, who otherwise would be sodomized. While this story has had ramifications for the tradition's understanding of homosexuality (suggesting something of the homophobia which characterizes the churches' failure to recognize *loving* same-sex relationships), what is primarily revealed is the deep-rooted misogyny of the Christian tradition. The story itself, the language used, the ultimate conclusion, suggests the male-centred bias of the tradition. What happens to women isn't important; the key figures in the stories are the men, who are to be protected at all costs – not the women, who are made their victims.

While such stories leave me deeply saddened, the failure of the church to accept its share of the blame for the structure of patriarchy and its cost in terms of human relationships leaves me frustrated and angry. To what extent is it possible to maintain faith in the 'God of Abraham', the 'God of our Fathers', when confronted with the violence and abuse perpetrated by 'his' followers? We are left wondering how similar acts of violence in the here-and-now are to be confronted if the biblical 'guidebook' fails to provide us with a categorical rejection of the abuse suffered by many women in a world where what happens to them still does not count for much.[5]

If the acceptance of Scripture as the word of God is problematic, the constant battle to fit my theology into a Christian framework has been both tiring and pointless. In 1996 the post-Christian feminist theologian Daphne Hampson published her first full account of her theology in *After Christianity*. Reading this work was something of a turning point. Hampson has rejected Christianity on the grounds that it fails to cohere with her 'ethical *a priori*' commitment to feminism. Its historicity, she argues, constantly reiterates and perpetuates the patriarchal context and values in which it was formed. In its place she offers her own account of God as 'a dimension of the totality that is' (Hampson 1996: 231). While her approach is not necessarily mine, it was immensely exciting and *liberating* to read a feminist theology unhampered by the constraints implied by doing 'Christian' theology. At that point, I decided the time for a break with Christianity was long overdue.

In achieving that break, I now have the freedom to think what I want to think, write what I want to write. Cupitt is right when he stresses the importance of creative self-expression for developing one's spirituality (Cupitt 1995). It is only by being true to one's self, and free to be one's self, that one finds one's spiritual centre. As Hampson puts it, a certain peace comes with being 'all of a piece' (Hampson 1992: 131). At the same time, I am aware that other women's choices may be different from mine: I have no desire to make all women 'post-Christians'. This is the right choice *for me*; but that does not mean that it will be right for other women – or indeed, men. For me, this *feels* right. And this is perhaps the crucial point: my own integrity demanded this decision. After years of disquiet that my beliefs were not at one with my sense of world and self, a resolution was needed. Am I a Christian, or am I not? Do I share the Christian beliefs of the vast majority of the church, or don't I? In the end there were too many contortions required to fit my personal beliefs to a framework which failed to match my key beliefs and ideals.

Concluding reflections

There remains a certain sadness that I have stepped outside of a community which has given me much for which I am grateful. I am pleased that as a young woman Christianity provided me with a moral framework which respected others and stressed the importance of a thoughtful approach to life. I enjoyed the youth activities that membership of my local Methodist church provided. Yet at the same time, I am pleased that I have found the courage to move on.

My main reasons for leaving the church could be described as intellectual, and it seems to me that this is an area the Methodist Church would do well to reflect upon. The emphasis on personal experience, on developing a personal relationship with God, can lead to a distrust of the intellectual expression of and reflection upon a faith. As a teenager deciding which degree course to take, I can well remember concerned members of the congregation advising me not to read theology as it was potentially faith-destroying. No doubt if they read this chapter they will feel justified in making such a comment; but ignorance is surely not the basis for a mature faith. Such anti-intellectual sentiments can leave those who want to consider their faith critically feeling isolated within a congregation.

In similar vein, the desire to make worship reflect the emotional elements of religious experience seems to me short-sighted. For a start, it is not necessarily what the church needs. My experience of worship within the church – both formal and informal – did little to cultivate any sense of the profound depths of human life. I find that a walk along a river, or in a park full of trees, has more spiritual power than the worship found within the church. At the same time, seeking to make worship more 'exciting' and 'attractive' to young people may mean that full-blooded theological discussion is neglected. Theology does not simply mean Bible study, and if Christianity, let alone Methodism, is to survive into the twenty-first century, a revolution in thinking is needed which few Christians may feel inclined to pursue. Such a revolution would entail questioning the traditional interpretation of creation, incarnation, and the role of Christ, and, as such, may prove painful.

Yet change is always possible, not only in the shape of the church, but also in my own life and situation. As such, I would not want to rule out categorically the possibility of a return to Christianity at some point. Perhaps if the church took more seriously Christ's words, 'why do you not judge for yourselves what is right?' (Luke 12.57), such change might be possible. A form of Christianity might evolve which was able to include images and ideas of the divine such as considered in this chapter, and which nourished and encouraged spiritual creativity. For now, I am aware of my new-found freedom for spiritual and creative expression, and it is a freedom I do not intend to relinquish in a hurry.

Notes

1. This sense of the importance of personal integrity seems to reflect some of the findings of Chapter 4 of Richter and Francis's study (1998), in which they suggest that people born post-1945 are less tolerant of perceived hypocrisy or inauthenticity than those born pre-1945.

2. Such a view is not, of course, without its parallels in Christianity (see e.g. Jantzen 1984 or McFague 1993).

3. For an earlier perspective on this tension between Christianity and feminism, see Clack 1994.

4. See for example my *Misogyny in the Western Philosophical Tradition: A Reader* (Macmillan, forthcoming).

5. For a recent example, see the lack of media coverage for the multiple murders of prostitutes in Glasgow over the last seven years. Jean Rafferty's 'Double jeopardy', *The Guardian Weekend*, 14 March 1998, 14–23, is a notable exception to the general silence.

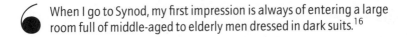

When I go to Synod, my first impression is always of entering a large room full of middle-aged to elderly men dressed in dark suits.[16]

Of course it is our aim to preach Christ and Christ alone, but, when all is said and done, it is not the fault of our critics that they find our preaching so hard to understand, so overburdened with ideas and expressions which are hopelessly out of touch with the mental climate in which they live. It is just not true that every word of criticism directed against contemporary preaching is a deliberate rejection of Christ and proceeds from the spirit of Antichrist . . . perhaps it would be just as well to ask ourselves whether we do not in fact act as obstacles to Jesus and his Word.[17]

Peter Kendall, a middle-aged ex-Methodist, complained that 'the church is a very, very simple organisation, with a very simple theology [that] nowhere goes to the root of people's deep, deep spirituality'. His disillusionment with the church went hand in hand with a disillusionment with its 'simplistic view of spirituality'. As a teenager he was inspired by the ground-breaking book by Bishop John Robinson (1963), *Honest to God*, but was disappointed to find 'no one thinking in those terms' in his church.[18]

Chapter 7

A training-ground for forgiveness: Methodism and 'fellowship'

Clive Marsh

Wherever you turn in Methodism, the emphasis is there. Talk to contemporary Methodists and many speak of the warmth of a church's 'fellowship'. Read an official report deriving from a national study group, and the word appears. Glance at a leaflet which seeks to summarize some of Methodism's key features, and the term is prominent. The form of Christianity embodied in Methodism treats fellowship as crucial. But what is it? When fellowship can be so easily criticized as a 'holy huddle', seen as a euphemism for an 'in-crowd', recognized as a way of dodging matters of belief through dealing just with social matters, it is worthy of closer scrutiny. For though the positive aspects of fellowship will be plain for all to see for those who have experienced them, the negative aspects are sometimes missed altogether. Furthermore, if the term itself carries little meaning outside of churches, and if churches themselves represent nothing more than mysterious gatherings of people who, it is assumed, are seeking to escape from 'real life', then the need to re-examine fellowship is an urgent one; it is a missionary task. Without fellowship being re-considered and re-defined for the present, one key aspect of Methodism – one of its strengths – may go unrecognized and remain unfulfilled in the present. And Methodism's contribution in this respect to contemporary understanding of, and participation in, Christianity more broadly may then be overlooked – to contemporary Christianity's cost. So what is 'fellowship'?

Understanding 'fellowship'

'Fellowship' is not a word which makes its way into dictionaries of religion or theology, or into handbooks of pastoral care. This is surprising given the importance of what the term is seeking to describe, not only in Methodism. But its lack of appearance indicates both its intangibility and the fact that it draws together many aspects of Christian theory and practice. Even though it would be a useful exercise to try and spell out a 'theology of fellowship', it is true that when Christians use the term, they don't often think first of all – if ever – in such lofty terms. A way must therefore be found which moves us from what people can readily identify as 'fellowship' towards theology more explicitly. I suggest that fellowship should be understood under six headings: belonging, having things in common, believing and searching with others, being open to and for others in a group, sharing joy, and being united in spirit (and the Spirit). I shall consider each of these in turn.

Fellowship entails belonging. You can't usually 'have fellowship', or be 'in fellowship' with people you don't know. Though the term is sometimes used in that way of the ease with which some Christians *can* easily get on with each other when they first meet, it's not a helpful use of the term. For the fellowship of which Methodists speak – when they are trying to put into words the significance of the quality of their congregational and/or small group life in their local church – is usually about sustained, committed belonging to a group, a body of people. It is in and through intense and sustained person-to-person contact that the love of God is believed to be discovered as present within human experience. Though the love of God for and within the world is by no means confined to such a context, whatever else 'church' might mean, it is best used for that form of Christian, human communal life within which the love of God can be enjoyed, discerned and named.

Inevitably, those who belong to each other and to God in this way will perceive that they have much in common. The notion of fellowship as belonging does not necessarily mean that only like-minded people, or those of the same social class, constitute a group to which people belong (though sadly at times Christian groups seem rather too uniform in their backgrounds, outlook and social habits). But it does raise the question of how much, or how little, people need to have in common with each other in order to belong together. Fellowship certainly includes the notion of 'having things in common'. Not for nothing do many English-speaking Christian groups use the Greek word *koinonia* (which literally means 'being in common') – the word which most closely relates to the word 'fellowship' – because there isn't quite an English word which describes what the 'having things in common' is about. Christians share a common faith, of course. But the detail of that faith (in terms of belief) is often not shared even by those who seem to espouse the same theological viewpoint. The same Lord, the same Christ, the same Spirit are worshipped and shared in. But there is quite likely to be considerable disagreement about matters of doctrine: there is likely to be greater agreement about patterns of ministry, baptism and communion practice within particular congregations than would be found across different denominations. But even here differences would not be far away.

Furthermore, not for nothing is there a strong tradition within early – and even in some later forms of – Christianity which refers to the sharing of goods and belongings. However idealistic the brief biblical accounts of this practice in the early church may be (Acts 2. 44–45; 4. 32–37), something important about the common ground between the believers, as expressed in very materialistic terms, is being stated. But even so, the 'having things in common' will (because it must!) also get tangled up with other matters: the being of the same age, political view, racial background, level of wealth, extent of local rootedness.

Such matters are far from mundane. They are part of who we are. But through them we also begin to see already the two-edged nature of fellowship: having things in common, as an aspect of fellowship, is vital to vibrant Christianity. It can also be one of fellowship's greatest dangers. We shall explore the extent to which 'fellowship as sharing a common culture' can become one of contemporary Christianity's greatest turn-offs in a later section.

The third aspect of fellowship is companionship: believing and searching with others. One of the most powerful (as well as most mysterious and rich) stories in the New Testament is the story of two travellers on the road to Emmaus, who are accompanied by a figure they don't initially recognize as the risen Christ (Luke 24.13-35). The passage is full of material pertinent to every aspect of Christian companionship (travelling, mutual confusion, questioning, Scripture-reading, moments of inspiration, disappointment, excitement, Jesus present one moment and absent the next). As an aspect of fellowship, companionship means that the group of Christians to which one primarily belongs are one's travel-companions, fellow-searchers, co-questioners, believers (who may believe differently from oneself) whose own faith and belief (in the form of both questions and answers) one can trust and make use of within one's own journey.

Fourthly, fellowship is about openness. By 'openness' here I mean a quality inherent in the relationships of people who belong to each other rather than to the question of who is 'in' a group and who is 'out'. 'Having things in common' can lead dangerously towards exclusivity and separateness. It can also all too quickly lead to a context within which answers to questions are assumed, party lines must be adopted and people's actual issues, questions, doubts and affirmations are not taken sufficiently seriously. But where fellowship is characterized by openness, then an element of uncertainty, surprise, discovery and mystery is maintained at the heart of a group experience. Those who belong to each other do not, in one sense, know where they are going. The openness cannot, in practical terms, be limitless: we are all committed to something, and the fact that a group calls itself 'Christian' in any sense presupposes at least a desire to work with common traditions. It will, however, always need to be broader than we expect it to be simply because God alone knows what theology it is best to have. But beyond the notion that people are journeying together – with God as known in and through Christ, towards God's kingdom, within a Christian community, in the world, guided by the Spirit – the precise meaning of all such religious terms has in many ways yet to be discovered. In that sense, the future is God's alone, and openness to the mystery of that future characterizes the fellowship in which travelling companions share together.

The fifth aspect of fellowship is one of the most overlooked features of Christian living: joy. When people speak of fellowship positively, then a depth and degree of contentment is being referred to which suffuses the whole of life. Fellowship with other believers becomes the focal point and primary means of discovering and gaining access to the resources for joyful living in God. In this regard it is perhaps no accident that there is a fundamental link between the Sabbath and joy. If the Sabbath means rest from work and the creating of space for 'holy convocation' (Lev. 23.3, NRSV), then the link between worship and joyful life, through the joyful fellowship enjoyed in worship, should be stressed. This is not a joy to be reduced to mere happiness (though Christians could often be a lot happier than they are!). And it is a joy which, through the link with the Sabbath, judges all notions of joy resulting from effort – even the hard work of preachers, musicians, readers and stewards in their respective roles in making worship happen. Joyful fellowship cannot be scripted: it is a gift.

Sixth and finally, fellowship is about being united in spirit (and in the Spirit). Whatever may be held in common is grounded in none other than the Spirit of God. This bond of unity is reflected in the inner bond which people 'in fellowship' experience one with another and which enables them to transcend difference. 'Transcend' does not mean 'ignore'. Nor does it mean avoiding painful difference, or dodging the need to 'agree to differ' on many things – even seemingly vital aspects of Christian belief. Being united in spirit/the Spirit means that though there clearly are Apollos and Cephas parties in every church, these distinctions will not become divisions. Fellowship at its best refuses to make do with a lazy, false unity and results from honest, open exploration of difference, under the guidance of the one God.

'Fellowship was the spiritual cement of early Methodism . . .' (Called to Love and Praise 1995: 4.2.14). It could easily be argued that it remains so now. The time has long since passed, however, when it can be assumed that everyone knows what the term means, or even that the term itself remains the most appropriate one to use. But at least, in these six headings, I suggest, we go some way towards identifying what that 'fellowship' is which Methodists are attempting to define when they signal its importance. If a summary statement were to be ventured, we can perhaps speak of a quality of human relationship which must also be *more than human* in order to *be* human. But we must yet do much more if we are to move towards re-asserting what these six headings amount to in practice, and what future 'fellowship' itself might have.

Forms of 'fellowship'

What forms, though, does 'fellowship' take? Or, more accurately, in what forms of Christian, human community do people speak of finding fellowship? I have so far fudged the issue somewhat as to what kinds of groups best enable people to discover or experience 'fellowship'. When I have talked of 'church', I have effectively done so in an ideal sense, in a way which people may not immediately be able to relate to through their actual experience of 'church'. This very point highlights a crucial aspect of 'fellowship': it may be spoken of in relation to churches of many different sizes, but those aspects which constitute 'fellowship' may more readily be found in relation to sub-groups within churches, or to patterns of belonging across churches. In other words, though there may well be particular types of churches – and particular types of activity – which foster the hallmarks of good fellowship, fellowship is more likely to be spoken of in relation to specific kinds of *group experience*. This is best illustrated through examples.

One of the most obvious examples of groups within which fellowship is fostered is church house-groups: stable groups which meet regularly and frequently in people's homes. Such groups essentially provide a Christian 'base group' in relation to which and out of which people can explore and develop their grasp of life and their Christian faith in the company of other people whom they get to know well. At their best, in such groups (potentially of mixed age, background and life-experience), people are mutually supportive and the group can carry members who are having a hard time, acknowledging that different people will need to be carried by the group at different times, and that most will need to be carried at some stage. In these groups, the deepest Bible study and prayer and the richest Christian character formation can take place.

'The best' is notoriously difficult to achieve, of course. More often than not, particular individuals dominate, awkward personalities become burdensome, opinions are rarely changed, the Bible is mused

upon or worshipped rather than studied and used. Yet even acknowledging such realism merely reminds us that humanity is flawed and if
there is to be fellowship at all, then it, too, will be flawed even though we
have a vision of something yet to be reached.

A second form of group overlaps with the first and provides a clear
case of what has, in recent Methodist history, proved a prime example of
successful small-group spirituality. In his recent book *Modern Methodism
in England 1932–1998*, John Munsey Turner devotes a whole section to
'University Methodist Societies' (Turner 1998: 76–8). These societies
enjoyed their heyday, perhaps, around the 1950s, though they continued
to be healthy right through to the 1980s. (Most of the contributors to
this book were members of a Methsoc at some stage. Indeed, collectively
we possess around 40 years' experience of Methsocs, in six different
British universities, from the period 1978 to 1989.) At their best, and as
Elizabeth Carnelley's chapter in this book bears witness, Methsocs are
examples of how a structure of small groups can enable Christianity to
flourish in a life-enhancing, socially and politically committed, and
intellectually credible way. (And, it might be added, Methsocs have thus
functioned very closely to the way in which John Wesley appeared to have
envisaged his 'class meetings' functioning within the 'societies' he set up
to supplement the church attendance of his eighteenth-century
Methodist Anglicans.) As Turner notes, not all those who came through
Methodist Societies in their heyday remained Methodist. Ultimately this
is not the main issue – and nor is it the main issue of this book. Indeed,
the example of Methsocs illustrates in a different way what is a main
point of this book: Methodism has fostered, and can foster, a particular
way of being Christian, in which small-group spirituality must play a key
part. Whether the results need to be called 'Methodist' is neither here nor
there. What matters is that God is worshipped in the midst of human life,
and if Christianity in this ('Methodist') form better enables that to
happen, then it should be encouraged.

Student societies had, and have, their drawbacks, of course. They are
always in danger of taking on an all-consuming character (as if the
wider world did not exist). They appeal to people at a particular stage of
life, intellectually and emotionally. And they are bringing together
people who, despite the fact that they may have very diverse social backgrounds, already have a lot in common. But these drawbacks merely
draw attention to what fellowship in small groups achieves. It possesses
a resourcing character, re-charging the batteries of the believer for
living the whole of life to the full. And though small-group fellowship
takes on different forms for different age groups (and perhaps indicates
that mixed-age groups may not always work very easily), it does not
alter the fact that people of all ages need groups of some kind.

A third example takes us in a different direction, one in which we often find people quite different from each other – more diverse than in the first example – experiencing 'fellowship' together. Many people who have been active in ecumenical Christian work (and even ecumenism more widely, across faiths) record experiences of having little success in fostering unity when discussing matters of belief, yet much success when undertaking a piece of practical socio-political action. Fellowship is therefore discovered and enjoyed in action. And by noting that the very example cited takes us beyond Methodism, we also highlight the fact that Methodism – itself a very activist movement, perhaps more inclined to stress right action over right belief – is very likely to want to foster an approach to fellowship which is action-oriented. A project, then, the focus of which might be land reclamation, opposition to road-building, or a campaign for better park facilities for children, could equally be the location for the emergence of fellowship in the quality of human relationship fostered between participants, as a major by-product of a basic task being undertaken corporately.

These are, of course, not the only forms of fellowship. But they are obvious examples. Readers should feel free to make connections with the above and add their own. The important feature across all such examples, however, is that though by no means peculiar to Methodism, they are nevertheless a hallmark of a Methodist way of being Christian. When seen as forms of Christian, human community in which the features of fellowship listed in the previous section come to light, then their importance, to Methodism and to Methodism's contribution to an understanding of what Christianity actually is and how it works, becomes evident.

Fellowship in contemporary context

The counter-cultural aspect of such an emphasis upon fellowship is, however, worth noting at this point. Whatever may be said about the extent to which human beings really are social animals (and, theologically speaking, reflect the fact that God is trinity – not an internally, isolated God but a constantly communing God, internally and externally), there is little doubt that individualism has reigned for long stretches in Western culture. It is readily assumed that we are self-sufficient, independent beings. Though we might quickly state that no one is an island, we dare not say that we *depend* on others, for that would be weakness. A focus, then, upon groups and group-relatedness, upon belonging as opposed to independent existence, is not a fashionable thing to say, despite the evident shift now happening towards a variety of forms of communitarianism in political life. Being out of fashion should not worry Christians, of course. The more pressing matter, though, may be that the fashion of inter-dependence seems about to return. Even if Methodism itself may not be resurgent as a result, then at least Methodism can make its important contribution to Christianity's part in the task of enabling creation to be as God wants it to be: as a fundamentally interconnected created order.

It is, however, important to broaden out our consideration of the theme of fellowship within the contemporary British context in order to clarify what a revised and reasserted emphasis upon it might have. Though this section can be at best sketchy within such a short chapter, its function is nevertheless important.

The first point to pick up relates to one of the general contextual factors which was highlighted in the introductory chapter to this work: the religious context, in which people may profess a spirituality, yet have little time for religion. The sociologist Grace Davie suggests that we live in an age of 'believing without belonging' (Davie 1994). By this term, Davie seeks to describe a religious situation in which the majority of people in Britain seem happy to continue to affirm belief in God (or a god of some sort), but are unwilling to join up with any group, or commit themselves in a particular way to an organized religious lifestyle. Whether or not Davie is right in her reading of the contemporary British situation with regard to religion – and she has her critics (see e.g. Bruce 1995a) – the discussion she is engaged in is a crucial one for any particular slant of Christianity which tries to stress the importance of commitment to a particular kind of social grouping as fundamental for the formation and development of a lively Christian faith in God. Fellowship, in other words, may simply be very hard to argue for in the present cultural climate.

But what about the converse: belonging without believing? This can be seen to take two forms. Clearly there are people who choose to be religious – even Christian – although their numbers may be lower than they once were. What is always likely to be unclear is the extent to which matters of belief are important too. At this juncture it is easy to generalize and it would be wrong to do so. It is no longer true to say that 'charismatic evangelicals will always be sticklers for doctrinal purity in a way that radical catholics are not'. As the opening chapters in this book illustrate, the boundaries between different church traditions and diverse theological persuasions are fuzzier than ever. The point to note here, though, is that 'belonging' – whilst crucial for Christian discipleship – is never enough. Methodism itself has often been guilty of implying that matters of belief mean little precisely because experience (the individual experience of personal salvation, and the corporate experience of fellowship) matters most. The challenge for any contemporary re-assertion of 'fellowship', therefore, is to work at specifying what aspects of belief lie at its heart. Ultimately, some form of 'theology of fellowship' will have to be spelt out.

It is not, however, only religious people who belong without believing. Rubbing alongside an evident individualistic tendency in British culture is, inevitably, the observation that people do in fact belong to all sorts of groups (e.g. families, sports clubs, work-teams, leisure groups). A key issue here, of course, is that some of the belonging is not by choice. But even this distinction is not ultimately decisive. The fact remains that it is within and through such communal contexts that people may have the nearest thing to the 'fellowship' described in the first section of this chapter. The greatest challenge for anyone seeking to re-assert the importance of 'fellowship', then, is to demonstrate what the practical difference will be to interpret normal, human social interaction through the lens of Christian faith and thought.

The problems of 'fellowship'

But before we get too carried away with a possible future for 'fellowship' we must examine some of its problems. These are many, and their weight should not be underplayed. Indeed, the fact that we include this chapter in this section of the book ('Questioning Methodism's effectiveness') rather than the previous section ('Perspectives on Methodist theology and tradition') is telling. As Elizabeth Carnelley will remind us in her chapter, many other traditions have stolen Methodism's clothes at this point. There are problems with fellowship, and there are problems with Methodism's handling of it. In this exploration we can mention only some of the main ones.

The first and most obvious problem with fellowship relates to a common critique of Methodism *per se*. Methodists, it is often said, are not terribly good with worship, but they know how to throw a good party. (Drinkers of alcohol would surely not agree!) But the point behind the quip is well made: 'fellowship' can too easily become a theological slogan covering up the private, cosy socializing of an exclusive group. The party – whether good or not – may actually not be open to very many people. And the 'fellowship', though it may well be quite advanced at a horizontal level (between the party-goers), may be less well developed on its vertical axis: God may not get much of a look-in. Furthermore, even the interaction between the party-goers may not be all that it seems, operating at a superficial level, and scarcely touching the depths at which one would normally expect faith to function. How, then, is human interaction to be seen as the place in which the presence of God is perceived and enjoyed?

A second, less obvious problem is far from only a Methodist ailment, though it is starkly present in Methodism. That is the problem of the relatively little time which we often assume we need to experience fellowship with other people. If the first problem is more likely to be associated with an over-familiarity brought about by regular meeting (though occasional parties can be exclusive and superficial too), then this problem is more commonly related to not knowing each other well enough. It is hard for a tradition which has so stressed good human relations at the heart of its expression of Christian faith, and which – for its older members – has meant in the past, and for many still in the present, considerable time in the company of their Christian friends, to consider the implications of Christians trying to be 'in fellowship with each other' when they may meet for only an hour a week. Even whilst it is undoubtedly true that more time has to be devoted to fellowship than the hour a week allows, creative ways need to be found for this. The simple critique that 'people don't commit themselves to things any more' won't wash.

A third, much more far-reaching, problem with an emphasis upon fellowship is connected to one of the most dominant forms within which that emphasis finds expression: via the image of the church as a 'family'. Many churches – Methodist churches included – choose to describe themselves as 'families' or 'family churches'. The latter term is even more problematic than the former, simply because it is ambiguous. Does it mean a church for families – and particular kinds of family at that – or a church which operates like a family? In all cases where the close association between churches and families is made, so much is left unsaid. The link is usually assumed to be a positive one. Churches which use the association are grasping after an image which goes some way towards expressing in less 'in-language' what this mysterious thing 'fellowship' might be about.

But, of course, the family image is profoundly problematic (on all this, see Selby 1996). Many people don't have happy experiences of families, and so the image is not positive. And even if the link between church and family is quickly qualified in terms of an 'ideal' family (assuming that agreement as to what 'ideal' amounts to can be gained) one of the key features of a family is that you cannot simply choose to belong to it. Furthermore, there are a number of different ways in which Christianity has understood God and family to relate. The theological notion that all human beings *are* already part of God's family could be argued to be decisive. It is also much more radical than most religious (let alone Christian) believers are able to cope with in practice. But it needs careful use at a practical, local level, when it so often feels that a 'family' church really does comprise people with blood relationships which cannot easily be broken into. In addition, the New Testament uses the language of adoption, suggesting that we may not automatically be 'in'. And then there are the hard sayings of Jesus which seem to put the immediacy of family ties firmly in second place, behind a yet more important grouping of people: those who are engaged in the work of God to build God's kingdom. So it is clear that we must be careful.

On the other hand, there are vitally important positive aspects to the image of church as family which can be noted, even if these often get overlooked when the image is used in its more cosy form. First, you don't choose most members of your family. Your family is largely a bunch of people you're landed with. In that sense, there could be no better image for the church, which is not – or should not be – simply a group of exclusive friends. 'Fellowship' is about being with, working with and travelling with people that you might not normally have chosen to accompany through life. Second, it has been said that families are places to which you go to have your arguments. The quip is misleading, but contains more than a grain of truth about how we learn who we are and how we relate to others. Because family life – of whatever form, and in the widest sense – is so formative, then it is usually within some form of family existence that people experience many of the most basic and essential aspects of human development. People move beyond one pattern of family existence in moving beyond childhood and adolescence. Their character forms and develops in different ways from then on and choices made become more prominent. But some pattern of family life will remain. And a clear relationship back to the earlier, formative phases of family life (whether via re-creation of those earlier forms, rejection of them, or a combination of both) will inevitably remain.

So churches *are* like families in at least these two senses, even if the way in which the church/family link is made usually relates explicitly only to other features (e.g. warmth, cosiness, security). A further challenge to a contemporary re-assertion of 'fellowship', then, must take on these more searching aspects of 'family life'.

A fourth problem for 'fellowship' is the obvious point that in English it is sexist language. Contained within the term is an implied – even if for many hearers, deeply hidden – notion of male companionship. Though the term is intended to be used in a general way as 'togetherness', 'companionship' or 'friendliness', the ways in which the term itself – and related terms, especially 'fellow' – have been used indicate that the headings under which fellowship might best be understood within the church (belonging, having things in common, believing and searching in company, openness, joy, unity in spirit/the Spirit) may not easily come to mind. 'Fellows' of universities were, for so long, always male. 'My dear fellow!' would never have been, or be, said of a woman. The 'right hand of fellowship [*koinonia*]' (as found in Gal. 2.9) may well be a Christian sign. But it has come to be a symbol of 'fraternity' or 'brotherhood' (and may, of course, have been so for Paul, Barnabas, Peter, James and John; early Christianity was far from free of sexism).

So even if, when we speak of 'fellowship', we might be tempted to say 'Yes, but we all know what we mean by it' (Selby 1996: 155), the matter is not so simple. The desire to reaffirm 'fellowship' – whatever Christians might wish to be the case – may simply sound like another example of the persistent re-assertion of a very male-dominated way of doing things.

I have suggested four main problems: cosy familiarity (yet superficiality), not giving it enough time, linking it too readily with family life and the word 'fellowship' itself. Is there, then, no way forward?

'Fellowship' transformed?

Despite all the negative points just listed, throughout this chapter has lurked the assumption that 'fellowship' is nevertheless worth holding on to and re-affirming, as if the only issue is 'How?' As I attempt in this final section to offer just one small suggestion for what has to be borne in mind as this is attempted, it is first necessary to collect together the challenges we have seen ourselves to be confronted with in examining 'fellowship' in our current context. The challenges are these:

- how to re-affirm fellowship when 'belonging' to anything is unfashionable and individualism is more the mood of the age;
- to identify what aspects of Christian belief specifically underpin any re-affirmation, so that any form of re-assertion of 'fellowship' is theologically informed;
- to clarify what difference an emphasis on 'fellowship' makes, in distinction from any other emphasis upon the social aspects of being human;
- to relate to the challenging aspects of the 'church as family' image, without 'fellowship' becoming exclusive;
- to try and find a less sexist term.

All these points, of course, present us with an impossible task. But readers may wish to stop at this point, disregard whatever I've got to say in conclusion, and simply take up for themselves the challenge of these five points on the conviction that it is vital for church and society that 'fellowship' be re-asserted. If readers were to do this, then it would be an appropriate Methodist response. Those who wish to continue reading before turning to their own action and reflection, however, will encounter – in sketchy, programmatic form – the exposition of one simple thesis: 'fellowship' must be re-asserted because at its heart lies salvation, central to which – in terms of human experience – is forgiveness. What does all this mean?

One of the most striking features of the small groups of Christians which the Wesleys were responsible for setting up was that their members met to 'tell each other their sins'. The opening lines of John Wesley's *Rules of the Band Societies* (1738), for example, begin with these words: 'The design of our meeting is to obey the command of God, "Confess your faults to one another, and pray for one another that ye may be healed"' (Davies 1989: 77). What such an exhortation sometimes meant in practice, of course – in Wesley's time and in many similar Christian groups of later periods, not only Methodist – was the creation of groups which were often extremely intense, sometimes morbid, frequently melodramatic, and at times not altogether psychologically healthy. But the importance of the centrality of confessing faults to the experience of salvation should not be side-stepped. If 'fellowship' rests upon a strong sense of belonging, mutual growth and exploration, being united in spirit and – most apposite of all – openness, then it is going to be important that people are present to each other in weakness as well as in strength. Some of what people have in common is very likely to be related to their weaknesses. And joy cannot be shared in all its fullness where there is no depth of self-knowledge and knowledge of one another.

There are, of course, still many steps needed, from confessing faults, to being forgiven and forgiving, and on to speaking in terms of salvation. My concern, however, is merely to observe and highlight the connections here. The link between such human experiences as 'feeling guilty', 'knowing one has done wrong', 'admitting to weakness', 'feeling one has been wronged', 'sensing that one needs to forgive another' and Christian exploration of salvation has to be made. This is an apologetic task: it is a way of showing how faith connects and is defensible. But it cannot be presumed that an experience and a theological idea are one and the same thing. A theological reading of such human experiences adds something to them by helping to transform them. But if the link is not made, then salvation is rendered idle talk. However, if salvation is to do with a fundamental characteristic of God's relationship with human beings, then the links have to be found. Such links would help those who may not have been enabled to use theological language to interpret their human experience, and who may therefore – from a Christian perspective – be experiencing a blockage to a fuller appreciation of the richness of human living.

At the heart of 'fellowship' then, I suggest, is salvation. And because joy-bringing forgiveness is located at the heart of salvation, then it is right and proper that 'fellowship' is a profoundly positive and life-resourcing human experience. Through 'fellowship' God is saving people. But because salvation is about forgiveness, then the joy which is intrinsic to salvation is not easily won. Forgiveness requires awareness of, and confrontation with, that which needs forgiving. Sometimes the people we ourselves know we need to forgive are close to us, and our forgiveness of them should not be wrapped in a prayer said at a distance from them, however important prayer may be. On the contrary, for-giveness should happen much more directly. However, forgiveness in such a direct way is far from always possible. So much of human living entails carrying hurts, and living on in spite of them. In the same way that the resurrected Christ always bears the marks of crucifixion, so followers of Christ are enabled to see that they too can live with their hurts – and may still discover a joyful resurrection. Indeed, it is precisely through observation of this link between Christ and the nature of 'fellowship' that the way in which human beings can live as forgiven and forgiving people becomes clear.

For who is Christ for us today, if not the very presence of God the Saviour in the form of the crucified and risen one, at the heart of any human community which is itself prepared to live between crucifixion and resurrection? This means that Christ *is* wherever God is saving. And God is saving where human interaction becomes the place for the emer-gence of divine community. *For that is what 'fellowship' amounts to: the kind of community created amongst human beings which reflects who God is and the way God wants the world to be.* Other words may be suggested too: spiritual community or the spirit of community. In some Christian circles, perhaps 'fellowship' will be deemed irreplaceable. But whatever term is used, it is important that the headings used in the opening section of this chapter are not played down, and the focusing of all those dimensions in terms of salvation is not lost.

If such an emphasis is maintained, then the heart of 'fellowship' – of divine community – in experiential terms is that of a training-ground for forgiveness. Human community which has the quality of 'fellow-ship' is a place where the profoundest of human interaction can occur, an interaction which reveals itself to be grounded in the saving action of a loving God.

The identification and articulation of such human interaction as grounded in divine action is the main (mission-oriented!) responsibil-ity of the church. But it is not the church's responsibility alone to create such interactions. For fellowship is a gift. And as such, it can emerge within many and diverse human communal contexts (e.g. work, local community, committee, friends, family). But because this is so, then it is therefore also a task of the church's mission to value and interpret such contexts as examples of fellowship, reflecting that quality of human and divine community to which the church itself aspires, and which Christians who speak of 'fellowship' are referring to by their use of the term. If at this point we find ourselves drawing distinctions between 'church' and 'kingdom of God' and noting the way in which the kingdom goes beyond and cuts through the church, then so be it. God's action has never been confined only to the church, let alone one particular church. Nor has that saving action ever been quite as starkly individualistic as even many strands of Methodism – including the emphasis upon the 'heart strangely warmed' – have suggested.

'Fellowship', then, is indeed a Methodist emphasis, though far from a Methodist preserve. The challenge, though, is how to recover a lost effectiveness: to participate with God in the renewed fostering of this divine community, which the use of the term 'fellowship' has sought to identify and maintain, in such a way that Methodism is but a means to an end and not the end itself. Can it be done, within and outside of British Christianity's future?

Holiness, then, was for Wesley 'religion itself' and he often referred to it as 'perfect love'. The goal of the Christian life, in other words, is not something achievable by an isolated individual, as theoretically 'perfect faith' might be, but something that binds the believer to others. As Wesley himself said, 'there is no holiness but social holiness'. ... Within the Methodist church, the contribution of small groups – whether known as 'classes' or 'bands' or 'house groups' – has been appreciated from the first. They are places where experience of worship, prayer and searching of the scriptures can promote spiritual growth. They are also places where individuals find challenge, acceptance and healing in the fullest sense. We need therefore to ask about our churches: Are they communities where, in such groups, people can grow and mature or do they stunt and maim people and leave them immature?[19]

Part III

Contemporary British Methodism in a wider context

American Methodism is surely only quite incidentally related to Christianity. (That is not to say that Methodists are without any convictions. Quite the contrary. For now that I am back among the Methodists, I have discovered that they do have a conviction: It is that God is nice. Moreover, since Methodists are a sanctificationist people, we have a correlative: We ought to be nice too . . .) [20]

Chapter 8

'Love the most distant': the future of British Methodism in a world church perspective

Stephen Plant

> You crowd together with your neighbours and have beautiful words for it.
> But I tell you:
> Your love of your neighbour is your bad love of yourselves . . .
> I exhort you rather to flight from your neighbour
> and to love of the most distant!
>
> (Friedrich Nietzsche)[1]

It has always been difficult for religious people properly to prioritize their responsibilities. Jesus can hardly have intended his parable of the Good Samaritan to be a criticism of the ritual duties of the priest, or of the liturgical duties of the Levite. Jesus insisted he had not come to remove the smallest part of the Jewish law. The parable of the Good Samaritan is rather a memorable answer to the question of the rich young ruler: 'Who is my neighbour?' Without an adequate answer to this question, Jesus suggests, the religious life of worship is as empty as a whitewashed tomb. This chapter begins by making two simple points. Firstly, British Methodists have neighbours for whom they are responsible and who are responsible for them, beyond the borders of the United Kingdom. Secondly, the British Methodist Church has no future unless it takes to heart the potential and meaning of living with its world church neighbours. I suggest that while the British Methodist Church has been reasonably successful in the first of these areas, over several generations inspiring enthusiasm amongst many Methodists, it has failed by and large to be affected by world church perspectives in the church's daily life. It has been, as Nietzsche wrote of the church of his own day, turned in upon its own concerns. Yet without a constant awareness that our mission is both within the British Isles and beyond, the British Methodist Church is scarcely a church at all but a self-serving friendly society fated to wither away in a parochial 'Church in England'.

Historical lessons from the world church

A favourite amongst my 'desk toys' is a Russian doll of President Boris Yeltsin. Pull him apart and Gorbachev is inside, inside him is Brezhnev and so on, with a miniature Lenin in the middle of them all. This satirical comment on Yeltsin's ideological ancestry makes a useful point about the relationship between the present and its historical context. To understand any political, ideological, or even theological innovator, and to evaluate their potential, one must place them in the context of their history. Yeltsin makes no sense without Lenin, nor Hitler without Bismarck. Moreover, what is true of individuals is also true of institutions: the life of an institution depends on its ability to treasure the past, and re-fashion it for the future. As George Santayana puts it: 'Progress, far from consisting in change depends on retentiveness . . . Those who cannot remember the past are condemned to fulfil it' (Santayana 1905: ch. 12). To understand how British Methodism has arrived in relation to Methodist and other partners in the world it is necessary to attend to its history.

Methodism was from its outset a missionary movement. All Methodists are, if the word is used properly, evangelicals. That is, Methodists have as their task the proclamation of God's good news. The Deed of Union (the Methodist Church's theological foundation) states unequivocally that the purpose to which God called the Methodist people into existence is: 'to spread scriptural holiness through the land'. The way in which Methodists 'propagate' this gospel has always had two distinct but inseparable elements: worship and mission. The Methodist Church, in other words, is always and everywhere both a *doxological* and a *missiological* church.

The notion of 'propagating the Gospel' had come to the Wesley brothers long before they began the Methodist revival. Both John and Charles Wesley served within the Anglican 'Society for the Propagation of the Gospel'. But it was a far from happy experience, particularly for John. His aim to preach Christ to native Americans had been frustrated by the realities of colonial Georgia. In the light of that experience John Wesley was understandably cautious about establishing fields of mission beyond 'the land' where the Methodist movement had begun. At the 1769 Conference, two Methodist preachers were sent to New York, but this was to a colony that still had strong cultural and, though not for long, political ties to England (Birtwhistle 1983: 2–3). Similarly, 'missionaries' designated by the Conference (though the term 'mission partners' is now preferable, I use 'missionaries' in this historical context) were sent to Ireland, Scotland, the Shetlands and the Channel Islands.

Even at this relatively early stage in the Methodist movement's life, several influential figures wanted to reach out in mission to other lands. In 1783 Dr Thomas Coke developed a 'Plan of the society for the Establishment of Missions among the Heathens', his own inclinations drawing him towards India. Wesley restrained this plan. His journal for 14 February 1784 records that he declined to send missionaries to the East Indies because there was, as yet, 'no invitation, no providential opening of any kind'. The decision at that point to focus work in the British Isles and America was, however, rooted in practical, logical, but scarcely theological reasoning. Thus, in 1787, Thomas Coke redirected missionaries intended for North America and set them to work amongst Black slaves in the Caribbean where Methodist communities had already been initiated by lay people (Birtwhistle 1983: 6). Caribbean missions led in turn to missions amongst former slaves in Sierra Leone, and from there into other African countries. Coke died *en route* to Ceylon in 1814, leader of the first group of Methodist missionaries to Asia.

As missions developed, raising interest in 'Overseas Missions' was often relatively straightforward. Africa and Asia were exotic and exciting to Methodists still living in a world closely confined to one small locality. Stories told by missionaries on furlough, or in the plenteous missionary magazines, caught the imagination. British Methodists wanted to send people and resources to 'win heathen souls for Christ'. It is easy now to sneer at some missionary attitudes and practices. With hindsight some of the attitudes towards 'overseas missions' in the past seem quaint, or embarrassing. Others seem racist, patronizing and shameful. Yet there is also much to admire in the courage and selfless devotion of some missionaries. In 1799 John Stephenson was imprisoned and fined in Bermuda because the island's white inhabitants resented any attempts 'to educate and elevate the slaves' (Birtwhistle 1983: 13). In China missionaries led the fight against the iniquitous practice of binding the feet of young girls. Methodist missionaries knew themselves to be called by God to their task as they knew themselves to be saved by his grace. The remarkable Thomas Birch Freeman, whose father was African, wrote on the eve of his departure for missionary service in West Africa: 'If I hesitate to go to a sickly clime at the command of the Lord of Hosts, because in so doing I may risk the shortening of my days in this life, cannot He who bids me go strike me here while surrounded with all the advantages of this sea-girt isle?' (Birtwhistle 1983: 56). Kenneth Cracknell's beautifully written account of several personalities involved in the 1910 Edinburgh missionary conference shows that amongst the tares of imperialist values, grew also the wheat of justice, courtesy and love (Cracknell 1995). Cracknell shows that many missionaries left Britain with one set of views but, after years of dialogue with other cultures and religions, returned with a quite different set of values.

At an early stage several patterns were set which continue today. One was that in their successive organizational incarnations the Methodist missionary societies have been able to generate a remarkable amount of support for 'overseas missions'. For much of the past 200 years the Wesleyan Methodist Missionary Society (MMS) was the largest Protestant missionary society in Europe. In 1840 the annual income of the Wesleyan MMS rose above £100,000 for the first time (roughly £3.5m today), a significant sum relative to a church with around 325,000 members, many with low incomes. Even in the late 1990s British and Irish Methodists gave nearly £3m a year to the Fund for World Mission. (This should, however, be put in perspective: of every £1 that people give to church funds, less than 3 per cent is spent in world mission or development.) Methodists recognized and responded to a sense of responsibility to share the Gospel with people they had never met. In the Minutes of the Methodist Conference of 1769 Wesley noted the question 'Who is willing to go?' to serve God abroad. Behind this question lies the challenge of Jesus to ask 'Who is my neighbour?'

Yet Methodist enthusiasm for what has been called 'overseas missions' contains two flaws which have made it very difficult for the full importance of belonging to a world church to be realized in the daily life of local churches. The first flaw is that most Methodists have been more willing to *give* to world church partners than to *receive*. A current example demonstrates this. One of the programmes which the World Church Office (the present incarnation of the Methodist Missionary Society) most values is its 'World Church in Britain and Ireland Programme'. Through this scheme Mission Partners from those parts of the world to which British and Irish Methodists have traditionally sent missionaries are invited to Britain and Ireland to serve. Most are ministers, invited for a fixed period to serve in Irish or British Circuits. As a rule such Partners are invited to serve in Circuits that are largely made up of White members. Through a living pastoral encounter with a minister from another part of the world, receiving Circuits experience the riches of a different perspective on the Gospel. Yet, though great efforts are made to publicize the scheme, few Circuits are willing to invite a Mission Partner. Many prefer not to have a minister at all than to 'risk' stationing a minister from abroad. The reasons given can be appalling. One Circuit complained that a Black minister wouldn't fit in, in a White Circuit. Another claimed that a minister from a non-English-speaking country would take too long to master English. Another declared that they didn't want to appoint someone without first having interviewed them. Such reasons appal because these same Circuits have for generations been part of a church which has *sent* British ministers to countries where they have been foreigners, which have welcomed them without first interviewing them, and where churches have patiently listened to ministers preaching through a translator.

A second flaw in British Methodist understandings of the significance of the world church to daily church life may be traced to the distinction which has often been made between 'overseas mission' and 'home mission'. Many British Methodists have failed to grasp that the task of mission is one, wherever it takes place. We have become so engrossed in our local context that we have neglected our global context. Organizationally at least, the Methodist Church in Britain has tried to integrate 'overseas missions' as few other churches. In the Church of England overseas missions was and is left to voluntary missionary societies (USPG and CMS). These societies depend upon Anglican members, but are structurally independent. In contrast the work of Methodist missionary societies has always been directly answerable to the Conference. Methodist missionary societies were integral to each Methodist Conference. Thus, when the United and Wesleyan Methodist Churches united in 1932, their Missionary Societies were also merged. Today, as has always been the case, every British Methodist member is a member of the Methodist Missionary Society (which still exists as a legal entity, though its affairs are run on a day-to-day basis by the World Church Office). Regrettably, this organizational integration of 'overseas missions' into the Church's life has not reached into the minds and hearts of most British Methodists. One Church Steward recently explained to me the absence at a Circuit missions event of members of another Circuit church by saying that 'We're an overseas mission church here, but they're a home mission church.' Until recently the church departmentalized 'home' and 'overseas' missions at the level of the Divisions, and usually at local church level too. Few British Methodists know that they are members of the Methodist Missionary Society and still fewer will exercise their right to attend its AGM which now meets during the Annual Methodist Conference. For many Methodist individuals and churches the world church remains an area for enthusiasts, poorly integrated into their daily Christian life. Arguably, those responsible for running the affairs of the Missionary Society have, in the past, colluded in this separation. They were content if their income was maintained. On the other hand, sometimes those engaged in 'Home Mission' have regarded jealously the apparent independence and strength of 'overseas missions'. Such divisions have prevented the Methodist Church from developing a full understanding and practice of mission. The insights of one side of the heretical division between 'home' and 'overseas' have not borne fruit in the other. The church must learn to think, worship and engage in mission at the local level with a global dimension. The British Methodist Church must incorporate the dimension of world church partnership into every level of its life.

Biblical and theological lessons from the world church

Partnership is a key word in the present vocabulary of the World Church Office. One biblical passage where the word 'partner' appears twice is Luke 5.1–11, the call of the disciples. For our purposes it is a striking and instructive story. In Greek two separate words are used for 'partner', but in this story, Luke uses them interchangeably. Following a fruitless night's fishing Jesus requisitions Simon Peter's boat to teach a crowd on the shore of Lake Gennesaret. When he finishes Jesus tells Simon Peter to let down his nets. The miraculous catch of fish is so great that Simon Peter and his colleagues have to summon their partners to assist them in bringing in the catch (v. 7). The partnership in which the fishermen share is a business partnership. There may well have been additional ties of kinship and certainly friendship, but the term 'partners' refers here only to a most concrete and practical kind of sharing. It is a sharing in the fishing project: a partnership of nets, of boats, of concrete property. It is also a sharing in trust and common purpose.

These glimpses into the economic and social conditions of first-century Palestine are interesting enough, but they are not what motivates Luke to write. Luke's interest is not at all in the fishing project; his interest is in God's project. The partnership which matters in this story is not so much the partnership of the disciples with each other, as their call to a radically new partnership in God's project. Their involvement with one kind of fishing project is to be replaced with involvement in a different kind of fishing project: 'Do not be afraid,' says Jesus, 'from now on you will be catching people' (Luke 5.10). Far from being the replacement of a mundane with a spiritual partnership, of fishing nets for prayer, this new partnership is also to be practical. Food must still be found to feed their stomachs, journeys must be planned, places found in which to sleep, crowds marshalled and the sick brought for healing. But crucially it will be a partnership with God in mission.

Can Luke's understanding of partnership be carried over into the context of world church partnerships? In this context too the partnership in which churches engage is not simply partnership with each other, but a common partnership with God. In calling the disciples, Jesus himself becomes their new partner. When churches engage together in partnership, their partnership with each other must always be rooted in their common partnership with Jesus in proclaiming the kingdom of God. The partnership they have with God – for Methodists expressed with particular clarity in the covenant service (MSB 1975: D1–D11) – precedes and defines the kind of relationship they have with each other.

A second New Testament passage which can help shape a proper understanding of partnership within the world church is Paul's account of the extraordinary collection taken by Gentile Christians for the ailing Jerusalem church (II Cor. 8 and 9; on all this, see Horrell 1995: 74–83). The details of the collection are hard to recover. In addition to Paul's account in the Corinthian correspondence some believe that Paul's meeting with the Jerusalem church described by him in Gal. 2.1–10 may be an occasion when part of the collection was delivered.

Whether or not Paul first began the collection project, it was very important in his view 'to remember the poor' as the Apostles also urged him to do (Gal. 2.10). Efforts amongst Christians in Antioch soon spread until funds were being collected in Macedonia, Galatia and in the province of Achaia in which Corinth was situated. Paul had great hopes of this collection. The dream of going up to Jerusalem replete with gifts for famine relief presumably recalled to Paul's mind prophecies of the redeemed of the Nations returning to Zion in the Last Days (Isa. 2.2–4, Mic. 4.1–3). A more pressing reason was the unity of the church. The collection physically demonstrated the unity of the Gentile Christian communities with the Jewish Christian church in Jerusalem, hence Paul's fear that the collection will not be accepted by those in Jerusalem (Rom. 15.30–31; Horrell 1995: 75). A third reason, the most obvious but not the most important, was to give financial assistance to those in need through a charitable redistribution of money.

Several points can immediately be extracted from these events which might provide scriptural guidance towards a theology of partnership. Amongst the most obvious are the eschatological resonances which always lie behind the gathering together of nations in one world church. In other words, partnership between nations in proclaiming the Gospel brings closer the dream of the book of Revelation of a holy city into which all the treasures of language, culture and faith will one day be brought to be consummated by the bridegroom (Rev. 21.22–27). Church life which does not include the dimension of belonging within a church of many nations is not moving towards this vision; it is eschatologically becalmed.

A second and equally obvious point is that financial assistance rendered by one part of God's church to another symbolizes the unity of the church. Paul is clear: Christians in Asia Minor and in Europe are responsible for Christians in Jerusalem. In a church which is one body with many members, individual Christians and individual church communities form part of a whole without which they cannot live and which cannot live without them. For Paul, humanitarian or charitable relief, though important, are subject to the primary task of expressing the unity of the church. The gift of one church community to another is not, then, simply a response to human need: it is also a response to Christ's prayer that the church may be one. Biblical authors consistently make clear that giving to the poor is an essential measure of true religion. Yet giving gifts, of money or other resources, of people and their skills, may be important between partner churches even where there is no humanitarian need.

Paul's account of the collection in II Corinthians yields further intriguing insights. Firstly, the relationship between churches embodied by the giving of money looks rather strange to modern mission agencies. In the collection of which Paul writes, it is the daughter churches which gather money as a gift for the mother church community in Jerusalem. Seniority of status and age are not in this instance accompanied by money. Indeed, as Paul makes clear, the collection is not even a collection by 'haves' for those who have not. It appears that at first Paul hesitated before allowing the church in Macedonia to collect for the Jerusalem Christians, for the Macedonians themselves were poor (II Cor. 8.1–2). In spite of their poverty, however, the Macedonians wanted to give. This was, according to Paul, because they understood that their giving was rooted in the model of the self-giving of Jesus Christ, who 'though he was rich, yet for your sakes he became poor, so that by his poverty you might become rich' (II Cor. 8.9).

In II Corinthians 9.8 Paul continues that 'God is able to provide you with every blessing [or 'grace'] in abundance, so that you may always have enough of everything and may provide in abundance for every good work'. For Paul, the 'grace' of the collection is grounded in the grace of the Lord Jesus (Horrell 1995: 77). The inter-church project of collecting and giving money had, for Paul, deep Christian meaning. It was as though the blessed-money which travelled along the roads of the Roman Empire in Paul's knapsack was the means of sharing God's grace between churches in the same way that, between tables, the bread and wine provided a sharing in the body and blood of Christ. When bread and wine are blessed they pass from being ordinary objects into sacramental ones. When money passes between Christians it becomes a grace or blessing.

The partnership of Irish/British Methodism with churches beyond the British Isles involves rather more than money: it involves people. Yet what Paul teaches about money can be applied to any resources which are gifts between churches. Paul suggests that giving is, for Christians, also a means to a mutual experience of God's gifts. When a gift passes between Christians it is not simply given by one and received by another. Both giver and recipient share in the gift of God's grace. *World church partnership is a necessary means of grace.* The former Presiding Bishop of the Kenyan Methodist Church, Lawi Imathiu, once indicated that the Kenyan Methodist Church would continue to seek co-workers from overseas 'even when we have enough ministers, doctors and nurses. Why? Not because they have anything new to give us, but they will be a kind of window to bring fresh air into our church. A church that does not receive people from outside becomes stuffy' (quoted in Pritchard 1998: 93).

The way forward

There are many areas in which British Methodism might integrate world church partnership into its life. I suggest three: the theology and practice of connexion, lay and ministerial training, and ecumenism.

'Connexion' (as other chapters in this collection point out) has a peculiar meaning for Methodists, which explains its distinctive spelling in the Methodist context. For British Methodists, 'connexional' means relating to the British Methodist Church in general and not only to one or more particular local churches, Circuits or Districts. British Methodists are 'in connexion' with each other. They do not belong in individual congregations, but to the Methodist Church in Britain. Members may be transferred from one church to another without re-examination by their new congregation. Ministers are received into 'full connexion' and are ordained by the Conference and not by individual congregations. Some maintain that these uses of connexion are the only uses which make sense, i.e. a British Methodist is 'in connexion' with other British Methodists, but strictly speaking with no other Methodists. This makes perfect sense organizationally but it is deeply problematic for world church partnerships.

To begin with, churches founded by Irish and British Missionaries were Overseas Districts of the British Methodist Church (or of those Methodist churches which proceeded into the Union of 1932). However, when the British Empire was dismantled and independence granted to former British colonies, the church, not surprisingly, followed suit. Overseas Districts became Autonomous Methodist Churches. Several, e.g. in India, and in Pakistan, entered new ecumenical church unions. In 1996 the Portuguese District became an autonomous church. Only two overseas Districts remain. Recent changes to the voting membership of the Methodist Conference mean that relationships with partner churches have been further weakened by depriving delegates from world partner churches to Conference of their vote. At the Conference it is difficult to escape the impression that representatives from world partner churches are wheeled on in their liturgical vestments like exotic star turns. Their view on 'domestic' issues (e.g. episcopacy, sexuality, new Methodist liturgies) is not sought, and they are often too polite to offer them.

A very different understanding and practice of connexion was followed by the United Methodist Church, the episcopalian Methodist family with its centre of gravity in the United States of America. For churches in the United Methodist tradition local autonomy has been granted but structural and organizational links have been maintained as an embodied expression of one theology of connexionalism. The United Methodist Church is thus one multinational connexion comprised of Central Conferences in the USA and other countries. Similarly, Anglican dioceses worldwide are self-governing, but retain a sense of identity within the Anglican Communion, with the Archbishop of Canterbury as head (though 'first among equals') of the Anglican Communion worldwide. Naturally, history cannot be re-written. But the result has been that world church partners who were once a part of the British Conference are now effectively merely visiting guests. In my view the British Methodist Church needs to form a new understanding and practice of connexionalism based on a theology of the Connexion of British Methodists with their world church partners.

A second area is training. In every layer of lay and ministerial training a world church perspective needs to be included. Including 'an essay', or a 'world church module' in every training course would not achieve this, and indeed would continue to departmentalize a world church perspective as a specialist subject, such as ethics, or pastoral theology. On every subject addressed in training, the world church perspective must be introduced. One means of delivering this is dramatically to increase the number of living encounters which those engaged in training have with Christians from other countries. All ministerial students should be encouraged to undertake part of their training abroad. Tutors, students and other 'Mission Live' visitors might be present in every college or course. In this way, when a British Methodist in training opens up a subject like ethics, they would have the opportunity to hear how issues appear to world church partners. Their own views would, in this way, be put into a far wider perspective. Though there are clearly cost implications here, some partnerships between British theological colleges and courses and institutions overseas already exist.

A third area in which a world church perspective has been ignored to the serious detriment of vital issues is ecumenism. A dictionary definition of ecumenism is 'of or relating to the Church throughout the world, especially with regard to its unity' (CED: 1994). In fact, for most British Methodists, ecumenism has an exclusively British, indeed *English* context. Recent talks between the British Methodist Church and the Church of England has taken little account of the contribution of international ecumenism. The Church of England and the British Methodist Church are in full communion with the same churches, for example the Church of North India. In Europe, a series of ecumenical agreements named after the places where the agreements were signed (Leuenberg, Meissen and Porvoo) have brought Anglican, Lutheran, Reformed and Methodist Christians into a complex web of relationships with each other. The expertise, experience and theological significance of these relationships has so far simply been ignored in the talks process. Moreover, the effects on Methodist and ecumenical partner churches of closer Methodist–Anglican ties has scarcely been considered. Alternative ecumenical relationships have not been part of discussions; many United Methodists in Europe dream of union with Irish and British Methodists. Such alternatives may well prove impractical or undesirable, but they ought to be considered. None of this is intended to devalue 'local' ecumenism which is indeed an urgent task. Local ecumenism too is an encounter with difference. Yet to conduct bilateral ecumenical conversations at the regional level without some consideration of wider perspectives mocks the term 'ecumenical'.

These areas, the theology of connexion, training and ecumenism are only three amongst others. Necessarily they are presented very briefly. But they are rooted in experience. Between a British Methodist and a Methodist from another country there are things held in common, theologically, culturally, experientially, which either of them does not hold in common with a Christian of another tradition in their own land. The connexion between them is real, and, by being a connexion across national boundaries, it is properly speaking an ecumenical connection. When British Methodists are enabled to meet Methodists from other countries invariably the experience is profoundly rewarding.

Conclusions

This chapter began with a quotation from Nietzsche, one of Christianity's most forceful and effective critics. Nietzsche expressed admiration for Jesus, but scorned the form of Christianity which he observed in the

Protestant church in which he had grown up. For Nietzsche the church was not merely sleek, tedious and complaisant (which would have been bad enough) but hypocritical and resentful of the strong. He challenged Christians to escape their introverted huddles, to flee the neighbour and to love the most distant. Loving those near to us may not challenge us nearly as much as loving those who are distant from us. As Jesus pointed out, everyone loves their friends.

Paul's message suggests not merely that relationships within an international church community are enriching. Paul insists that world church partnership is a means of the grace of Christ. Indeed, without world church partnership the British Methodist Church is not a *church* at all, just as a church which is not a missionary church is not a church at all. According to one statement concerning mission: 'there is no participation in Christ without participation in his mission to the world' (quoted in Newbigin 1983: 1). It is a view which echoes John Wesley's most famous words, recorded in his journal entry for 11 June 1739: 'I look upon all the world as my parish.'

Note

1. Nietzsche 1969: 86–7.

For the first time since the World Church in Britain Partnership began about 20 years ago there will be no new mission partner families from overseas joining circuits of the British Connexion this September . . .

The purpose of the World Church in Britain Partnership is to foster a more complete awareness in both the British and Irish Churches that they are part of the World Church and of opportunities to be enriched by the insights of Christians from other parts of the world.

Consequently, the lack of response from British circuits raises a question about the British Church as a receiving Church being equipped to share more effectively in God's global mission.[21]

Chapter 9

'Water from the rock': Methodism and other faiths

Nicholas Sissons

The challenge of a multi-faith society

In an article entitled 'Teaching Tolerance' (Romain 1996: 16) the Reform rabbi Jonathan Romain tells the following well-known joke: Two holidaymakers in Africa suddenly find themselves in the path of a charging rhino. One turns to the other and says 'What shall we do?' 'Don't worry,' comes the reply, 'rhinos are vegetarians.' 'You know that and I know that,' says his friend, 'but does the rhino know that?' Romain goes on to make the point that Britain is a multi-faith society. You know that and I know that. But has anyone told the rest?

As far back as 1977 the British Council of Churches affirmed that it 'believed the presence in Britain of significant numbers of peoples of faiths other than Christian to be within God's gracious purposes and welcomed the new opportunities this presented to Christians both to learn from those of other faiths and to bear witness to their own faith'. Have the majority of people in the Methodist Church in Britain even begun to come to terms with this basic fact? Has the Methodist Church as an institution started to think through what this might mean?

To answer the second question first: Yes! In 1993 the Methodist Conference published its 'Principles for Dialogue and Evangelism' which took a positive stance towards the diversity of British society; the first four principles read:

1. Our multi-ethnic society is a gift from God, an expression of the sort of society God wants us to establish, within which all human beings can flourish.
2. Meeting with people of other faiths is essential for building relationships of trust through mutual understanding.

3. Opportunity must be given to Methodists to learn about the beliefs and practices of people of other faiths.
4. Methodists engaged in working among people of other faiths should be encouraged in their work and assured of the Methodist Church's warm support for what they do.

But to answer the first question: No! Although, as a Conference statement, this might be taken to represent the view of Methodism, the vast majority of Methodists have not been given the theological tools, the liturgical resources or the necessary encouragement to act on this statement. For it demands something of a revolution in our traditional perception of church and of the relationship between Christianity and other faith traditions – it means we can no longer simply speak with 'biblical authority' of the exclusivity of Christianity, as if this were an objective fact that gives us the right to discount from the start those who understand the world differently. Out-of-hand appeals to such authority (what Bishop Rowan Williams once called 'an alibi for thinking') and the presumption that revelation stopped with 'Revelation' do Christian faith no justice, if we resort to them as undeniable truths. In the post-modern age, it is rightly argued that we must do better than that. The time has come when we must speak for ourselves as people whose faith is forged in the realities of twentieth-century British culture and society and not lifted wholesale out of the Middle East of two to four millennia ago.

But to sustain any such development in our thinking, our resources for worship and study (hymns; liturgies; Sunday School material; Local Preachers' material, prayers etc.) must encourage us to reflect deeply on our context. Yet these have not changed enough; they reveal for the most part an uncritical faith, which has little regard for the complicated challenges posed by other faiths and which often reinforce a comfortable Christian world-view that is both out-of-date and, for a growing number, intellectually untenable. The message that we live in a society of many different faiths, which cannot be easily dismissed as either misguided or devilishly tricky, is not being heard. Yet the problem will not go away – reality will catch up with us all in the end. You can only ignore a charging rhino for so long.

Other faiths and how to survive them

Despite Jesus' charge that those who try to save their life will lose it, many of us continue to think that faith is about 'being saved'. As long as this instinct for survival dominates our approach, for so long we shall probably fail to rise to the challenge that other faiths pose. In my own experience our obsession with survival means that as a church we adopt one of three main responses towards those people of different faith traditions:

1. we pretend they don't exist or aren't different;
2. we consciously keep them out;
3. we sally forth to convert them.

Beneath such responses lies a basic human difficulty of relating to those who are different. All three responses seek to remove or reduce the disruption which difference poses, because it is seen as a threat to survival, to being safe and saved. To pretend the difference does not exist is to try to remove the fact of the problem; to keep those who are different out is to minimize the disruption their presence would cause; to convert those who are different is to make them like you, and what is the same is no longer different.

The first response comes in two forms – the more widespread is a simple refusal to face the issue: 'there's no place for mention of Muslims from a Methodist pulpit' is the way one person expressed it to me after a preacher had done just that. Such a view wishes that Islam did not exist. But in a country where there are now more Muslims than Methodists, that view is intolerable; it is tantamount to saying that church is not meant to relate to the reality of the outside world. Many of those who have recently left Methodism, when asked why they left, replied that the church was simply irrelevant (Richter and Francis 1998). We live in a multi-faith society and that's relevant to each of us.

The less widespread form of this first response is more insidious, because it appears to have thought through the issues and reached a conclusion: 'We all believe the same things, don't we?' 'We're all heading up the same mountain, aren't we?' Such statements are often couched in question form, because people who make them are looking for the reassuring answer that says: 'Yes, of course, we're all the same really. Life isn't as complex and hard as it seems.' But the truth is we are not the same; life is hard and complex. This shallow approach, by appearing positive, hopes not to be challenged. In an incisive cartoon Simon Bond argues that those who ask such questions will be very disappointed should they finally reach the top of their mountain: he pictures an answering machine on the very summit saying: 'I am sorry I'm not here to answer your question . . . if you would care to leave . . .' (Bond 1990).

For me it is vital we give due recognition and weight to the differences that exist between people. Brought up on the Universal

Declaration of Human Rights we tend to assume that humans will treat one another better once they acknowledge what they have in common, their sameness. In contrast, other faith traditions confront us with un-sameness: Jacob Neusner startled many people when he described Judaism and Christianity as 'different people talking about different things to different people' (Neusner 1991: 1). I believe he was right and the fifth principle in the Methodist Guidelines tends to agree: 'The faiths of humankind are diverse and do not all share the same goals.' If we can approach, acknowledge and accept this difference then we shall have laid a far firmer foundation for the survival we all desire.

Faiths are not all about the same thing and we are called to meet people of other faiths not to discover we are all the same, but precisely to find out that we are all different and then live together with that knowledge. In the case of Judaism and Christianity, Christians should not meet Jews so that they may understand their own Christian roots better (many Jews rightly find this offensive) but so that Judaism might stand on its own and for its own sake, and reveal the great differences between the two faiths. Jonathan Sacks pointed out that on only one occasion does the Hebrew Bible command us to love our neighbour (Lev. 19.18), but in 37 places it commands us to love the stranger. This, he says, is the heart of the matter: 'neighbours are those we love because they are like ourselves; strangers are those we are taught to love precisely because they are not like ourselves' (Sacks 1995: 74–81). And although in the New Testament mention of loving neighbours appears half a dozen times, it is always in the sense in which Jesus used the phrase in Luke 10, to speak of the neighbour as the stranger, i.e. as someone, like the Good Samaritan, who is entirely different from us and not the same. Ironically, it is this fact of difference that unites us deeply with other people.

The second response I outlined above spoke about the way we try to keep difference at arm's length. The police recently fixed a sign on a lamp-post directly outside a church in the Mid-Sussex Circuit, which read: 'We catch burglars here.' 'Burglars are not wanted here', the police assert. And how like the church, I thought: despite our wayside pulpit promises of welcome and acceptance to all, little we do is geared towards our accepting people who are radically different from what and who we are. We simply assume that 'we' and 'they' will by definition be different. Whilst we appeal to a diminishing number of people within a narrowing section of the social spectrum, the majority of society remain outsiders who do not understand us and are not understood by us. Like burglars, they do not belong.

And what is more, this attitude has a good biblical text to support it: Jesus in the gospel of John says 'I am the gate' and proceeds to warn the flock about the thieves and bandits who have tried and will continue to try to break into their sheepfold (John 10); such a Jesus might well have stuck up the same notice as the Sussex police outside his pen. Many churches adopt this attitude, with no critical understanding of themselves or the context of John's gospel. Why is it they are less inclined to take notice of the words of a different Jesus in a different gospel, who promises Paradise to the condemned thief crucified next to him (Luke 23.43)? Paradise clearly has a less stringent entry policy than John's sheep-pen; do the Pearly Gates carry the notice: 'We let burglars in here'?

Then there is the third response – converting those who are different. To me this is the most honest of the three approaches, for three reasons: it acknowledges that differences exist between faith communities, it seeks to meet those who are different, and it realizes that the church is as much about going out as it is about coming in. Much of the rest of what I want to say concerns this response (even if I am effectively offering a modified version of it), because it rightly places mission at the heart of what the church is about.

The ambiguity of Christian identity

What I have said so far reveals a basic ambiguity in our understanding of church, which has become acute in recent years. It may be summed up in this question: to whom does the church belong – to those on the inside or those on the outside? The fourth Methodist Principle mentioned above was about encouraging and supporting Methodists who work among people of other faiths. In reality most who do are often dis-regarded with suspicion. When an insider takes a positive stance towards anyone on the outside, who, like a burglar, falls into the wrong category, the ambiguity is plain. It becomes plainest when the outsider belongs to a different faith community. People who believe nothing pose little threat; but people who believe something do, especially if what they believe differs from what you believe. Therefore, in the world of religious belief, alternative convictions and truth claims pose the greatest threat of all.

There is a powerful poem by the Israeli Yehuda Amichai (Amichai 1988: 34) which best portrays the bleak terrain such a clash of convictions can cause, where one group cannot admit the possibility of another one's rightness and rights, because such an admission undermines their own convictions and stability:

From the place where we are right
flowers will never grow
in the spring.
The place where we are right
is hard and trampled
like a yard.
But doubts and loves
dig up the world
like a mole, a plough.
And a whisper will be heard in the place
where the ruined
house once stood.

What in matters of faith appears at first sight to be a position of strength, the poet exposes as fundamental weakness and barrenness. But, says the poet, loves and doubts, like a mole or a plough, are the means by which these sterile certainties can be undermined, allowing the whisper of fertility to break through. Poetry, however, is not history; and history tells us that religious communities have generally suspected and usually condemned doubts, whilst suspicion of the outsider makes love relatively uncommon, because it is hard to love someone you have never met. History is not on the side of poets, but the ambiguous language of poetry remains central to our faith: a vast proportion of the Hebrew Bible is poetry and whilst the New Testament offers us little poetic language, Jesus' parables are a notable exception. They stand out by their remarkable ambiguity and open-endedness, pointing towards the possibility of a faith that can live with the complexities of life.

The Christian Church, however, has always preferred an unambiguous reading of the ideas and expressions of belief that have been handed down to us. Martin Luther, for example, deliberately mistranslated Amos 5.15 to omit the Hebrew word meaning 'it may be' because it did not fit in with his own theological certainties. The canonization of Scripture and the drawing up of the Creeds (with important capital letters) sanctified such an approach and, by becoming so central to Christian self-understanding, made things difficult for poets, prophets and creative thinkers. The argument runs that if all theology is fraught with blasphemy and if the identity of the group is threatened the minute its underlying beliefs are challenged, then it is better not to think too much. This is why any religious group that can persuade its people to limit ambiguity and reduce the threat of difference, will cohere well in times of uncertainty, such as we now experience in secular multi-faith Britain at the end of a millennium. But I would not call this renewal or revival. Conversely any group that encourages critical thinking and poetic ambiguity and engages positively with those outside, may be in danger of undermining its existence. But I would not call this disaster or defeat.

The church needs to embrace the fundamental precariousness of what it means to be the Body of Christ. Precariousness is linguistically derived from the root word for prayer (derived from *prex* in Latin) and we are meant to exist in this threatened prayerful state. Our present dilemma today may lie less in our being in decline and more in our not following the prayerful example of Jesus. Along with his precarious existence we need to mirror Jesus' constant stance of self-criticism towards his own (Jewish) community. This means being similarly self-critical towards our own (Christian) community and at the same time open to the faith to be found outside of it (e.g. as Jesus was with the centurion in Matthew 8 and the Canaanite woman in Matthew 15).Whether Methodism can embrace the outsider positively will depend on whether it can find within its tradition or its present situation the courage and resources to face up to this basic ambiguity and fragility of faith. Before I consider whether the present weaknesses of Methodism may be helpful in this regard, I want to speak of the kind of new language we need to discover, if we are to be able to respond positively to those who are different and who, by their difference, pose a threat to our beliefs and existence.

A new language

As we have seen, it is an instinctive human reaction for religious groups to erect barriers to protect themselves from outside threat. In rabbinic Judaism the idea is enshrined in the first chapter of the ancient and influential *Sayings of the Fathers*: 'The Men of the Great Assembly said three things: be deliberate in judgement, develop many disciples and make a fence for the Torah' (Scherman 1984: 545). But the poet responds that unambiguous identity and self-protection are human and not divine concerns:

> a fence is a fence.
> A defence.
> A pretence.
> An offence ....
> (Dickens 1991: 171)

So what are the theological tools with which we could think about different faiths in a more positive way? At present many Christians feel bound to approach other faiths with what I call a 'Cluedo' mentality:

God sets up life like a game of 'Cluedo' in which our job as players is to try and guess the one right solution – was it Moses up Sinai with the Torah, Mohammed in the Cave with the Qur'an or Jesus on Calvary with the Cross and so on. Death is the end of the game, when God will open the little black envelope and we shall all go off to our respective places depending upon whether we got the answer right or not. People looking in at religious groups from the outside rightly ridicule this kind of attitude: Simon Bond, the cartoonist, pictures an Anglican priest, now a newspaper seller, standing beside his stall which bears the headline: '*Church Times*: the Muslims are right; 140,000 jobs lost – everything must go' (Bond 1990).

If there is to be a change in our approach to other faiths it will only come about when ordinary Christians are given a new way of conceiving the non-Christian world. Out must go the 'Cluedo' approach and with it the 'Cluedo' language. In his book *I Am Right, You Are Wrong* (the cover of which is symbolically half black and half white), Edward de Bono calls such an approach and such language 'Rock Logic' (de Bono 1991: 290). We find it often in the stark and unfair contrasts with which Christians compare the New and Old Testaments: Law v. Grace; God of Wrath v. God of Love; Works v. Faith etc. What we need is something far more fluid, more flexible, better able to cope with difference, with the ambiguities of faith and the complexities of life – what we need, says de Bono, is Water Logic. Here, this kind of logic is illustrated by a story, which appears in most religious traditions:

> A man came to the great Turkish sage Nasreddin Khodja with a complaint against his neighbour. The sage listened to him and to his case and finally said: 'You are right.' The man went away happy and then his neighbour came up and put his other side to the story and the sage listened and then said: 'You are right.' The wife of the sage had been listening all this time to her husband and now turned to him and said: 'I heard what you said to both men – how can they both be right? It is not possible.' And the sage turned to her and said: 'You are right.' (Traditional tale, here in its Muslim version)

Our Western church has for centuries ignored Water Logic and been dominated by Rock Logic, expressed in what has been called 'solus' language. 'Solus' is the Latin word for 'only' and is found in a great many of the statements of the Reformation church: *solus Christus, sola scriptura, sola fide, sola gratia* (*only* Christ, Scripture, faith, grace etc.). This language is very helpful in focusing people of faith upon what is distinctive and central to their belief in God and what gives them identity:

> Thy hand, O God, has guided thy flock from age to age;
> The wondrous tale is written full clear on every page;
> Our fathers owned thy goodness, and we their deeds record;
> And both of this bear witness: One church, one faith, one Lord.
> (E. H. Plumptre 1821–91; *Hymns and Psalms* 1983: No. 784)

But the problem with such language is that it cannot help us begin to understand how the life of a people in another religious tradition may also be a life lived for God. Indeed, historically Christianity has had to misrepresent Judaism in order to strengthen its own identity; thus, in the hymn above, the church's 'wondrous tale' can only be thought to be 'full clear on every page' by denying the existence of an authentic but different Jewish interpretation of scripture. To live with another tradition's difference we need to employ a different language, some-thing that springs from the approach of Water Logic. This is what the theologian Paul Varo Martinson called a 'simul' language, from the Latin for 'at the same time as' (Martinson 1990: 12). We need a 'simul' language that has the possibility of saying 'both/and', to our Christian hopes and the hopes of other people of faith.

For example, since the Holocaust, mainstream church statements have allowed for a radically different conception of the relation between the Jewish and Christian covenants by seeing how the 'Old' covenant between God and Israel and the 'New' covenant in Christ can be regarded as 'both/and', not simply 'either/or'. They talk of one covenant extending the other rather than replacing it; of the church not super-seding the Jews, but carrying on their witness to the Gentiles. And they express necessary caution about language such as 'Old' and 'New', which is more traditionally associated with the Rock Logic of 'either/or'.

Nor is this 'simul' language something alien to our Christian think-ing. We have, until recently, simply never brought it to bear upon our relationships with other faiths. Martinson recognizes that it is deeply rooted in our understanding of God as both hidden and revealed, transcendent and immanent; it is there in our talk of Christ as both fully human and fully divine; it is there in Communion when wine and bread are also body and blood and it undergirds our claims that the kingdom is both now and not yet. This is not logical talk at all, but it is the ambiguous way that many faiths articulate their beliefs.

One excellent example of this is the Jewish prayer which includes the words: 'May God's peace come on earth as in heaven.' Long ago the rabbis asked the important question, 'What sort of peace is this that exists in heaven?' They found a clue in the word for 'heaven' which in Hebrew is *shamayim* and seems to be made up of two other familiar

Hebrew words: the word for fire (*esh*) and the word for water (*mayim*). So, they concluded, the peace in heaven that people are asked to bring about on earth is a peace where fire and water live together, but where the fire does not vaporize the water and the water does not douse the fire; both are held together by God in tension and harmony although they are completely different. Linguistically and logically this explanation is a nonsense, but theologically it offers great insight.

In such a 'simul' approach lies the challenge for our own way of living – can we be united with those who are different, by a vision that is greater than the things that divide us? When the writer of the biblical book of Revelation tried to give a glimpse of what Jesus was like in heaven he says 'his eyes were like a flame of fire . . . and his voice was like the sound of many waters'(Rev. 1.14–15). Here the heavenly Christ unites in himself fire and water; Christ who once spoke ambiguous parables to his followers has now become an ambiguous parable himself, which we wrestle with and urge others to join in..

The Jewish prayer referred to above has much in common with the Christian Lord's Prayer, in which we ask that God's kingdom and God's will may be done on earth as in heaven. But do we ask, 'What is it like in heaven?' For the answer to this question, our picture of heaven, will dramatically affect what sort of kingdom we try to bring about here on earth. So often we regard heaven as a place where everyone thinks and acts and looks the same; where, as the hymns say, all distinctions are 'rendered void', where 'everyone in white shall stand around'. What a bland and impoverished place that sort of heaven would be! Where in that picture is the celebration of the richness and diversity of cultures and peoples that the first Methodist Principle called 'a gift from God'? I believe that if there is richness here, heaven must be richer; if there is diversity here, heaven must be more diverse. And I and many others seek a Christian faith that embodies such a belief and a language that can express it.

Mission as dialogue

'Simul' language is a tool to help us think some hitherto unthinkable thoughts. It helps put to rest the false understanding of the relationship between mission and dialogue, which so hinders people from engaging fruitfully with other faiths. Too often this relationship is considered in the form 'mission or dialogue' and encourages the pursuit of dialogue as tantamount to a rejection of mission: 'If you wish to talk to other faiths (dialogue) then you must first set aside any possibility of witnessing to the truth of God as you have seen it in Jesus (mission).' It is because of this misrepresentation that many people suspect those

Christians who engage in inter-faith activity. Ironically, the first real challenge to such an antagonistic view of mission and dialogue came from Christian overseas missionaries, who found, not the benighted paganism they expected, but advanced, spiritually sensitive religions, that they could not dismiss as easily as they wished; now they needed to re-think their faith as John Wesley before had done: 'I who went to America to convert others, was never myself converted to God.'

To accept, therefore, the relationship between mission and dialogue, as a straightforward 'either/or' is a false choice, which does not relate to the realities of the past or the present. So is 'mission and dialogue' a better expression of the relationship? In other words, are we to regard these two activities as both valid and in some sense complementary, but operating separately? So we have people who call themselves 'missionaries' and people who call themselves 'practitioners of inter-faith dialogue' – they do different things, but there is a need for them both to be there. Is this the proper relationship?

The Birmingham Multi-Faith Resource Unit (MUFRU – presumably with a silent 'B') says in its Mission Statement: 'If proclamation is concerned chiefly with presenting Christ, dialogue seeks also to find Him already present in a given situation.' But it is then made clear that these are both missionary activities and furthermore, that dialogue is implied in all genuine missionary activity. So whilst the expression 'mission and dialogue' is a distinct improvement on 'mission or dialogue', many would still want to argue that any separation of the two areas in this way still avoids the crucial issue. Churches need to grasp the nettle and assert that mission and dialogue are not two separate activities, but that dialogue in all its variety – what S. Wesley Ariarajah calls dialogue of life, dialogue of discourse, dialogue of spirituality and dialogue in action (Ariarajah 1993: 17–19) – is the means by which we communicate our faith and witness to Christ. In other words I would argue for the relationship being expressed thus: mission as dialogue; and at the same time and by the same token, dialogue as mission.

To claim that dialogue is mission presumes not only that I have something of God to share with the other, but just as importantly, that the other might have something to teach me about God. This is a biblical model as we have already noted from Jesus' own ministry, where outsiders teach insiders. It is embodied most clearly in the fictional character of the Good Samaritan, whom Jesus invents to show his hearers that those beyond the pale in Jewish eyes can yet teach God's chosen people, the Jews, about God. It is good to discover that such an idea is becoming more acceptable within churches, as is the insight that by meeting those who differ from us we are helped in clarifying our own beliefs: dialogue not only helps us to be authentic to our beliefs, but also to articulate what those beliefs are:

> I believe the truth is dialogical. Only in dialogue can we discover the truth because only in relationship to others do we form our own identity. We need the eyes of others to understand ourselves. When encountering another person and hearing the words 'I see you' and 'I know you', we begin to see ourselves and understand ourselves. Otherwise we would sit incarcerated in our prejudices and our anxieties. One does not lose one's authentic identity in dialogue with others, but rather one gains a new profile over against the other. (Moltmann 1993: 77)

The Methodist response

What has been written so far applies to all churches. This closing section deals more directly with Methodism, asking whether it may not be better placed than other churches to respond to the needs I have identified. That it might be, would be a combined result of its ambiguous theology, non-conformist nature and even its present difficulties, each of which create a potential space in which inter-faith practitioners can work.

Meeting people of other faiths is not some optional extra for Christians, but an essential element in spiritual growth and faith development. It should not, therefore, be entered into for aggressive or defensive reasons. A church which is over-confident and assured in the rightness of its views is unlikely to allow its members to engage in the kind of open and compromising activity that dialogue demands. If they are encouraged to go out to meet the outsider it will probably be from an unassailable platform and not involve any re-assessment of traditional beliefs and assumptions.

Methodism could be very defensive about its present position and try to concentrate its energies inwardly, not from a desire to protect its ideas from outside influence, but simply to conserve its numbers. Yet as a smaller church and a long-time shrinking one, if Methodism could embrace a humble perception of itself, this should better equip it to reach out across the fence to fellow-pilgrims. And as a relatively recent institution it could regard itself as free from the tiring demands of protecting its past and re-direct those energies into more positive areas of mission.

Along with an acknowledgement of its relative insignificance, Methodism should embrace the essential provisionality of faith; it has, after all, never gone in for rigid definitions of itself and since the Union of 1932 has had a distinctly pluralistic feel. Even in the Deed of Union's statements on Purpose and Doctrine, which would be the place to find the most rigid expression of what Methodism believes, we encounter 'principles' and 'standards' rather than any closely-defined doctrinal basis of faith. Some regard this ambiguity as a weakness and wish to have the principles and standards spelled out; but for many Methodists this offers the liberty to enter into dialogue with one's own tradition and those outside it.

Full-time Methodist inter-faith practitioners are few in number, but it is vital that the church gives them its blessing and a hearing to voice their peculiar challenge. The irony of their position is, of course, that they highly value an institution which gives them the freedom to wander outside its boundaries and query some of its basic assumptions. Because their energies are not directed at maintaining the continued existence of the institution to which they belong there is an advantage in their remaining a minority; their witness, however, to the majority is crucial, for dialogue is about the willingness to be continually changed and converted. Like the Desert Father who gave away his Bible because it told him to give away everything he had, so the radical call of Christ to lose oneself must mean being prepared to lose even that through which you have found yourself. Although it is a fair criticism of dialogue that many people do not enter the real and dangerous territory of authentic witness, but prefer to stay on the fringes of courteous behaviour and respectful curiosity (both important places to begin), nevertheless to be open to change is the real stuff of meeting those who are different – this is where one learns what one is and what one might yet be. Nothing is safe in such a meeting, but faith is not about being safe, any more than it is about protecting institutions.

When Vincent Donovan, the Roman Catholic missionary, was in Kenya working with the Masai, the Vatican sent someone out to see what on earth was going on; they had heard rumours about things not being done properly, procedures being broken, doctrine being fudged, the proper lines of authority being undermined. The priest who came began to talk to some Masai Christian converts: 'So you know padre Donovan,' he said. They replied that they knew about him. 'But didn't he baptize you?' said the priest. 'No,' they answered, 'the tribesmen in the next village baptized us.' Later on the priest took Donovan aside: 'These people are illiterate, they are not even able to write their names in a baptismal register let alone baptize – this whole situation is out of control.' To which Donovan replied: 'Yes, it is out of control and it should have been out of control a long time ago. Because this is where the Spirit works – the time of chaos is the time of the Spirit – in the beginning God created the heavens and the earth and it was chaos – and that's where we find the Spirit of God moving over the surface of the deep – we are constantly trying to control the Holy Spirit; but the playful unpredictable Spirit is always out of control. And will be so' (Donovan 1997).

The Spirit is the non-conformist element in the Trinity, blowing where it will; and following the daring demands of such a Spirit is part of Methodism's self-perception and heritage. When one considers the general ethos of Methodists, there is a distinct impression that what attracts many to the church is its freedom from authority and dogmatism and its ability to be flexibly innovative. From its origins the movement was highly pragmatic, adapting boldly to contemporary needs and circumstances – one thinks of Wesley's use of women lay preachers or the ordination of missionaries for America. Early Methodism was also highly eclectic, unashamedly taking what was best from those around (e.g. hymn-singing from the Moravians, field-preaching from the Franciscans via the Lollards and Quakers, and the idea of Methodist Societies from the many seventeenth-century antecedents), and putting it all together to create something distinctively different. Today's society requires Methodism to display a similar pragmatism and eclecticism.

Our multi-faith society is here to stay and we must acknowledge that as a fact. Christianity must also recognize it is but one of a number of small faith communities within a largely secular society that does not share our basic assumptions of faith. There is therefore a practical urgency to work hard at making allies of all those who hold similar values to us and who recognize the same spiritual dimension to existence. In doing so we will find that we must learn as well as teach, listen as well as talk and in learning and listening we shall, like the master of the household, bring out treasures old and new (Matt. 13.52). If we engage in such authentic witness and relationship with other faiths we shall certainly become something different to what we now are. But this should not be confused with some move towards a new syncretistic religion forged by human will: 'the aim of dialogue is not reduction of living faiths and ideologies to a lowest common denominator, nor only a comparison and discussion of symbols and concepts, but the enabling of a true encounter between those spiritual insights and experiences which are only found at the deepest levels of human life' (WCC 1979: 13). What the result of this encounter will look like will be impossible to predict: it is what Kenneth Cracknell referred to as 'You ain't seen nothing yet' (Cracknell 1994: 16).

So Methodism opens up the possibility of creating many spaces in which to meet those who are different, without the fear that one is compromising all that it is to be Christian or Methodist. One might even enlist the support of John Wesley himself; for although he was certainly far from systematic in his thinking about other faiths, he did not share entirely the general bigotry of his day, which dismissed non-Christian faiths out of hand. Thus the voice of Wesley, which was sympathetic to the authentic faith of the non-Christian, could be taken as a prophetic voice for today, since it was prepared to recognize the activity of the Spirit beyond what Wesley himself regarded as the proper channels.

Without this recognition the urgent millennium call for the churches to 'start again' may fail to address the central challenge posed by a multi-faith Britain. The Churches Together in England pamphlet entitled *A Chance to Start Again* calls on the churches nationally to step across this threshold with an attitude that 'owes more to parable than propaganda' (we might say 'more to poetry than prose; more to Water than Rock'), where the Christian message is not tied down in pre-packaged answers but is thrown open to stir people's imaginations (CTE 1996: 9). Alongside this must go an acute appreciation of Christian history in relation to other faiths, a proper sense of repentance for the horrors that have been perpetrated in the name of Christ and a desire to establish a different relationship in the future, one of mutual witness, where we stand and speak together as people of faith on the immense social issues facing all of us.

In this respect we need to acknowledge a change of direction from the past. The Deed of Union in 1932 declared that the Methodist Church 'ever remembers that in the providence of God Methodism was raised up to spread scriptural holiness through the land by the proclamation of the evangelical faith and declares its unfaltering resolve to be true to its divinely-appointed mission'. My concern is that to be ever mindful of what God did with Methodism in the eighteenth century, may well leave twenty-first century Methodists less mindful of the present world and less capable of fulfilling their urgent call to witness within it. Is it not time to leave behind this rather defensive 1932 version of providence and embrace in its place the 1993 version found in the 'Principles for Dialogue and Evangelism'?: 'We commend a theology of providence which believes that God has created the whole diverse human race and wants all human beings to live together in justice and peace, whatever their religious beliefs or ethnic origin.'

Dialogue is not in contradiction to persuasion. On the contrary. When dialogue is truly free, Christians will affirm their own convictions passionately. And those convictions normally include the view that their partners in dialogue should share these convictions. Christians will be as persuasive as they can. Christians also listen to what their partners say, and they want their partners to be as persuasive as possible in the way they present their beliefs. It is only thus that Christians can gain the most from the interchange. Real dialogue consists in the effort of both sides to persuade the other. [22]

Chapter 10

'A time to be born and a time to die'?: a historian's perspective on the future of Methodism

Martin Wellings

Contemporary Methodists are, according to position and tempera-
ment, informed, inspired or exasperated by the *Methodist Recorder*, but
for denominational historians it fulfils an additional purpose as a rich
and vital source of evidence for the complex realities of our connexional
past. Reading the *Recorder* for the Edwardian years at the beginning of
the present century, it is possible to find two tendencies side by side, two
fascinating and contrasting impressions of Methodism in the apparent
heyday of English Nonconformity.

First, there is an impression of a movement characterized by great
internal strength and growing social influence. In purely denominational terms, 1907 saw the successful union, after long negotiations, of
the Methodist New Connexion, the Bible Christians and the United
Methodist Free Churches, creating a nationwide Connexion of 'liberal'
Methodists to complement the Primitives and the Wesleyans (Currie
1968: 217–47; Thorne 1997: 73–95). Despite the misgivings of
Wesleyan conservatives, talk of wider Methodist Union was in the air,
to say nothing of R. W. Perks' schemes for international Methodist co-
operation. In the political and social sphere, the Liberal landslide in the
1906 General Election brought in a House of Commons with a strong
Nonconformist element (Munson 1991: 282), and two years later the
Recorder was pleased to report the presence of two Wesleyans, Walter
Runciman and Sir Henry Fowler, in the Cabinet. Fowler's elevation to
the peerage as Viscount Wolverhampton in 1908 made him the first
Methodist member of the House of Lords. When the Wesleyan
Methodist Conference met in London in 1907, representatives were
able to see in the massive structure of the Westminster Central Hall,
then taking shape as 'the new Church House', a symbol of connexional
confidence and prestige at the heart of Britain's imperial capital.

The second impression, however, qualifies this picture of success.

From the mid-1880s onwards the *Methodist Recorder* published an annual 'Methodist Church Census', based on the statistical returns of members, members on trial and junior members in the Wesleyan Connexion submitted by superintendent ministers to the May Synods. 1907 saw the twentieth century's first recorded numerical decline, and somewhat sanguine reactions from connexional officials broke down when the 1908 statistics painted a still bleaker picture, showing the greatest drop in members since 1854 (*Recorder* 18 April 1907: 3; 2 May 1907: 17; 16 April 1908: 3). Membership figures continued to fall until the early 1920s, prompting a variety of suggested remedies, from a crusade against Modernist theology and worldliness in the Connexion via 'humiliation, prayer, thought and redoubled effort' to calling in the totals of the buoyant Foreign Districts to boost the sagging statistics at home (*Recorder* 18 April 1907: 3; 23 April 1908: 3). Confidence and strength, therefore, co-existed with a measure of anxiety about the future at the beginning of a century whose closing decade has brought lurid predictions of imminent denominational 'meltdown' as the triennial statistics have once again made gloomy reading. In this context, it may be asked whether Methodist history sheds any light on the prospects for the next century and the new millennium.

'What hath God wrought?': a sketch of Methodist history

Historians tend not to be builders of grand systems and purveyors of sweeping generalizations, much less predictors of the future in the light of the past. Beautiful theories and all-encompassing explanations have a sad tendency to fall victim to ugly facts! A survey of Methodist history may, however, help analysis not only by tracing the evolution of the movement, but also by evaluating in the light of available evidence some of the theories brought forward to explain the course of events this century. While space clearly precludes a full discussion of nearly three centuries of Methodist history, a number of points need to be made about the development of the movement over time, not least to dispel some of the hardy myths which cluster around the story.

It is worth noting at the outset that the Wesleys' Methodism in the eighteenth century was just one manifestation of a widespread move-ment of religious revival which was international and transatlantic in its scope (Ward 1992). Contrary to popular tradition, the revival did not begin immediately after John Wesley's 'evangelical conversion' in Aldersgate Street in May 1738, with Wesley jumping on his horse and galloping off in all directions. There were both earlier and parallel movements, and arguably part of Wesley's genius lay in his ability to draw into his 'Connexion' networks of voluntary religious societies which owed their origins to other preachers and leaders (Heitzenrater 1995: 147).

Methodism during Wesley's lifetime, moreover, remained compara-tively small. In 1791 the movement in Britain had some 71,000 members, 300 preachers and 400 preaching houses (compare the 919,099 members, 4,370 ministers and 15,408 chapels at Methodist Union in 1932, and the 380,269 members, 3,660 ministers and 6,678 chapels returned in the 'meltdown' statistics of 1995) (Davies, George and Rupp 1988: 648–9; Agenda 1996:16). The eighteenth century was not an era of unruffled progress and constant expansion. Methodism grew by fits and starts, and there was controversy within Wesley's Connexion on questions of doctrine, discipline and organization, as well as fierce debate within the wider revival movement as the Wesleys defined their position against the Moravians and against the Calvinist Evangelicals (Heitzenrater 1995: 120–2, 188–90).

Methodism faced a crucial test when John Wesley died in 1791. Although the transition from the authority of the founder to the author-ity of the Conference was negotiated successfully, tensions within the movement made the period from the 1790s until the early 1850s one of conflict, schism and secession. The thread of Wesleyan tradition expanded into a cat's cradle of connexions large and small, competing for support, developing their own emphases and building vigorously. The Wesleyan movement coped with the expulsion of the New Connexion (1797), the Primitive Methodists (1808–10), the Bible Christians (1815) and other groups through the 1820s and 1830s, and even survived the vicious conflicts of the 1840s which gave painful birth to the United Methodist Free Churches and the Wesleyan Reform Union (Wilkinson 1978: 276–329). During these years competing strands within Methodism repositioned themselves in relation to one another, establishing a legacy of distrust which endured into the era of reunion schemes early this century. Methodism also adjusted its stance within the wider ecclesiastical scene, finding itself increasingly alienated from the Church of England and making common cause with Evangelical Dissent. This half-century of conflict, moreover, was also one of rapid numerical growth and of chapel building: in 1850, in the midst of the reform agitation, the Wesleyans alone claimed a member-ship of 358,277, while the various Methodist bodies combined mustered 11,007 places of worship (Davies, George and Rupp 1988: 497–8). Vigorous outreach in this period was a function not only of evangelical theology, but also of denominational competition, an inter-esting point to a generation schooled to see ecumenism as essential to effective evangelism.

The second half of the nineteenth century, held in popular mythology to be the high point of English churchgoing, saw all the mainstream Protestant denominations decline relative to a rising population. It has been argued that in both rural and urban areas, in terms of church attendance, the Church of England was in decline from the 1850s and the Free Churches from the 1880s (Gill 1993: 44–7, 76). An awareness of a need for more organized evangelism prompted a range of measures in Methodism, from the extension funds of the 1860s and 70s to the city missions of the 1880s, and the activities comprehended under the vague title of the 'Forward Movement'. District Missionaries, Connexional Evangelists and lay workers trained by Thomas Champness on the proceeds of the newspaper *Joyful News* were among those commissioned to take the Gospel to the unchurched. The symbol of the new approach was the central hall, with its blend of social, evangelistic and educational work. There were 41 such mission centres by 1909, but their effectiveness, lauded by contemporaries, has been subjected to a searching critique by modern scholars (Rack 1983: 129–30, 132–40).

A scheme for comprehensive Methodist reunion was launched in the 1910s. Despite an initial lack of enthusiasm, particularly among the Wesleyans, the negotiations eventually bore fruit in the Union of 1932. The tortuous process defies easy analysis, but a couple of points need to be made. First, the scheme drew to itself many hopes, some of which were mutually incompatible, and therefore bound to be disappointed. For some, for instance, Methodist union was a step on the road to the reunion of all the churches in England; for others, its aim was to create a bulwark against the Church of England, or against a doctrinally ambiguous United Free Church. Second, although concern about over-provision of chapels and the duplication of effort ('overlapping') formed part of the background to union, the drastic steps needed to streamline three national denominations into one were found to be politically impossible; even the amalgamation of Circuits and the adjustment of District boundaries proved highly contentious. The high hopes of 1932 for a revival of Methodism proved illusory, and the Conference of 1957 despondently rejected a memorial proposing the celebration of the Silver Jubilee of the Union (Currie 1968: 248–89, 300).

For the purposes of the present chapter, the general theme of recent decades has been continuing numerical decline. Falling membership and financial constraints, as much as agreed strategy, have reduced the total number of chapels, although it remained the case in 1996 that almost 40 per cent of Methodist chapels were cared for by fewer than twenty members (Agenda 1996: 297). Remedies for the present situation, sometimes sounding remarkably like those advocated in 1907–08, have been put forward, together with substantial analysis and interpretation of the statistics (Bartholomew, Barber, Beck and Horner 1997: 48–61). It is to this task of explanation that attention may now be turned.

Explanations for decline

The analysis of decline is itself part of our history, and at intervals over the last 250 years use has been made of the alleged poor state of Methodism in one or more of its branches for denominational, partisan or polemical purposes. When decline has been perceived, three broad strands of causation have been advanced to account for it.

The first strand of explanation might be labelled, for convenience, a 'spiritual' understanding. On this argument, Methodism declines when the heart grows cold, the spiritual fires are quenched and believers fall away from their first love. This was a recurrent concern to John Wesley, especially as the Connexion seemed to grow and to prosper. It was manifested, for example, in his repeated exhortations to sustain the 'morning preaching' (the service at 5 a.m.), lest the glory should depart from the Connexion (Burdon 1991: 19). A sermon published in Wesley's *Arminian Magazine* towards the end of his life, and given the title 'Causes of the Inefficacy of Christianity', rebuked the Methodists for their failure to uphold Christian discipline, especially with regard to the use of wealth (Outler 1987: 86–96). Wesley was aware of the ebb as well as the flow of his societies, and he looked to spiritual discipline and zeal as key factors in determining the health of Methodism.

An appeal to spiritual causes may be traced through the subsequent history of Methodism: in nineteenth-century debates on the desirability of ministerial training, where there were fears that 'lettered learning' would replace fervent experiential preaching; in connexional agonizing over the retention of the requirement for members to attend their weekly class meeting; in the early twentieth-century polemics sparked by the official toleration of biblical criticism; in periodic calls in the denominational press for a return to a 'Bible-believing' message, or some other pet scheme (Macquiban 1995: 83–107; Davies, George and Rupp 1988: 571–5; Bebbington 1984: 421–33). In the minds of the fundamentalists of the Wesley Bible Union in the years around the First World War, departure from traditional conservative theology had incurred divine wrath, visibly manifested in a declining membership. A more nuanced interpretation might connect a cooler spiritual temperature with diminishing commitment, leading to a gradual drift away from church and faith.

At this point, where an attempt is made to account for changing beliefs, the second broad strand comes into play: a 'cultural' interpretation of decline applying to all denominations and linked to the sociological model of secularization. Secularization theory draws together a range of causes which, it is argued, make religious faith and practice less plausible and more difficult in modern societies. Elements of the picture might include social changes like industrialization and urbanization promoting the breakdown of traditional communities and behavioural norms, the spread of a scientific world-view diminishing the scope of the supernatural and the role of God, and greater toleration of different ideas leading to religious pluralism and waning commitment (Gill 1993: 2–8; Bruce 1995b: 125–35). Robert Currie has applied this model to late nineteenth- and early twentieth-century Methodism in his study *Methodism Divided*, seeking to show that Methodism was transformed from within by the gradual acceptance of biblical criticism and the theory of evolution, by a growing repudiation of traditional doctrines of hell and judgement, and by a switch from the zealous piety of the class meeting and the enthusiasm of revival preaching to a blend of dignified worship and tepid 'fellowship' (1968: 112–40). According to Currie, as Methodists ceased to be a 'peculiar people' and as the distinctive beliefs, values and patterns of behaviour of the chapel culture were broken down, so 'belonging' ceased to matter and attendance slumped. For some historians, the First World War marked the watershed in religious faith and practice in Britain, bringing together the cumulative social and ideological effects of several decades. On this view, Nonconformist allegiance was the major casualty, and Methodism, as the largest of the Free Churches, the greatest sufferer.

The secularization theory, with its deterministic progression from social change through ideological repudiation of Christianity to declining church attendance, has been challenged recently by Robin Gill. In an amply documented study Gill argues for a third strand of causation, a 'structural' strand related to the policies and strategies of the churches themselves (Gill 1993). Gill's case is that declining attendance pre-dated 1914, that secularization was as much a consequence as a cause of decline, and that a major factor in undermining the position of the churches in the late nineteenth century was denominational competition which produced an over-capacity of seating, sometimes against a background of rural depopulation or urban migration from the town centres to the suburbs. As a result, the stock of churchgoers and ministers was divided between more and more debt-ridden buildings, creating an impression of failure which then fuelled demoralization and actual decline.

Conclusions

Having accomplished a rapid survey of Methodist history and exam-ined the main theories invoked to account for the present situation, it remains only to draw some tentative conclusions. First, it should be recognized that Methodism does not stand alone: the trends and pat-terns discernible in our history over the last century or more are paralleled in other denominations, which have also experienced numer-ical decline. This applies to the other Free Churches, to the Church of England, and even to the Roman Catholics, who seem to have resisted twentieth-century trends more effectively than other churches. Gill's research has shown that the new denominations of the late nineteenth century, like the Salvation Army, soon manifested the same tendencies as older groups. It remains to be seen whether the contemporary 'new churches' will go the same way (Gill 1993: 218–19).

Second, careful historical analysis bids us beware explanations relying on single causes. As noted above, perceived decline has often been a wonderful opportunity for people seeking to promote particular theological, liturgical or church-political agendas. According to personal preference, administrative reorganization, liturgical change, ecumenical amalgamation, a favoured brand of conservative, liberal or radical theology, an attempt to recreate a traditional culture in an ecclesiastical theme park, a shotgun wedding to the spirit of the age, or any number of other 'solutions' may be justified on the basis of a simplistic reading of the evidence. The three strands of interpretation outlined in this chapter all have obvious strengths. Clearly, no Christian would wish to discount a spiritual framework for historical study. Faith does not operate in a vacuum, so social trends and ideologies cannot be ignored. Furthermore, the identification of the role of structures and strategies is supported by a wealth of evidence which repays thoughtful consideration.

Third, careful attention to detail and to the untidiness of historical events encourages us to resist the pure secularization model. Secular-ization is an elegant theory, and a beguiling one for those within the churches who are tempted to see decline as inevitable, and therefore not amenable to any form of remedial strategy. To be locked into a pattern of decline controlled by irresistible forces may be disheartening – or it may absolve us from any sense of responsibility. Our theology, with its emphasis on the 'optimism of grace' and its openness to God's providential leading, let alone our history, should close this option to us, but it is not difficult to discern a lack of purpose, a loss of identity, an absence of hope and a failure of nerve in the Connexion which readily link up with a perception of terminal decline. Bringing Robin

Gill's structural model into play at least serves to modify the picture of irreversible collapse, and bids us plan intelligently for the future, a theme developed elsewhere in the present volume by Andrew Hindmarsh.

Fourth, such planning requires clear thinking about Methodism's current strengths, weaknesses and opportunities. Inevitably these are historically as well as contextually influenced, and many raise issues which have recurred at various points in the long evolution of the movement. Understanding the past does not offer a blueprint for the future, but reflection on our history may pose helpful questions to contemporary planners. Taking up, for brevity's sake, just three burning issues, the following points may be made.

In relation to *ecumenism*, as the Anglican–Methodist waltz staggers into a new phase, there is little historical justification for the belief that denominational amalgamation will, of itself, make for more effective mission. As seen above, nineteenth-century competition produced mixed results: Methodism expanded rapidly at a time when the movement was going through a series of secessions and expulsions, but it may also be argued that rivalry sowed the seeds of structural weaknesses which have come to fruition since the 1880s. The case for a new attempt at Anglican–Methodist union may be made on biblical or theological grounds as a Gospel imperative, or perhaps argued in pragmatic terms of economies of scale (although the prospect of a drastic downsizing of Methodist plant to fund the preservation of Anglican listed buildings would perhaps diminish connexional enthusiasm for the scheme). What cannot be said is that 'Christian unity', here defined as institutional mergers, makes a decisive positive contribution to church growth; indeed, the indications are that the opposite is true. Methodist history since 1932, and the trajectory of URC membership since 1972, makes that point clear (Bruce 1995b: 68).

If being, in Reg Ward's provocative phrase, 'sucked uncomplainingly into the ecumenical Hoover' (Ward 1996: 248) does not appeal, a sharp question may be posed about the rationale for *Methodist survival*. John Horner has argued that Methodism has fulfilled its historic task, and that it is time for it to die (Bartholomew, Barber, Beck and Horner 1997: 59). The option for continuing existence as an autonomous body needs justification, not simply to be taken for granted. In a recent history of twentieth-century Methodism, John Munsey Turner advances nine components of an important continuing role. Several emerge specifically from our history: a prophetic witness to society; a reasoned defence of the Christian faith, building on the so-called 'Epworth quadrilateral' of Scripture, Tradition, Reason and

Experience; the use of groups to nurture faith; a flexible church structure geared to mobilizing resources for mission (Turner 1998: 157–65). Methodism has evolved as a complex organism over the last two and a half centuries, and some aspects of the tradition have ceased to be applicable, for instance, the exclusively ministerial Conference and some of the ethical norms associated with the late-nineteenth-century phenomenon of the 'Nonconformist Conscience'. At the movement's core, however, a theology which underlines that the Gospel is 'for all' and which holds out a vision of humanity transformed by Perfect Love, a spirituality, characteristically expressed in hymns, which is both catholic and evangelical, and a church structure driven by mission rather than maintenance, remain fundamental, and, where neglected, worthy of re-appropriation.

While Methodism has gained and sometimes lost distinctive features since the eighteenth century, an enduring characteristic since the movement's origins has been *connexionalism*. Various attempts have been made to define the connexional principle theologically (Rigg 1887: part V; Beck 1991; Carter 1997), but it is now challenged practically by an insidious creeping congregationalism. Small churches with energy only for maintenance and large churches safe in their self-sufficiency pay scant heed to the tradition of mutual responsibility and accountability, and do little to foster a wider vision. Ironically, at a time when Anglicans are being urged to use deaneries for strategic planning, Methodists are neglecting the key resource offered by the Circuit system. A healthy future for Methodism depends on checking this isolationist tendency at local level, and on reversing national policies which effectively 'disconnect the Connexion'. Methodism cannot function on a congregational model without radically changing its historic understanding of the church, accepting a programme of swingeing closures of local chapels (thus deserting broad tracts of the urban and rural landscape), and abandoning any claim to speak prophetically from a national position in British life. Meaningful connexional ecclesiology is well worth fighting for!

History does not offer glib answers to hard questions. It can provide tools for understanding the forces that have shaped the present, and it can suggest resources with which we may face the challenges of the future. W. T. Davison's advice, offered in April 1908 to the anxious readers of the *Methodist Recorder*, may form an apt conclusion: 'the one thing which *should* be done is to face the facts with such breadth of view and spiritual insight as may help to convert a source of discouragement into an abiding and helpful . . . lesson' (*Methodist Recorder*, 9 April 1908: 12).

I say 'those who are called Methodists', for let it be well observed, that this is not a name which they take to themselves, but one fixed upon them by way of reproach, without their approbation or consent. It was first given to three or four young men at Oxford, by Mr John Bingham, then Student of Christ Church – either in allusion to the ancient sect of physicians so called (from their teaching that almost all diseases might be cured by a specific *method* of diet and exercise), or from their observing a more regular *method* of study and behaviour than was usual with those of their age and station.[23]

... the Circuit, rather than the local church, has been the primary church unit in British Methodism.[24]

Popular enthusiasm for the raw edges of spiritual authenticity, however irksome to those with more traditional views of the role of religion, is remarkably resilient to secularizing forces.[25]

Part IV

Responses

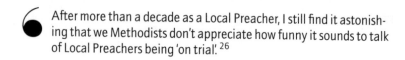

After more than a decade as a Local Preacher, I still find it astonishing that we Methodists don't appreciate how funny it sounds to talk of Local Preachers being 'on trial'. [26]

Christians who come to Methodism from other churches often find the close care of its members . . . both attractive and questionable. It is attractive because it can be pastorally very effective when, for example, people move home or students leave home for college. But it is more questionable when it leads Methodists to exaggerate the importance of membership figures, especially in estimating a church's strength. [27]

This original organization of Methodism as a voluntary order . . . has been of great moment for her subsequent life. In a true sense she has ever been a society in search of the Church . . . [28]

Chapter 11

The future of British Methodism: an Anglican perspective

Elizabeth Carnelley

How many Anglicans does it take to change a light-bulb?
Two – one to write a liturgy for it, and one to do it.

How many Methodists does it take to change a light-bulb?
One – but why does it need to change?

An Anglican raising critical questions about the Methodist Church may seem to be a case of the pot calling the kettle black. However, as I write this, both the Methodist Conference and the Church of England General Synod have now agreed to have formal talks about unity once more, and so it is perhaps appropriate for an Anglican to make some comments. I do so from an entirely personal viewpoint. I cannot claim to represent the Anglican Communion nor the Church of England. I do, though, have a slight Methodist pedigree.

I grew up in Mosborough, Sheffield, in one of the first Local Ecumenical Projects, where a new ecumenical church school was being built in a new housing development. It was one of the Methodist ministers who gave the address at my mother's funeral. My father was one of the Anglican clergy in the team. There were lots of joint services and 'doing things together'.

At Durham University, in my first two weeks I met some very keen members of 'Methsoc', the Durham Methodist Students' group, and soon found myself a regular member. There was no Anglican Society, and I found the Student Christian Union a bit too hearty and evangelical. I also objected to the fact that women were never asked to speak at the weekly teaching session because of the 'headship' issue! But in the Methodist Society I found sensible, open questioning and highly committed people. There were several strengths which drew me in:

1. The tradition of singing and music.
2. The small cell group system of which we were all part.
3. The commitment to living out faith each day and to mission.
4. The lay-led nature of our meetings and worship.
5. The equality of women and men.

As a result of my friendship with those I met, I became Secretary, and attended the Presidents' and Secretaries' Conference in my second year.

Singing and music

I joined the Methodist student choir and found the congregational singing and Methodist hymnody very attractive. (Middle-of-the-road Anglicans mumble hymns.) I still love 'And Can It Be', which I did not know before Durham, having been brought up largely on the Anglo-Catholic *English Hymnal*!

It seems now, though, fifteen years later, that the tradition of hymns and songs which might capture a generation is not now a distinguishing feature of Methodism. I agree with Adrian Burdon that all denominations share a variety of music, and it seems it is the music of the house church movement and the huge evangelical Anglican churches with their OHPs and Spring Harvest/Vineyard/New Wine songs, or the music which has come from ecumenical communities such as Iona and Taizé, which are capturing the hearts of churchgoers today. (It is ironic that Adrian's chapter concludes with a fine modern hymn – by a non-Methodist!) The various chapters in this book all struggle, I would argue, to find something distinctive in present-day British Methodism. Adrian's analysis of worship is a case in point, despite the direction in which he has taken his conclusion. I think many evangelical Anglicans, for instance, would echo the features in worship that Adrian highlights such as fellowship, the rehearsal of the whole story of salvation, the concern for evangelism and the tension between catholic and evangelical expressions.

The small cell group system

The class system has, I understand, largely disappeared from Methodism in the UK. And Clive Marsh examines some of the issues around this in his chapter in relation to Methodism's understanding of 'fellowship' (significantly placed in the section of this book on 'Questioning Methodism's effectiveness'). But it was in such a small group as a student that I met and learnt from three older women, and their Christian journeys have subsequently influenced me a great deal.

Richard Woolley points out that it is the evangelical churches which have understood the potential of small cell organization for the purposes of teaching and nurturing, fellowship, and care for one another. Churches which rely on Sunday worship alone to be the place where people learn, meet one another and grow in faith and fellowship will probably find people take a long time to get to know one another and will have a poor knowledge of the Scriptures and of their church tradition even after an attendance of several years. My own experience in the Church of England is that some people can have attended church regularly for a lifetime and still not know whether I Corinthians is in the Old or New Testament. That the class system has almost died must be to the detriment of the Methodist Church as a whole. This is surely something the Methodist Church in Britain needs to rediscover and revitalize.

The commitment to living out faith and to mission

As students we took part in a mission every summer. I was a member of two of these, to small struggling churches in the Durham area coalfield (this was in 1982–85 when there were still a few pits open). I was highly impressed by the commitment of the other students I met in my first few weeks who met in threes to pray daily, and privately had times of Bible study and prayer each day. The mission gave a focus to our prayer and there was a weekly prayer meeting for our mission.

The missions were very encouraging to the congregations of the local church who had approached us to do such a mission, and it was a busy week of children's workshops, school visits, door-to-door invitations to special events, Christian music nights for young people, worship, preaching and late-night conversations. The impetus of the others, both to live out each day their beliefs, and their hunger to share the Gospel with others, made a lasting impression on me.

It is clear that there are many Methodist churches whose response to dropping numbers and feeling beleaguered has been to look inwards and simply to care for those who are members and ignore those who are not. Mission has not been high on the agenda. And yet a church which is not engaging with those outside is not breathing. This is Nicholas Sissons' point about insiders and outsiders. Mission is the life-blood of the church. I am not simply talking of evangelism; but mission in its widest sense: to be involved and engaged with the local context and the people in your community. This is the sort of vision that Christopher Shannahan puts forward with such vigour.

It is instructive to note that Christopher in his chapter takes as one of his examples of good practice the action local churches took on the Isle of Dogs when a British National Party (BNP) candidate was elected to the local council. This was a genuinely ecumenical movement of people together. Roman Catholic, Baptist, URC and Anglican churches joined together to work for reconciliation and to campaign against racism (see Carnelley 1998). The Methodist-funded Island Neighbourhood Project consisted of two workers, one of whom was Muslim and one of whom was a non-practising Methodist. Though they were certainly part of the 'rainbow' alliance there was no local Methodist congregation on the Island itself which might have rooted the work of their 'red shop', as it was known, in the local community. Any Methodist ecclesial presence on the Island had gone long ago. As a contrast to this, the Baptist, Roman Catholic, and Anglican churches were thriving, growing and engaging with the issues of local people and which brought together Eastenders and yuppies, Blacks and Whites, Islanders and incomers in their congregations.

There has to be some serious thinking as to why and how the Methodist Church has declined so fast in its traditional heartlands. Martin Wellings' chapter helpfully suggests some possibilities. The fact is that there are now many communities (such as my own parish in Bury) where the nearest Methodist church is too far away for the elderly, or those with small children, who have no transport. *John Wesley went to the poor people that the Anglicans ignored; a case could be made out to argue that the reverse is now true.* To quote an Anglican bishop I heard speaking recently: 'When you go to the inner cities the other churches have already pulled out – we are the only ones left.' It has to be admitted that there are strengths in the Church of England's system that everyone in England lives in an Anglican parish and is therefore a parishioner of the local Anglican church. As such they are able to elect the churchwardens, and to be married, baptized or buried there – whether a churchgoer or not. There is no place in England, no local community, that does not have an Anglican parish church. Whether there is actually any effective mission to the people there is another question; but the fact remains that the Anglican parish church is not simply made up of the churchgoing congregation; the parishioners are those who live in the parish, and the church, including both clergy and laity, has a duty to serve those local people.

The Island Neighbourhood Project was a very good small-scale project working with women on the Isle of Dogs, particularly Bangladeshi women, and it is crucial that the Methodist Church supports projects such as these. But at the same time they were not able to motivate local people to take part in the vigil for peace on the day of the election, for example, because they were not part of the local church community – and neither of the workers actually lived on the Island.

Mission – living out the Gospel of Jesus Christ and proclaiming good news for the poor and freedom for those in chains – has to be done *by* local people *for* local people.

I am not arguing that there should now be a programme of church planting so that there is a Methodist church planted in every community. But I am saying two things: one is the importance of the local church, which I shall return to, and the other is to say that churches must at grass-roots be prepared to work together if mission is to be effective. It means responding to the local context – together. If the Methodist Church is declining into nothing there is no point bravely standing firm and saying: 'We are distinctive – let us die distinctively.' Nicholas Sissons' chapter argues for a response to the fact that we live in a society made up of people from different ethnic backgrounds and faith positions. Surely this is best done ecumenically. The vision Christopher Shannahan has of theology responding to local stories is a vision which Christians can share together in communities – it is not just for Methodists. Christopher argues that if the Methodist Church was indeed 'raised up by God to "spread scriptural holiness" . . . Our future must not be found in the maintenance of the Methodist Church as an institution as if that institution was the Kingdom itself.' The spreading of scriptural holiness may be done more effectively as Wesley intended – from within the local Anglican parish church.

Lay-led meetings and worship

At Durham the local Methodist minister actually took little part in the running of Methsoc. He encouraged, enabled, advised and presided at our occasional prayer breakfasts, but it was run by the students for the students.

Although one of the strong traditions in the Methodist Church has been the strength of local congregations and the participation of lay people in the structures, and leadership, I actually think that the Local Preacher system and the 'preaching plans' *prevent* local lay involvement and flexibility. I have at one stage in my own ministry been 'recognized and regarded' as a Methodist minister. This was when I undertook my first curacy (the Anglican church I served there now worships in a Methodist church as an ecumenical congregation) and it is my experience that going to a local church to take a service means that since you have to structure the service yourself, there is hardly any opportunity for the actual congregation to participate in leading the worship (except maybe doing the notices) since they don't know what you are going to do until you arrive there. Contrast this to an Anglican church where the same staff are there every week and therefore it is possible to do long-term planning of lay people to plan worship, lead prayers, to do dramatic presentations, to lead a meditation or whatever. This was the strength of the student Methsoc. Everyone was drawn in and involved in the worship and discussion which was informal, lively and creative. I can still remember a dance/mime to Fleetwood Mac's song 'O Daddy'. In contrast to this the services at the local Methodist church were often deathly dull; we sat as if we were in a cinema facing a blank wall in rows, waiting to be entertained; but we were not entertained: instead someone at the front stood and talked to us while we listened. That is not the authentic worship which Adrian Burdon speaks of which 'brings heaven and earth together'.

The other issue is about being local. A minister or lay leader who is present each week knows the people and can respond to the local situation and be flexible. When the BNP were elected in Millwall Ward on the Isle of Dogs, the following Sunday the whole service at the Anglican church was geared to that situation. People were asked during the prayers to go and write on sheets of paper on the wall their feelings about the situation and their hopes for the future. We reflected together on what it meant for our local community. A Methodist preaching plan made up months ahead with people coming from elsewhere means that local flexibility and ability to respond to context and local need is not possible. Further, the local people themselves are hardly able to participate except as 'pew fodder'.

I know that some Methodist churches have responded to this by having worship leaders who are members of the local church who share in planning and worship; but this is circumvented by some Local Preachers who do not bother to contact them to liaise about worship and insist on preaching the same thing they did this time last year in another church. The fact that some local churches therefore have two morning services – one led by the worship leaders of the church, and the other by whoever is on the plan – to me sounds the death knell of the plan. It is not helpful or creative, and does not assist liturgy to be as Adrian Burdon argues it should be, truly *leitourgia*, the work of the people.

The equality of women and men

It was in the Methodist Society I met feminist Christians for the first time, and as I began to study for my theological degree this shaped my growing understanding of Scripture and tradition in the light of feminist thinking. Unlike the Christian Union, or indeed the Anglican Church, women and men were, in theory, accepted and equal in the structures of the Methodist Church. And yet, as we know, the fact that women have been able to be ordained as ministers in the Methodist

Church for some considerable time (since 1974, in fact) has not meant an end to patriarchal structures, androcentric language about God, sexism or the glass ceiling for women. Like Beverley Clack, many women have indeed left the church. However, this does not mean the church is irredeemably patriarchal. I have now been ordained myself as an Anglican priest and I can trace this back to the Methodist women and men I met as a student at Durham who showed me that power and authority can be used well, that women and men can share leadership, that women too are acceptable, valuable, made in the image of God. Beverley Clack mentions Phyllis Trible's book *Texts of Terror*. This brilliant book does not, however make me want to leave the church. Rather, it makes me want to struggle with the tradition and the Scripture and to make it speak to our condition. Trible herself compares the unnamed concubine of Judges 19 to the body of Christ, broken and shared out (Trible 1984). She looks at the texts in a creative way and makes them resonate with the Christian story of Jesus. For her the concubine is a Christ figure, the victim of oppressive violence. The anger we experience as we read this story and others like it in our tradition should fire us up to work for justice and freedom in our church and in our world – because we know that oppression in any form is not what God wants. That is the shock of Scripture; we wrestle with it as Jacob did the angel and find ourselves dislocated.

Clack is frustrated and made angry by the violence and abuse that followers of Christ perpetrate on women. I am angry too; but there is also violence against children, against other ethnic groups, against our planet, done by Christians – and Jews – and Muslims. This is a deeper problem than merely patriarchy. It is a network of violence in a society where oppression, greed, and the thirst for power and easy gratification are endemic. It is for such a society that Christ died. If the church really listens to God's Spirit, and can really respond to the life-changing presence of Christ in the church, there may yet be hope for both the human race and the planet.

It seems to me that the Methodist Church in Britain may be able to help the Anglican Church in its own deliberations about women's ministry. As we know, the Church of England embodies the song 'Like a mighty tortoise moves the Church of God' (sung to 'Onward Christian Soldiers') and five years on from the priesting of women we still appoint bishops who will not recognize that women can be priests. This issue will be one of the stumbling blocks in formal talks between us – or at least I hope it will, because it may wake the Church of England up to reality.

Conclusion

As I was preparing to write this chapter I read a book written out of the context of the Roman Catholic Church in Britain. It is interesting to compare and contrast that book with this one. Mary Grey's *Beyond the Dark Night* (Grey 1997) sees the church as going through a dark night of the soul, but there is for her a glimmer of light at the end of the tunnel – communities working together for justice, those looking to save the planet, those journeying with the oppressed, those seeking a different way of sharing power-in-relation. The same exodus of young people, of structures which stifle, of empty churches, and lack of resources, which she identifies in her own church, is echoed in other churches. Yet she sees a hope of resurrection.

The question must be asked: is there, in the Methodist Church, the capacity to be transformed into a living church of the community which can engage with, challenge, support, and make sense of, the lives of the people around? It seems to me that the things once distinctive and attractive for me in the student Methodist Society of Durham University are things which are either as well or better expressed in other denominations (for example local relevant lay-led cutting edge worship, or cell-groups), things which would be done better shared with other Christians at a grass-root level (like effective mission), or shared with other Christians at a national level (like the struggle for equality between women and men, Black and White).

I have argued that one must struggle to find something distinctive in Methodism which cannot be found in other denominations, or would be better done with others. However, that is not to say that the Methodist tradition has nothing to offer other churches. As we consider Anglican–Methodist unity, there are clearly some things which the Methodist Church *would* offer to the Church of England in particular. For example: the long period that women have been ordained ministers in Methodism in Britain, and a tradition of equal participation by men and women; the strong network of youth in MAYC which has no parallel in the Church of England; an emphasis on preaching; and the participation of selected and trained lay people in leading worship and preaching.

Part of my job is to train Anglicans to be Readers in the Church of England. One difficulty is the numbers of clergy – and lay people – in the diocese who do not know what Readers are (they are authorized to preach, teach and lead worship, in a way similar to Local Preachers in the Methodist Church). You would be hard pressed, I think, to find a Methodist lay person who had not experienced the ministry of a Local Preacher. The participation of lay people in teaching, preaching and leading worship is a strong focus in the Methodist Church which is simply not present in the Church of England as a whole. That is not to say that lay people do not do those things at all; there are 8,000 Readers in the Church of England, and many other Anglican lay people are involved in leading worship in different ways. But generally the emphasis in the Church of England is on 'priest and parish'. Whilst I have expressed reservations about the outworking of 'the plan', the life-blood of the Methodist Church is the laity, and the local preacher tradition is crucial and to be celebrated and shared.

Thus there would be several strengths that the Methodist Church would bring to a closer working together, or a reunion, with the Church of England. It does seem to me that rather than dying distinctively, it would be better for the British Methodist Church to offer its strengths to the mission and ministry of the kingdom through a closer collaboration with the Church of England.

Methodism has had an important part in the story of God's church in Britain, and the Methodist Church abroad, (like the Anglican), is growing in many places. Yet perhaps the British Methodist Church has now to accept that its future may well be where it started – in the arms of the Anglicans. If that is not to be the case, then the alternative is radical change, perhaps along the lines that some of these chapters have argued. Can the Methodist Church meet either challenge? It would mean painful change. But it might be that cutting off the leg is the only way to save the patient.

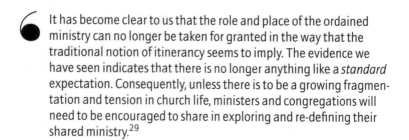

It has become clear to us that the role and place of the ordained ministry can no longer be taken for granted in the way that the traditional notion of itinerancy seems to imply. The evidence we have seen indicates that there is no longer anything like a *standard* expectation. Consequently, unless there is to be a growing fragmentation and tension in church life, ministers and congregations will need to be encouraged to share in exploring and re-defining their shared ministry.[29]

We need some more copies of the Local Preachers' Training Course provided by the Connexion.[30]

'What does Headquarters think it's doing?'[31]

Chapter 12

The threads with which we weave: towards a holy church

Jane Craske

It is time to review where we have got to in the course of this book, and in the process that has culminated in this book. In this short chapter I shall try to tease out some of the threads which have run through the chapters of this book, and now appear as central concerns to be highlighted. Focusing on these threads must not appear to unravel the complex arguments in separate chapters, or obscure the differences in emphasis between chapters. But it is helpful to draw attention to certain shared, often implicit, concerns. The postscript which follows this chapter focuses explicitly on the future.

In this book, we have concentrated on British Methodism, but tried to put it in context by looking at British Methodism's place in world Methodism, at our role in a multi-faith society, and at the way one particular ecumenical partner might review our concerns. We have tried to examine the present in the light of the past, and to assess where individuals and churches find themselves theologically, liturgically and organizationally. The Methodist story is a whole series of narratives, and is a story worth telling and re-telling. It includes the emphases we have highlighted in this book, and the ways in which those emphases were arrived at. It is important for British Christianity's future that Methodism's particular adventures in Christian discipleship should not be lost, because they are examples of how people have reflected, in their own contexts, on the primary Christian story. They encourage us to similar reflection on both our context and the Christian good news. There are 'dangerous memories' in the Methodist story about the ways in which past forms of Christianity have had to be called to account, needing reform and renewal. There are further 'dangerous memories' about the ways in which Methodists too have got it wrong. All of this is an important narrative strand, to be re-told again and again within British Christianity.

Connexionalism

I wonder how many readers will find it strange that a group of Methodists under the age of 40 have kept returning to such a tenet of Methodism as 'connexionalism'. To use the word 'connexionalism' is to assert that the Methodist understanding of what it is to be the church is all about relationships and networking (a word implying the activity of making relationships). Relationships and the interdependence of people (and of people with the rest of creation), have become key concerns in much modern theology, as well as in other fields. Contemporary trinitarian theology helps us to see that the God who is three persons relating in one empowers us to relate better to others. It can never be a question of whether local Christians and local churches should be in relationship, but only what sort of relationships. Methodism, of course, is not even a network of local churches; it is a network of *Circuits*. Methodism (in theory) simply cannot conceive of the local church aside from relationships with other local churches. It might be argued that the lack of Circuit consciousness which many Methodist people exhibit is about people not wanting relationship, and thereby denying something fundamental not only about Methodism but also about Christian faith.

The relationships of Circuits within the British Methodist Connexion are like basic and extended family relationships. They are important as somewhere to start, but become damaging if we only remain there and never venture beyond the extended family. Wider relationships are needed, just as they are needed for individuals and for families. So we have explored relationships with world Methodism, with our ecumenical partners, in Britain and around the world, and with other faith groups. These are the networks which expand our vision; they grow out of love and they express love. They are expressions of the vitality in us and of our interest in others. Churches, like individuals, have to be interdependent in order to be whole, and to grow. Only when death or despair are near do people withdraw from relationships, or only when they are kidding themselves about life, and trying to pretend to a stand-alone independence which they do not possess.

In the Methodist heritage connexional relationships are embodied practically, in the sharing of resources. That is perhaps at its clearest in the stationing of presbyteral and diaconal ministers. It is also shown in many forms of training, through the funds the Connexion distributes, and the gifts of District and Connexional officers. But relationships are never one-directional. The relationships of churches within a Connexion *live* in the giving and receiving of support, in the mutual learning and interest of every local church with others, in the sharing of insights that come from the grassroots of the church, and from those who have an overview out of experience of a large number of churches.

Connexionalism bites, to take one example, in an issue such as that of Local Preachers, which Elizabeth Carnelley highlights. In particular at present, many churches are working with the difficulties of balancing the relatively new possibilities of worship leaders with the more traditional Local Preachers and the sacramental ministry of presbyters. Who does the local church's worship belong to? Should it not be the local congregation? But Local Preachers represent the sharing of resources and gifts which is at the heart of the relationships the local church needs if it is not to be insular in a way that will deny its mission and its being in Christ with others. The conflict over the word 'local' becomes immediately apparent. In fact Local Preachers bear the particular tensions of an inversion of local and itinerant roles. It now seems that the minister is regarded as more local than the Local Preacher. Circuit-based Local Preachers are struggling to be both local, and therefore relevant, and also to embody a wider perspective than the local congregation.

'Insidious creeping congregationalism' in British Methodism (to use Martin Wellings' phrase) has developed at a time when individualism has become stronger in British society, when there has been demonstrably less sharing between rich and poor, yet also at a time when the importance of decentralization has been recognized, and talk has been of 'subsidiarity' (taking decisions at the most local level possible, closest to those who will be affected). At the same time, we are also recognizing that communities are not only formed on a geographical basis, nor is the community where people live necessarily their primary community, when, for some, interest-group communities or work-related communities are equally powerful. What practices would be most positive for the local church's worship, in the light of this? It must surely be those which are based firmly in the local congregation when it is aware of itself as necessarily, and with delight, involved with others. So local worship leaders, Circuit-based 'local' preachers, and Connexion-appointed presbyters, are all precious and necessary resources, but none must represent an 'outside' or 'individualist' control of worship. Worship must not become (as it so often has) a spectator event in which people participate as little as they choose.

Connexionalism means relatedness and entails mutual support. Much of contemporary Christianity's weakness is to do with people inside churches being debilitated by the sheer number of churches and church buildings, and by people outside the church being baffled as to what such denominational diversity actually means. What if insights about relationships between churches, as they have taken concrete structural shape in Methodism, were to be argued for theologically, and actually worked out practically in ecumenical settings at all levels? Here is something to offer to British Christianity as a whole.

Diversity

Other relationships are possible beyond the structural ones of churches, circuits and national organizations. There are numerous networks to which individual Methodists or, sometimes, local churches belong, which represent interest groups. They may be theological networks (e.g. Headway), or networks that represent specific ethnic (Black Methodists' Group) or gender (Methodist Women's Forum) interests. Can British Methodism, with or without that label, offer a space which sees why such groups (based on similarity of interest) are important, and yet celebrates difference or diversity? Can we develop relationships which celebrate what we share while recognizing that what we share is both our similarities and our differences?

Diversity has become a crucial word in our discourse. Nigel Collinson, in meetings during his Presidential year (1996–97) challenged the Connexion to think about diversity. But we have tended to think about it in such restricted contexts (principally human sexuality and credal confessions) that we have narrowed our discussions to 'the limits of diversity'. That immediately puts a negative cast on any discussion. That cast is even more negative when the discussion is further limited to the subject of theological diversity. As soon as that happens, we have lost the sense of so many other aspects to a welcome diversity within the church. The contributors to this book share a generational similarity and are a theologically diverse group of people, with diverse roles in and out of church life. We are far from representative of Methodism as a whole. But it was very clear to us that our theological diversity did not easily fit with a simple 'liberal' versus 'evangelical' agenda, though some have tried to force those labels on us. We want to celebrate diversity in a greater variety of forms. This book comes at a time when we have become very aware of British Methodism losing its generational diversity. 'All ages' together in Christian discipleship is a cause for celebration. Likewise we can celebrate gender and ethnic diversity. It is crucial that we are a diverse church.

If our discussion of diversity could centre on celebration, rather than on anxiety about the limits we should be setting, we would be considerably better off. Perhaps then we would realize that we cannot set limits apart from people, for limits unrelated to actual people and situations are destructive. We are taken back to our relationships, to the joy of relating to other people in their differences and samenesses, rather than trying to exclude people by setting doctrinal limits. Since ideas do not exist separately from people, when we discuss the limits of diversity we do not outlaw ideas, we exclude people. A celebration of diversity within the church might then lead to the recognition and acceptance of difference more widely.

If we are intent on the vision of a diverse church which is a delight, to us and to God, we must be seeking a theologically educated church as one aspect of that. Such a church would be a body of people prepared to ask questions, knowing the traditions, but not prepared to make idols of them. Richard Woolley's chapter more explicitly than any other shows up the desire for resources which enable people to ask questions and find their own answers, rather than being force-fed with other people's answers. That is clearly something that our contemporaries find important as part of the search for personal integrity. Such questioning is not a sign of weakness, as some suggest, but the principal sign of vitality, vigour and even loyalty. Why bother to challenge what you don't care about? This searching is what goes on in the broad, diverse church which it seems to me has been pictured by most of the contributors to this book.

The kind of diversity I am exploring is not, though, to be understood as 'each to his or her own'. That would lead to even more denominational divisions than we have now, and the Protestant tendency to support the free spirit would indeed then have issued in the individualism from which Western culture is reeling. Instead it needs to be held together with the previous thread of 'connexionalism' and relationship. Looking at the two together helps us to ask how Christians in Britain as a whole can handle their differences and build together, seeing diversity as positive and necessary, rather than turning to ecumenism only as a survival strategy.

This book has sought not to create a false unity, but to recognize the differences among the contributors. Yet our experience, for all our diversities, was of increasing closeness as people, precisely in the exploration of our differences. Can others not testify to that experience?

Mission

We are moving towards the end of a Decade of Evangelism (or Evangelization) in which the membership of the Christian church in Britain (in whatever ways that is measured) has continued to decline. So if we expected the Decade of Evangelism somehow crudely to boost numbers we have obviously failed. But, perhaps the Decade has achieved something completely different. Perhaps it has taught the church about mission. During the 1990s, all sorts of churches have begun to talk much more consistently about mission. Our structures have been reorganized to emphasize mission, however far Andrew Hindmarsh's chapter suggests there is still to travel. It has become normal to talk about 'mission rather than maintenance', or to concentrate on 'getting out there' without first having to 'get our house in order' (since we won't do the latter if we don't do the former). Perhaps we have even begun to realize that the purpose of mission is not to 'get our own house in order', or boost our numbers: it is not in fact *for us* at all. This Decade has also given us a chance to become more aware of a multiplicity of models for evangelism, and to focus on an 'Emmaus Road' style of growth into faith, and growth within faith, rather than solely concentrating on 'Damascus Road' sudden conversions and imagining that is the end of the matter.

Within this book too, from the past and into the present, we have highlighted the essential Methodist emphasis on mission, out of Arminian 'for all' theology, which is quite clearly the language of mission. We have seen it reinterpreted for the present and future in the idea of mission as dialogue. Mission makes the church tick. It is the lifeblood of the church, because it is about bringing new life into the church.

We have to recognize again the origins of the word 'mission' in the idea of 'being sent', and to concentrate not just on the God who sends us, or on ourselves as sent, but on those we are sent to; interested in people for who they are. Again, the image is one of a church that wants to reach out beyond its own walls, that wants relationship. But if that is our predominant attitude, we will not be able to determine the outcome of our mission activity. Instead we will be promoting the kind of exploration which assumes we have learning as well as teaching to do. And we need to be organized for this, conscious of our purpose and direction, with clear strategies for achieving the next few steps towards that purpose. Both the sense of clarity, and the fascination with which we explore the unknown are necessary to mission.

Contemporary Christianity's mission must face the apparent loss of confidence within and beyond Christianity about what *religion* is for. We need to work harder at clarifying what religion is and does, and what our form of religion is and does, otherwise we haven't got a chance of introducing others to it. Is not part of mission a simple, educational task to open up the riches of the Christian religion, not as an end in itself, but in order to demonstrate how a Christian approach to life actually functions? If we can't point people to the principles behind our practice (even if, as Methodists accused of being pragmatists, we are always more likely to stress the practice), then God help us. Again, this is not just a Methodist issue. Ultimately it's about recovering some theology (even if we are wary of using the word 'theology'). It is not coincidental that the Alpha course is so successful, that Christians of other theological persuasions cry out for similar alternatives, or that the numbers of people on adult education courses in theology and religious studies are so staggeringly high. Even if church-going may be culturally odd, those who go (and others beyond the fringes) are actually wanting to know more about what it is they believe, and why they do what they do. Perhaps part of our mission is to ensure that that could be said of all Christians.

Adrian Burdon's chapter highlights the place of worship for mission, but challenges us in that very emphasis to reassess the worship in which we participate. Is it the celebration of some 'in-group', alienating to everyone else (and does it ever feel like celebration?), or is it celebration in which others find it possible to join? Is it welcoming to women as well as to men, to children as to adults, to Black as to White? Will all people find in our worship words, music, silence, actions, and the God they point to, which they can access from their own experience of the world and of themselves, as well as the resources to be stretched beyond themselves?

Given Methodism's origins, it should be at the forefront of mission. But since Methodism originated as a challenge to British Christianity's tendency to be socially exclusive, Methodism should equally be at the forefront of enabling British Christianity today to see what the contemporary equivalent of that past Methodist calling should be in its mission. Christopher Shannahan, Richard Andrew and Nicholas Sissons in this book have all in their ways pressed powerfully the link between mission and diversity. Within our mission the concern for social exclusion remains part of Christianity's agenda simply because we understand it to be part of God's agenda.

A vision of holiness and the possibility of change

At present British Methodism is participating fully in the problems of most of British Christianity – decline, tedium, lack of care, lack of intellectual credibility, lack of emotional credibility, an inability to answer the questions of minority groups, or of many women. But, if we have heard the cry to be more conscious of our purpose, what is it we are here for? What can sum up so many of the concerns above? Perhaps we can find renewed vigour for the word 'holiness' to match our concerns. It may be possible if we can rid it, in our own minds, from associations of self-righteous, 'holier than thou' attitudes. That project would be aided if we remember the links between the words 'holy' and 'whole' (originating from the same Germanic root), and 'healing'. The primary meaning of holiness is about dedication to God. But it links also to a range of concepts about healing, being complete, having integrity. It is about salvation (that word also so closely linked with healing in its Greek origin). That 'healing holiness' is what our mission is for, in the church and in the world. It is a word which covers the whole vista from personal piety to the creation of a new heaven and a new earth, dedicated to God. It sums up the effect of the personal, spiritual experience of God in Christ in the life of the individual, as well as how that individual relates to others. It includes the dimension of socio-political action. Such a vision, shared, provides a rationale for connexionalism. It is properly rooted in our history, but extends its meaning into the everyday life of Christians today, their 'private' and 'public' lives. We should be hearing it as an umbrella word for diversity, echoing all the diversity of a holy God.

If a vision of holiness can inspire us afresh, we must come back to the shape of the church demanded by that vision. It will be a church firmly in society, a church which stays close to everyday life, and recognizes the diversity of everyday life. The church can only be that sort of church if its people are that sort of people.

So many of the ideas, arguments and assertions in this book are old ones, or at least ones well worn in the public domain, even if we hope they are seen in a different perspective because of the place in the church and in today's society from which they come. But if all this has been said before, why isn't it getting through? Why do things in the church not change? Somehow there is a failure to convince people, or a failure to know how to put ideas into practice. We are constantly living between the real and the ideal church and that is a place of tension. Our hopes and dreams are ahead of us, and seeing them often only ahead of us, we focus on the frustrations of the present. That may mean we fail to see the seeds of the future in the present, the seeds of the ideal in the real.

It has become increasingly noticeable – and important – that we have not felt the need in this book to concentrate on issues of specialized ministries in general, and ordained ministries in particular. Yet eight out of twelve of the contributors are ordained. It does, however, seem relevant here, from 'inside' ordination, to ask whether those of us who have been trained recently have focused more on the ideal than the real church, looking deliberately and properly towards the future, seeking to develop vision for local Methodist churches and for the church as a whole, in such a way that we are bound to experience and focus many of the particular tensions of change. It is painful trying to live towards the future.

Change is always difficult, but perhaps we don't face it enough. There is more than a suspicion that we don't really communicate with each other at depth in our churches. We have become acclimatized to the idea of the church and Christian experience as 'for me' and have failed in our relationships. Some have become so acclimatized to relationships with the same people, that they have lost the drive to build other relationships and reach out. So often we don't share our stories, we don't think strategically, we refuse to analyze our situation, and we certainly don't expect anything to change. All we can be bothered about is whether people turn up to join us on Sundays. None of that makes for a holy people.

One of the things that we want to point to, in response, is the process by which this book came about. Many of us were able actually to meet together to explore, even to explore negative experiences, which is how many of us characterize some of our experiences of the church. Most of the contributors are still in the British Methodist Church because we believe it has something precious in its past, present and future. We have all rejoiced in the hopeful conversations that have attended the writing of this book, even as we have felt bound to say that we are struggling and that many of our contemporaries have given up the struggle with the church because they feel they can live more authentic lives outside it. Yet our model of communication is ultimately what we can offer. It has entailed reflection, challenge, disagreement, deep articulation of things that matter to us, meeting to spend time together where possible, hard slog and a profound respect for what each of us has to impart to the others.

Holiness is not a state to be achieved; it is activity, and direction, and process. It is the process of exploration and dialogue which is part of living the consequences of being a broad church. The church that lives that process will be a holy, healing church, celebrating diversity and relationship in the name of the Triune God. That celebrating activity will make us reach out beyond ourselves in Christ's name. And that is our holy purpose.

It is being caught up in the Connexion that saves me and the churches I serve from being small minded, introverted Christians, who would turn our churches into little religious clubs. The Connexion is always obliging us to think big as well as supporting us when we attempt great things for God, or at least we attempt little things in a great way.[32]

Chapter 13

The challenge for contemporary Methodism: a postscript

Clive Marsh and Jane Craske

So where is British Methodism to go in the light of all this? It is important to emphasize that the contributors to this book did not set out to work as a group towards a common understanding of what the British Methodist Church should do about its own institutional status. Such a decision can only follow on from the kind of considerations offered here. What we have tried to do is offer from a limited range of perspectives a collection of insights into what seem to be major issues in Christianity, from our respective (mostly Methodist) standpoints. As a collection, these chapters therefore suggest what Methodism should contribute to any understanding and practice of Christianity, whatever be the shape of Christianity in Britain in the future, and whether or not Methodism continues to exist as a separate institution.

What we have done (and had done already, in fact!) is precisely what the Methodist Council in Britain asked for in offering guidelines for responses to a discussion paper about British Methodism's future, circulated throughout the Methodist Church in October 1998. We have not 'got bogged down in detail'. We have, effectively, identified 'a few broad issues which are essential to the nature and purpose of the Christian church as understood in the Methodist tradition, while at the same time remembering that Methodists are a "catholic" community' (*Methodist Recorder*, 23 October 1998: 24). We have, via Andrew Hindmarsh's article, asked some questions about church structures. But even there, we were speaking broadly. And, if anything, a main conclusion of that very chapter was the suggestion that Methodism should ask the question of what it is actually trying to do. Given that contribution's foresight, it suggests that some of its other points may be worth scrutiny.

We set out neither to be definitive nor especially original. If there is novelty here, it pertains simply to the fact that the insights derive from a surprising minority group – the under-forties. What we are doing is reflecting what Methodist emphases and interests look like from where we stand. We half expect readers, Methodist or not, to say: 'But isn't Methodism *more* than that?', to which we can then respond (to Methodists) 'Then make it so' and to all 'Well, we are not experiencing it in this way'. We cannot make Methodism something it isn't, especially given our numerical weakness in the church. What we are doing is reflecting the particular strengths and interests of Methodism which relate significantly to us. We are (most of us) inevitably going to imply that Methodism (as a movement, though not necessarily as a separate institution) is a 'good thing' because we are within it. But it commits us neither to arguing for its continuing independence nor its demise in institutional terms. That was not our purpose. Our challenge – to Methodists and others who are interested – is to note and 'dwell on' some of what we see to be important about it, in relation to Christianity as a whole.

This postscript will do three things:

1. emphasize how the book's structure and content should be understood in relation to Methodism's present and future;
2. link the book's contents to a further recent proposal for the future of Methodism, that by John Munsey Turner;
3. lay out in direct fashion for the reader what the concrete options for British Methodism are.

So how does Methodism's present relate to its future?

The question 'What is British Methodism about?' has in effect been answered in a number of ways by this present book. In the first part, four writers offered readings of Methodism's theology, worship, socio-political activity and its relationship to its evangelical heritage from a variety of angles. Different theological persuasions and church traditions were represented. These persuasions and traditions cut across the chapters and the effect of the whole first part of the book is to compel the reader not to label these chapters and writers as 'liberal', 'radical', 'catholic', 'evangelical' or 'post-evangelical' too easily. For the threads which Jane Craske spoke about in the previous chapter were all interweaving across the chapters. Methodism has been – and still is – about all the features presented in those chapters, caught up within more embracing headings such as 'connexionalism', 'mission' and 'catholicity'.

Elizabeth Carnelley, looking in on Methodism from the outside, offered her own reading of what she had experienced Methodism to be about. Clear links can be discerned between her expectations and features of the book as a whole. Martin Wellings' material invited us to see what has sustained Methodist distinctiveness throughout its history, in the context of noting the persistent ambiguity about Methodism's self-confidence as an institution. But it would be useful for readers to do their own checking at this point. Whether you're a Methodist or not, it would be worth your asking what's missing from our exploration as a whole? In other words, you could compare your own understanding of what you think Methodism to be about with some of the emphases to be found throughout the book, but especially in the first part, and in Martin's and Elizabeth's chapters.

Other chapters in the book's second and third parts took us into further challenging territory. In Part II, we had to face up to some tough questions, and we could have multiplied the examples. Beverley Clack was talking about Christianity generally. Her story invites our consideration both of the way in which Christianity seems increasingly less plausible for people in the contemporary world, as well as the way in which, for a whole variety of reasons, twenty- and thirty-somethings have drifted from the churches. Methodism cannot escape this fact, and no amount of expression of regret that the 'young don't come any more' can replace the need for churches to do some serious thinking about what this all means for the future of Christianity.

Clive Marsh's chapter focused upon an aspect of Methodist practice which is readily identifiable and rarely examined. In addition to the discussion it may itself provoke, there is a wider issue: are there other aspects of Methodist practice which would merit such close examination, because they have been insufficiently scrutinized?

In the case of Andrew Hindmarsh's chapter, there is again a broader issue beyond its own immediate content: how ready is any church, in practice, to receive and learn genuinely from the actual experience of the majority of its people in the wider world?

Any form of Christianity in Britain in the future has also got to ask questions of itself such as those posed by Stephen Plant and Nicholas Sissons. In other words:

- What account is being taken of the fact that Christianity is a world faith, and far from only a Northern Hemisphere faith? What sense are we to make of Christianity no longer being a Eurocentric religion? And how should that affect British Christianity in any form?
- What account is being taken of Christianity's place alongside a range of other faiths, in such a way that Christianity's own insights and practices are not flattened or stunted, but that its members are more mindful of what it means to be one religion among many?

These reflections all derive from the actual practice of Methodists undertaking their respective work, and living their lives as Christians. But we must stress: these are not questions for Methodism alone. It therefore makes no real sense for Methodism to be addressing them alone. An ecumenical imperative is again sounded. And yet they are also real issues for Methodists, as Christians. If they are not on our agenda, we are simply living in the past, or pretending that these questions are not live (and in turn effectively wishing Christianity dead).

So what of the future? John Munsey Turner has recently put forward his own suggestions as to what Methodism should focus on if it is to make any significant contribution to the future (Turner 1998: 90–6). Two of his nine points focus on a new style of ecumenism, one on the institutional level, one on the individual. In this volume, we have come at things largely from a Methodist angle, but none of us has wanted to stop there. If our resources are not to be offered to and shared with the whole of the church, then we are not using them aright, and they will become useless even for us. Turner highlights the particular resource of our style of worship, and in this volume we have faced the difficulties of telling the story of our distinctiveness, while recognizing the extent of modern ecumenical sharing, particularly in resources for worship.

As Jane Craske's chapter highlighted, we agree with Turner's reminder of the importance of mission to Methodism. Turner follows that by emphasizing the importance of offering a reasoned defence of the Christian faith, and, interestingly for us, expounds his call for the development of theological education for all with particular attention to the needs of young adults. Throughout this book runs the call for space to ask questions, and for resources with which to search out answers. That is not just relevant to personal faith, but includes the socio-political commitments highlighted by a further two of John Munsey Turner's keys to Methodism's future. Finally, he emphasizes the importance of small groups for the development of mature faith. It seems we have arrived at the end of this book with very similar concerns to Turner's. Our concern – which we know to be shared by some of Turner's generation – is why we all continue to observe these strengths and weaknesses of Methodism without moving towards the more dynamic, inclusive church which we sought to present here.

So where is British Methodism to go? There are at least four options:

1. Methodism continues as it is and fizzles out some time in the next century.
2. Methodism continues independent of other Christian traditions with a clearer focus on what justifies it being separate.
3. Methodism disbands and becomes re-incorporated into the Church of England.
4. Methodism prepares to disband itself, whilst working towards a new, more fully ecumenical Church *in* England.

From our perspective, only Option 1 is to be excluded altogether. For clearly, as the Methodist Council recognizes, something must be done. It is, though, worth saying that from our own small-scale survey among ourselves, most of the contributors to this book believe that Methodism will have an independent future, whilst only half of the contributors think it should. As a group, then, we may well not be wholly representative of our generation. But we may perhaps be uncomfortably representative of our generation in the church. If so, then there is more of a willingness among us than may have been supposed, or even shown by the contents of this book itself, to suggest that we should at least actively consider ecclesiastical euthanasia, in order to preserve the insights and future of the Methodist form of Christianity within British Christianity's future.

So perhaps it is time to bow out gracefully, and relinquish the separate denomination John and Charles Wesley would have so disliked. Option 3 would then not be about mere dissolution into the Church of England, but more a case of a prodigal returning. For the father surely learnt something, too, from the younger son's departure. Methodism, for its part, might want to rue the sheer length of time it had stayed away, and how many of its precious resources could have been put to greater effect.

On the other hand, perhaps a vision of resurrection for British Methodism is possible. That picture could take us in two possible directions. The resurrection body of Christ was in some way familiar, but also so unfamiliar that some could see the risen Christ and still doubt (Matt. 28.17). So the form of the British Methodist Church might be a denomination renewed, altered, passionate, life-filled and life-giving. That might be unfamiliar, yet recognizable, because for some, that's what the church is managing to achieve, if fitfully. Or perhaps the resurrection body is a body of British Christianity far more united than at present, recognizable because of what it has incorporated from many denominations, unrecognizable because we cannot yet imagine the shape such a body might take. But, either way, an image of resurrection is an image of what there might be *beyond death*. Whether that does or does not mean the end of the institution, it recognizes the pain of what we are going through, perhaps worse pain to come, and the necessity of giving up at least some aspects of what we have been.

Our interest – to preserve the insights and future of the Methodist form of Christianity within British Christianity's future – does not of itself, then, resolve the issue of whether Option 2, 3 or 4 should be chosen. Only readers can do that. Our simple hope is that the material in this book has given readers, Methodist or not, enough to chew on to reach an answer for themselves. More than that: we hope that the book has encouraged you to do something about British Christianity's future.

The calling of the Methodist Church is to respond to the gospel of God's love in Christ and to live out its discipleship in worship and mission.

Worship in the Methodist Church is expressed in many ways. In worship the Church

- gives praise to God in Christ through the Spirit
- opens itself to God's transforming love
- receives and reflects on the gospel of God's ways in the world
- offers itself to share in God's costly action in the world.

Methodism endorses many dimensions and methods of Christian mission. In particular it affirms that mission includes:

- telling the good news of Jesus
- calling people to faith in Jesus Christ and to Christian discipleship
- caring for individual people and communities
- sharing the task of education and social and spiritual development
- struggling for a just world
- being alongside the poor
- becoming friends with people of different cultures and faiths
- caring for the earth
- building partnerships with other churches and other groups who share some of our mission aims.[33]

List of quotations used

1. Elaine Storkey, 'Change and Decay in British Society?' in M. Eden and D. F. Wells (eds) *The Gospel in the Modern World* (Leicester and Downers Grove: IVP, 1991), 109–10
2. Adrian Hastings, *A History of English Christianity* (London: Collins, 1986), 660.
3. By 'The Serpent', in *Movement*, the SCM magazine for University Chaplaincies, Issue 93, Summer 1996, 24.
4. Methodist woman in her twenties, when organizing a youth group reunion.
5. Dietrich Bonhoeffer, *Letters and Papers from Prison* (London: SCM, 1971), 382.
6. Geoffrey Wainwright, *Methodists in Dialog* (Nashville: Kingswood Books, 1995), 114.
7. Richard Heitzenrater, *The Elusive Mr. Wesley (Vol. 1)* (Nashville: Abingdon Press, 1984), 27.
8. Albert Outler, *John Wesley* (New York: Oxford University Press, 1964), iv.
9. Howard Mellor, 'New Methodism – New Millennium' in *The Handbook of the Methodist Conference, London '97*, 18.
10. Philip Richter and Leslie J. Francis, *Gone But Not Forgotten* (London: DLT, 1998), 96.
11. Gavin White, *How the Churches Got to Be the Way They Are* (London: SCM/ Philadelphia: TPI, 1990), 38.
12. *Called to Love and Praise*. The Methodist Church Faith and Order Committee's Report to Conference, 1995, 49.
13. John Munsey Turner, *Modern Methodism in England 1932–1998* (Peterborough: Epworth Press, 1998), 91.
14. *Called to Love and Praise*, The Methodist Church Faith and Order Committee's Report to Conference, 1995, 52.
15. Methodist man in his thirties, working in the Midlands.
16. Methodist woman presbyter, in her thirties.
17. Dietrich Bonhoeffer, *The Cost of Discipleship* (London: SCM, 1955), 29–30.
18. Philip Richter and Leslie J. Francis, *Gone But Not Forgotten* (London: DLT, 1998), 62–3.
19. John Munsey Turner, *op. cit.*, 44–5.
20. Stanley Hauerwas, *Wilderness Wanderings* (Westview Press: Boulder and Oxford, 1997), 29.
21. *Methodist Recorder*, 11 June 1998.
22. John B. Cobb Jr, 'Dialogue' in L. Swidler *et al.*, *Death or Dialogue?: From the Age of Monologue to the Age of Dialogue* (London: SCM/Philadelphia TPI, 1990), 9.
23. Nichola Jones, Extract from an Address to the Methodist Conference, June 1996; quoted from the Methodist Church's website (www.methodist.org.uk).
24. John Wesley, Preface to 'The Character of a Methodist' (1742), in *The Works of John Wesley (Vol. 9)* (Nashville: Abingdon Press, 1989), 32–3.
25. Colin W. Williams, *John Wesley's Theology Today* (London: The Epworth Press, 1960), 216.
26. *Called to Love and Praise, op. cit.*, 50.
27. Methodist man in his thirties.
28. *Called to Love and Praise, op. cit.*, 41–2.
29. David Hempton, *The Religion of the People* (London: Routledge, 1996), 70.
30. From the report 'Role and Place of the Ordained Minister in a Modern Church', presented to the British Methodist Conference, 1998 (Agenda, 1998), 588.
31. Said at a Circuit Local Preachers' Meeting early in 1998.
32. *Ibid.*
33. The current Mission Statement of the Methodist Church, as featured in the Methodist Church's website (www.methodist.org.uk).

Glossary

Definitions of Methodist terms in this list are largely taken from introductory leaflet PB226 *The Methodist Church: Its Roots, How it Works, The Words it Uses* produced by the Methodist Church in March 1998, in which the definitions of many further Methodist terms are provided.

Aesthetic: pertaining to what is beautiful; appreciating the beautiful.

Agenda/Conference Agenda: programme for a meeting; specifically, as a publication, the large book (complete with all relevant discussion documents) produced for all representatives at the Methodist Conference in June/July each year.

androcentric: putting men at the centre.

catholic/catholicity: though this word is used in a variety of senses, its main use in this book is as 'universal', 'comprehensive', or 'inclusive of a wide diversity', rather than 'Roman Catholic' or 'orthodox'.

Christology: branch of Christian theology dealing with understandings of the Christ, especially in relation to the figure of Jesus.

Circuit: one or a number of local Methodist churches in the charge of one or more ministers. Several Circuits make up a District.

communitarianism: term currently used for any social or political movement which stresses the importance of community, and the priority of the communal over the individual. Often opposed to 'individualism' or (political or economic) 'liberalism'.

Conference: governing body of the Methodist Church which meets in a different District in June/July each year.

Connexion/connexionalism: term used to describe the way in which the Circuits and Districts of the Methodist Church in Britain are linked together.

CPD: The Constitutional Practice and Discipline of the Methodist Church: a compendium of the rules and regulations of the Methodist Church, amended and updated each year by the Methodist Conference.

Deed of Union: one of the basic constitutional documents of the Methodist Church. Adopted when different Methodist denominations united in 1932, and revised regularly since then. Available as part of CPD (Volume 2).

Deists: prominent in the seventeenth and early eighteenth centuries, though still represented today, Deists support the view of God's creation of the world, but reject the possibility of God's continuing intervention in it.

dialectic/dialectical: a way of arguing, which proceeds by noting directly opposing viewpoints. Often accepts that two opposing views have to be held in tension, as there may be no resolution of a conflict.

District: a collection of Circuits. There are currently 33 Districts in the Methodist Church in Great Britain.

doxology/doxological: literally: relating to 'glory' or 'praise'. Used more generally as relating to worship in its widest sense.

ecclesiology: the branch of Christian theology dealing with understandings of the church.

episcopal/episcopalian: literally to do with oversight, and therefore relating to bishops (who are primarily 'overseers'); also refers to denominations (Episcopal Churches) which have bishops.

eschatology: the branch of Christian theology dealing with understandings of the 'end' including, traditionally, death, judgement, heaven, hell (often known as 'the four last things'), but more generally also of all aspects of 'ultimacy', including the kingdom of God.

existentialism: pertaining to matters of human existence; often identified as a form of philosophy which prioritizes human experience (usually individual experience); exists in Christian forms, where the close relationships between self-understanding and understanding of God are explored together.

fundamentalist/fundamentalism: term first used early in the twentieth century of a particular branch of evangelicalism which emphasized the inerrancy, as opposed merely to the supreme authority, of the Bible.

ideology/ideological: literally, to do with ideas; also used to indicate the way in which all forms of thinking and acting are affected, even controlled, by particular patterns of thought.

Latitudinarians: a group of seventeenth-century Anglican theologians who were willing to permit 'latitude', or flexibility, in matters of doctrine, ecclesiastical organization, and liturgical practice.

Memorials/Memorials Committee: refers to the submissions (usually in the form of questions or proposals) which may be made to Conference by any Circuit or Synod, and the Committee which deals with such enquiries.

Methodist Council: acts on behalf of the Methodist Conference between meetings of the Conference, and initiates and makes policy recommendations to Conference. Every District is represented on it.

missiology/missiological: the branch of Christian theology dealing with understandings of mission, evangelism and dialogue.

modernity: term used for all forms of thought influenced by the European Enlightenment.

platonic: relating to the Greek philosopher Plato (c.429–347 BCE); denotes a form of thinking which places emphasis upon the non-material, and views objects as forms of a non-material essence.

postmodernism/postmodernity: sometimes called 'late modernity'; much-used and much-maligned term seeking to denote the present climate in Western culture, in which 'modernity' is being criticized; these reactions against Enlightenment-influenced thinking stress flux, diversity, the particular, the individual, the consumer, the visual, and oppose any effort to offer total explanations.

praxis: referring to action, especially action contained within a thought-out, reflective strategy.

priestly authors: refers to some of the writers who contributed to the first five books of the Bible (collectively, the Pentateuch) and whose work makes up the so-called 'P' document, which interweaves with the documents J, E and D within these five books.

secularization: the process in which religion (especially in Western culture, and expecially Christianity) has lost its social, political and cultural power, being replaced by widespread assumptions which neglect or reject attention to any theistic belief.

soteriology/soteriological: the branch of Christian theology dealing with understandings of salvation, redemption or liberation.

Bibliography

Agenda (1996) *Agenda of the Methodist Conference*, Peterborough: Methodist Publishing House.

Agenda (1997) *Agenda of the Methodist Conference*, Peterborough: Methodist Publishing House.

Agenda (1998) *Agenda of the Methodist Conference*, Peterborough: Methodist Publishing House.

Amichai, Y. (1988) *Yehuda Amichai, Selected Poems*, Harmondsworth: Penguin.

Anderson, Pam (1998) *A Feminist Philosophy of Religion*, Oxford: Blackwell.

Andrewes, L. (1841) *Ninety-six Sermons by Lancelot Andrewes*, Oxford: Parker.

Ariarajah, S. Wesley (1993) 'Pluralism and Harmony', *Current Dialogue*, 25.

Bacon, Francis (1620) *Novum Organum*, trans. Robert Leslie Ellis and James Spedding. London: Routledge (1905).

Balasuriya, T. (1984) *Planetary Theology*, London: SCM.

Bartholomew, David, Barber, Peter, Beck, Brian and Horner, John (1997) 'Membership Matters', *Epworth Review*, 24/2, 48–61.

Beardwell, Ian and Holden, Len (1994) *Human Resource Management: A Contemporary Perspective*, London: Pitman.

Bebbington, D. W. (1984) 'The Persecution of George Jackson: A British Fundamentalist Controversy', in W. J. Sheils (ed.) *Persecution and Toleration*, Oxford: Basil Blackwell, 421–33.

Bebbington, D. W. (1989) *Evangelicalism in Modern Britain*, London: Unwin Hyman.

Beck, Brian (1991) 'Some Reflections on Connexionalism', *Epworth Review*, 18/2, 48–59; 18/3, 43–50.

Beckford, R. (1998) *Jesus Is Dread*, London: Darton, Longman & Todd.

Bennett, Alan (1994) *Writing Home*, London: Faber & Faber.

Birtwhistle, N. Allen (1983) 'Methodist Missions', in R. Davies, A. R. George, and G. Rupp (eds) *A History of the Methodist Church in Great Britain, Vol. 3*, London: Epworth Press, 1–116.

Bond, Simon (1990) *Holy Unacceptable*, London: Methuen.

Bonhoeffer, Dietrich (1978) *Christology*, London: Fontana.

Borgen, O. E. (1972) *John Wesley on the Sacraments: A Theological Study*, Nashville: Abingdon.

Bosch, D. J. (1985) 'In Search of a New Evangelical Understanding', in B. J. Nicholls (ed.) *In Word and Deed – Evangelism and Social Responsibility*, Exeter: Paternoster Press, 63–83.

Bosch, D. J. (1991) *Transforming Mission*, Maryknoll: Orbis.

Brierley, Peter (1991) *'Christian' England*, London: MARC Europe.

Bruce, S. (1995a) 'Religion in Britain at the Close of the 20th Century: A Challenge to the Silver Lining Perspective', *Journal of Contemporary Religion*, 11/3, 261–75.

Bruce, S. (1995b) *Religion in Modern Britain*, Oxford: OUP.

Bruce, S. (1996) *Religion in the Modern World: From Cathedrals to Cults*, Oxford University Press.

Buckley, James (1992) *Seeking the Humanity of God: Practices, Doctrines, and Catholic Theology*, Collegeville: The Liturgical Press.

Bultmann, Rudolf (1960) *Jesus Christ and Mythology*, London: SCM.

Burdon, Adrian (1991) *The Preaching Service – the Glory of the Methodists*, Nottingham: Grove Books.

Called to Love and Praise (1995) 'The Methodist Church Faith & Order Committee *Called to Love and Praise*, A Report to the 1995 Bristol Conference', Peterborough: Methodist Publishing House.

Calver, C. (1993) 'The Evangelicals', in M. Eden (ed.) *Britain on the Brink*, Nottingham: Crossway Books, 143–56.

Calver, C. (1995) 'Afterword', in J. Wolffe (ed.) *Evangelical Faith and Public Zeal*, London: SPCK, 198–210.

Caputi, Jane (1992) 'On Psychic Activism: Feminist Myth-Making', in Carolyne Larrington (ed.) *The Feminist Companion to Mythology*, London: Pandora Press, 425–40.

Carnelley, E. (1998) 'Prophecy, Race and Eastenders: Ministry on the Isle of Dogs and Celebrating the Difference', *Modern Believing*, 36/1, 1995, reprinted in M. Northcott (ed.) *Urban Theology*, London: Cassell, 318–22.

Carter, David (1997) *Some Methodist Principles of Ecumenism*, Unpublished paper, given at the Tenth Oxford Institute of Methodist Theological Studies.

CED (1994) *Collins English Dictionary*, London: Collins.

Checkland, Sir Michael (1997) 'Vice-President's Address to Liverpool Synod' (Unpublished).

Clack, B. (1994) 'Salvation and Feminism', in D. English (ed.) *Windows on Salvation*, London: Darton, Longman & Todd, 153–65.

Coates, G. (1983) *What on Earth Is the Kingdom?*, Eastbourne: Kingsway.

Cone, J. (1975) *God of the Oppressed*, San Francisco: HarperSanFrancisco.

Cracknell, Kenneth (1994) 'The Theology of Religious Pluralism', *Current Dialogue*, 26, 10–22.

Cracknell, Kenneth (1995) *Justice, Courtesy and Love*, London: Epworth Press.

CPD (1997) *The Constitutional Practice and Discipline of the Methodist Church, Volume 2*, Peterborough: Methodist Publishing House.

CTE (1996) *A Chance to Start Again: Marking the Millennium*, London: Churches Together in England.

Cuming, G. J. (1966) 'Two Fragments of a Lost Liturgy?', in G. J. Cuming (ed.) *Studies in Church History*, Leiden: Brill, 247–53.

Cupitt, Don (1980) *Taking Leave of God*, London: SCM.

Cupitt, Don (1988) *The New Christian Ethics*, London: SCM.

Cupitt, Don (1995) *Solar Ethics*, London: SCM.

Currie, Robert (1968) *Methodism Divided. A Study in the Sociology of Ecumenicalism*, London: Faber & Faber.

Daly, Mary (1993) *Outercourse: The Be-Dazzling Voyage*, London: The Women's Press.

Davie, G. (1994) *Religion in Britain Since 1945*, Oxford UK and Cambridge USA: Blackwell.

Davies, R. and Rupp, G. (1965) *A History of the Methodist Church in Great Britain, Vol. 1*, London: Epworth Press.

Davies, Rupert, George, A. Raymond, and Rupp, Gordon (eds) (1988) *A History of the Methodist Church in Great Britain, Vol. 4*, London: Epworth Press.

Davies, R. E. (1989) *The Works of John Wesley, Volume 9: The Methodist Societies – History, Nature and Design*, Nashville: Abingdon Press.

de Bono, E. (1991) *I Am Right, You Are Wrong*, Harmondsworth: Penguin.

Dickens, L. (1991) 'The Fence', in V. Zundel (ed.) *Faith in Her Words – Six Centuries of Women's Poetry*, Oxford: Lion.

Donovan, Vincent (1997) *Gospel and Cultures – Where Have We Got To?*, an unpublished paper presented to the Churches' Commission on Mission meeting in Edinburgh.

Finney, J. (1992) *Finding Faith Today*, Swindon: Bible Society.

Fiorenza, Elisabeth S. (1983) *In Memory of Her*, London: SCM.

Freire, Paulo (1972) *Pedagogy of the Oppressed*, Harmondsworth: Penguin.

Frost, Rob (1997) *Which Way for the Church?*, Eastbourne: Kingsway Publications.

Gibbs, E. (1993) *Winning Them Back*, Tunbridge Wells: MARC Europe.

Gill, Robin (1993) *The Myth of the Empty Church*, London: SPCK.

Gill, Robin and Burke, Derek (1996) *Strategic Church Leadership*, London: SPCK.

Goldenberg, Naomi (1991) 'The Return of the Goddess', in A. Loades and L. D. Rue (eds), *Contemporary Classics in Philosophy of Religion*, Illinois: Open Court, 421–41.

Greet, Kenneth (1985) 'The Role of the President', in Daphne Pickford (ed.) *The Future of Methodism – Approaching End or New Beginning?*, Birmingham: NACCCAN, 31–3.

Grey, M. (1997) *Beyond the Dark Night: A Way Forward for the Church?*, London: Cassell.

Gutiérrez, G. (1974) *A Theology of Liberation*, London: SCM.

Hampson, Daphne (1992) 'On Being All of a Piece/At Peace', in T. Elwes (ed.) *Women's Voices – Essays in Contemporary Feminist Theology*, London: Marshall Pickering, 131–45.

Hampson, Daphne (1996) *After Christianity*, London: SCM.

Handy, Charles (1990) *Understanding Voluntary Organisations*, London: Penguin Books.

Hefner, Philip J. (1984) 'The Church', in C. E. Braaten and R. Jenson (eds), *Christian Dogmatics:Volume 2*, Philadelphia: Fortress Press, 179–247.

Heitzenrater, Richard P. (1995) *Wesley and the People called Methodists*, Nashville: Abingdon Press.

Higginson, Richard (1996a) *Transforming Leadership – A Christian Approach to Management*, London: SPCK.

Higginson, Richard (1996b) 'Affirming Lay Ministries', in John Nelson (ed.) *Management and Ministry – Appreciating Contemporary Issues*, Norwich: The Canterbury Press, 59–65.

Horrell, D. (1995) 'Paul's Collection: Resources for a Materalist Theology', *Epworth Review* 22/2, 74–83.

Hymns and Psalms (1983), London: Methodist Publishing House.

Jacob, W. M. (1996) *Lay People and Religion in the Early Eighteenth Century*, Cambridge: Cambridge University Press.

Jantzen, Grace (1984) *God's World, God's Body*, London: Darton, Longman & Todd.

Kelly, J. N. D. (1958) *Early Christian Doctrines*, London: A & C Black.

Landry, Charles, Morley, Dave, Southwood, Russell and Wright, Patrick (1985) *What a Way to Run a Railroad – An Analysis of Radical Failure*, London: Comedia Publishing Group.

Lash, Nicholas (1986) 'Theologies at the Service of a Common Tradition', *Theology on the Way to Emmaus*, London: SCM, 18–33.

Long, Asphodel (1992) *In a Chariot Drawn by Lions*, London: The Women's Press.

McCulloch, N. (1992) *A Gospel to Proclaim*, London: Darton, Longman & Todd.

McFague, Sallie (1993) *The Body of God: An Ecological Theology*, London: SCM.

McGrath, Alister E. (1994) *Christian Theology: An Introduction*, Oxford: Blackwell.

McGrath, Alister E. (1996) *A Passion for Truth*, Leicester: Apollos.

Macquiban, Tim (1995) 'Practical Piety or Lettered Learning', *Proceedings of the Wesley Historical Society* 50, 83–107.

Macquiban, Tim (1996) 'Does Methodism Matter Enough?', *Epworth Review*, 23/2, 67–75.

Martinson, Paul Varo (1990) *Salvation and the Religions: From Sola to Simul*, St Paul, USA: LWF Group on Other Faiths.

Meeks, M. Douglas (1985) 'The Future of the Methodist Theological Traditions', in M. D. Meeks (ed.) *The Future of the Methodist Theological Traditions*, Nashville: Abingdon, 13–33.

Micklethwait, John and Wooldridge, Adrian (1997) *The Witch Doctors*, London: Mandarin.

Milburn, G. and Batty, M. (1995) *Workaday Preachers*, Peterborough: Methodist Publishing House.

Moltmann, J. (1993) 'Christology in the Jewish–Christian Dialogue', in *New Visions*, New York: Crossroad.

Mosedale, S. E. (1994) 'What is an Evangelical?', *Epworth Review*, 21/3, 56–8.

MSB (1975) *Methodist Service Book*, London: Methodist Publishing House.

Munson, James (1991) *The Nonconformists. In Search of a Lost Culture*, London: SPCK.

Nelson, James (1988) *The Intimate Connection*, Pennsylvania: The Westminster Press.

Neusner, Jacob (1991) *Jews and Christians: The Myth of a Common Tradition*, London: SCM.

Newbigin, L. (1983) *The Open Secret*, Grand Rapids: Eerdmans.

Nietzsche, F. (1969) *Thus Spoke Zarathustra*, Harmondsworth: Penguin.

Outler, Albert C. (1964) 'Do Methodists Have a Doctrine of the Church?', in D. Kirkpatrick (ed.) *The Doctrine of the Church*, London: Epworth, 11–28.

Outler, Albert C. (ed.) (1984) *The Works of John Wesley. Sermons I*, Nashville: Abingdon Press.

Outler, Albert C. (ed.) (1987) *The Works of John Wesley. Sermons IV*, Nashville: Abingdon Press.

Pannenberg, Wolfhart (1972) *The Apostles' Creed in the Light of Today's Questions*, London: SCM.

Pattison, Stephen (1997) *The Faith of the Managers*, London: Cassell.

Pelikan, Jaroslav (1984) *The Christian Tradition: A History of the Development of Doctrine – Vol. 4 Reformation of Church and Dogma (1300–1700)*, Chicago: The University of Chicago Press.

Pickford, Daphne (ed.) (1985) *The Future of Methodism – Approaching End or New Beginning?*, Birmingham: NACCCAN.

Plumwood, Val (1993) *Feminism and the Mastery of Nature*, London: Routledge.

Pritchard, J. (1998) 'Missionary Concepts and Procedures: Time for a Review', *International Review of Mission*, 87/344.

Rack, Henry D. (1983) 'Wesleyan Methodism 1849–1902', in R. Davies, A. R. George and G. Rupp (eds) *A History of the Methodist Church in Great Britain, Vol. 3*, London: Epworth Press, 119–66.

Rack, Henry D. (1992) *Reasonable Enthusiast: John Wesley and the Rise of Methodism*, London: Epworth Press; 2nd edn.

Radford Ruether, Rosemary (1983) *Sexism and God-Talk*, London: SCM.

Ranke-Heinemann, Uta (1991) *Eunuchs for the Kingdom of God*, Harmondsworth: Penguin.

Reddie, A. (1998) *Growing into Hope* (2 vols), Peterborough: Methodist Publishing House.

Richter, P. and Francis, L. (1998) *Gone But Not Forgotten*, London: Darton, Longman & Todd.

Riddell, M. (1998) *Threshold of the Future*, London: SPCK.

Rigg, James H. (1887) *A Comparative View of Church Organizations, Primitive and Protestant*, London: T. Woolmer.

Robinson, John A. T. (1963) *Honest to God*, London: SCM.

Robinson, M. (1992) *A World Apart*, Crowborough: Monarch.

Robinson, M. (1994) *The Faith of the Unbeliever*, Crowborough: Monarch.

Romain, Jonathan (1996) 'Teaching Tolerance', *Common Ground*, 2, 16.

Rowe, Trevor (1987) *Uncomfortable Chairs*, London: The Methodist Church.

Sacks, Jonathan (1995) *Faith in the Future: The Inter-faith Imperative*, London: Darton, Longman & Todd.

Santayana, George (1905) *Life of Reason, Vol. 1*, London: Constable.

Scherman, Nosson (1984) *The Complete ArtScroll Siddur*, New York: Mesorah Publications.

Segundo, J. L. (1976) *The Liberation of Theology*, Maryknoll: Orbis.

Selby, P. (1996) 'Is the Church a Family?', in S. C. Barton (ed.) *The Family in Theological Perspective*, Edinburgh: T. & T. Clark.

Sobrino, J. (1978) *Christology at the Crossroads*, London: SCM.

Storkey, Elaine (1991) 'Change and Decay in British Society?', in Martyn Eden and David F. Wells (eds) *The Gospel in the Modern World*, Leicester and Downers Grove: IVP, 108–23.

Strawson, William (1983) 'Methodist Theology 1850–1950', in R. Davies *et al.* (eds) *A History of the Methodist Church in Great Britain, Vol. 3*, London: Epworth Press, 182–231.

Tabraham, Barrie (1995) *The Making of Methodism*, London: Epworth Press.

Telford, John (1931) *The Letters of the Rev. John Wesley Vol. 3*, London: Epworth Press.

Thorne, Roger F. S. (1997) 'All Together Now! The United Methodist Church 1907–32', *Proceedings of the Wesley Historical Society*, 51, 73–95.

Tidball, D. J. (1994) *Who Are the Evangelicals?*, London: Marshall Pickering.

Tillich, Paul (1962) *The Shaking of the Foundations*, Harmondsworth: Penguin.

Tomlinson, D. (1995) *The Post Evangelical*, London: SPCK.

Townsend, W. J., Workman, H. B. and Eayrs, G. (eds) (1909) *A New History of Methodism*, London: Hodder and Stoughton.

Trible, Phyllis (1984) *Texts of Terror*, London: SCM.

Turner, J. M. (1983) 'Methodism in England 1900–1932', in R. Davies *et al.* (eds), *A History of the Methodist Church in Great Britain, Vol. 3*, London: Epworth Press, 309–61.

Turner, J. M. (1998) *Modern Methodism in England 1932–1998*, Peterborough: Epworth Press.

Vincent, John (1984) *OK, Let's Be Methodists*, London: Epworth Press.

Vincent, John (1986) *Radical Jesus*, London: Marshall Pickering.

Vincent, John (1992) *Liberation Theology from the Inner City*, Sheffield: Urban Theology Unit.

Wainwright, G. (1995) *Methodists in Dialog*, Nashville: Kingswood Books.

Walker, Barbara (1983) *The Woman's Encyclopedia of Myths and Secrets*, London: HarperCollins.

Wallwork, N. (1988) 'Wesley's Legacy in Worship', in John Stacey (ed.) *John Wesley: Contemporary Perspectives*, London: Epworth Press.

Walton, H. (1985) *A Tree God Planted: Black People in British Methodism*, London: Ethnic Minorities in Methodism Working Group.

Ward, P. (1997) 'The Tribes of Evangelicalism', in G. Cray *et al.*, *The Post Evangelical Debate*, London: Triangle, 19–34.

Ward, W. R. (1992) *The Protestant Evangelical Awakening*, Cambridge: CUP.

Ward, W. R. (1996) 'The Dissenters, Volume 2', *Proceedings of the Wesley Historical Society*, 50, 246–8.

Watson, J. R. (1997) *The English Hymn: A Critical and Historical Study*, Oxford: Clarendon Press.

Watty, W. (1981) *From Shore to Shore*, Kingston: UTCWI.

WCC (1979) *Guidelines on Dialogue with People of Living Faiths and Ideologies*, Geneva: World Council of Churches.

Wellings, M. (1994) 'What is an Evangelical?', *Epworth Review*, 21/3, 45–53.

White, Lynn (1967) 'The Historical Roots of Our Ecological Crisis', in M. H. MacKinnon and M. McIntyre (eds) *Readings in Ecology and Feminist Theology*, Kansas City: Sheed & Ward, 25–35.

Wilkinson, John T. (1978) 'The Rise of Other Methodist Traditions', in R. Davies, A. R. George and G. Rupp (eds), *A History of the Methodist Church in Great Britain, Vol. 2*, London: Epworth Press, 276–329.

Wilkinson, J. (1993) *Church in Black and White*, Edinburgh: Andrews Press.

Willey, Basil (1965) *Spots of Time*, London: Chatto and Windus.

Wright, N. (1996) *The Radical Evangelical*, London: SPCK.

Wright, N. (1997) 'Re-imagining Evangelicalism', in G. Cray *et al.*, *The Post Evangelical Debate*, London: Triangle, 96–112.

Index